ENGINEERING

Engineering with Excel
Custom Edition for University of British Columbia
APSC 160

PEARSON

Please visit our website at *www.pearsonlearningsolutions.com*.

Attention bookstores: For permission to return any unsold stock, contact us at *pe-uscustomreturns@pearson.com*.

Pearson Learning Solutions, 501 Boylston Street, Suite 900, Boston, MA 02116
A Pearson Education Company
www.pearsoned.com

ISBN 10: 1-256-57585-2
ISBN 13: 978-1-256-57585-6

Table of Contents

Introduction to Excel

Objectives

After reading this chapter, you will know

- What an Excel worksheet is
- How to start using Excel
- How the Excel screen is laid out
- The fundamentals of using Excel
- Some options for organizing your worksheets
- How to print your worksheets
- How to save and reopen Excel files

1 INTRODUCTION

Spreadsheets were originally paper grids used by accountants and business people to track incomes and expenditures. When *electronic spreadsheets* first became available on personal computers, engineers immediately found uses for them. They discovered that many engineering tasks can be solved quickly and easily within the framework of a spreadsheet. Figure 1 shows how a spreadsheet can be used to calculate fuel efficiency.

Figure 1
Calculating fuel efficiency using a spreadsheet.

	A	B	C	D	E
1	Vehicle Mileage Calculation				
2					
3		Miles Traveled	Gallons of Fuel		Miles Per Gallon
4					
5		435	16.4		26.5
6					

Powerful modern spreadsheet programs like Microsoft Excel[1] allow very complex problems to be solved right on an engineer's desktop. This text focuses on using Microsoft Excel, currently the most popular spreadsheet program in the world, to perform common engineering problems.

Excel is now much more than just an electronic implementation of a spreadsheet, and this is reflected in a change of nomenclature; what used to be called a spreadsheet is now more commonly referred to as a *worksheet*, and a collection of worksheets is called a *workbook*.

1.1 Nomenclature

Some conventions are used throughout this text to highlight the types of information:

- Key terms, such as the term "active cell" in the example below, are shown in italics the first time they are used.

    Press [F2] to edit the *active cell*.

- Variables, formulas, and functions are shown in Courier font.

    `=B3*C4`

- Individual keystrokes are enclosed in brackets.

    Press the [Enter] key.

- Key combinations are enclosed in brackets.

    Press [Ctrl-c] to copy the contents of the cell.

- Buttons that are clicked with the mouse are shown in a bold font.

    Click **OK** to exit the dialog.

- Ribbon selections are indicated by listing the Tab, group, and button (or text box) separated by slashes. A boldface font is used for Ribbon selections to help them stand out in the text.

    Use **Home/Font/Underline** to underline the selected text.

- Menu options for prior versions of Excel are indicated by listing the menu name and submenu options separated by slashes.

    [Excel 2003: File/Open]

- Excel built-in function names are shown as follows:

    Excel can automatically calculate the arithmetic mean using the **AVERAGE** function.

1.2 Examples and Application Problems

We will use sample problems throughout the text to illustrate how Excel can be used to solve engineering problems. There are three levels of problems included in the text:

- *Demonstration Examples:* These are typically very simple examples designed to demonstrate specific features of Excel. They are usually single-step examples.

---

[1] Excel is a trademark of Microsoft Corporation, Inc.

- *Sample Problems:* These problems are slightly more involved and typically involve multiple steps. They are designed to illustrate how to apply specific Excel functions or capabilities to engineering problems.
- *Application Problems:* These are larger problems, more closely resembling the type of problem engineering students will see as homework problems.

The scope of the text attempts to include all engineering disciplines at the undergraduate level, with emphasis on topics appropriate to freshman engineering students. There has been an attempt to cover a broad range of subjects in the examples and application problems and to stay away from problems that require significant discipline-specific knowledge.

1.3 What Is a Spreadsheet?

A *spreadsheet* is a piece of paper containing a grid designed to hold values. The values are written into the *cells* formed by the grid and arranged into vertical columns and horizontal rows. Spreadsheets have been used for many years by people in the business community to present financial statements in an orderly way. With the advent of the personal computer in the 1970s, the paper spreadsheet was migrated to the computer and became an *electronic spreadsheet*. The rows and columns of values are still there, and the values are still housed in cells. The layout of an electronic spreadsheet is simple, making it very easy to learn to use. People can start up a program such as Excel for the first time and start solving problems within minutes.

The primary virtue of the early spreadsheets was *automatic recalculation*: Any change in a value or formula in the spreadsheet caused the rest of the spreadsheet to be recalculated. This meant that errors found in a spreadsheet could be fixed easily without having to recalculate the rest of the spreadsheet by hand. Even more importantly, the electronic spreadsheet could be used to investigate the effect of a change in one value on the rest of the spreadsheet. Engineers who wanted to know what would happen if, for example, the load on a bridge was increased by 2, 3, or 4% quickly found electronic spreadsheets very useful.

Since the 1970s, the computing power offered by electronic spreadsheets on personal computers has increased dramatically. *Graphing capabilities* were added early on and have improved over time. *Built-in functions* were added to speed up common calculations. Microsoft added a *programming language* to Excel that can be accessed from the spreadsheet when needed. Also, the computing speed and storage capacity of personal computers has increased to such an extent that a single personal computer with some good software (including, but not limited to, a spreadsheet such as Excel) can handle most of the day-to-day tasks encountered by most engineers.

1.4 Why Use a Spreadsheet?

Spreadsheets are great for some tasks, but not all; some problems fit the grid structure of a spreadsheet better than others. When your task requires data consisting of columns of numbers, such as data sets recorded from instruments, it fits in a spreadsheet very well; the analysis of tabular data fits the grid structure of the spreadsheet. But if your problem requires the symbolic manipulation of complex mathematical equations, a spreadsheet is not the best place to solve that problem.

The spreadsheet's heritage as a business tool becomes apparent as you use it. For example, there are any number of ways to display data in pie and bar charts, but the available X–Y chart options, generally more applicable to science and engineering, are more limited. There are many built-in functions to accomplish tasks such as calculating rates of return on investments (and engineers can find those useful), but there is no built-in function that calculates torque.

Spreadsheets are easy to use and can handle a wide range of problems. Many, if not most, of the problems for which engineers used to write computer programs are now solved by using electronic spreadsheets or other programs on their personal computers. A supercomputer might be able to "crunch the numbers" faster, but when the "crunch" time is tiny compared with the time required to write the program and create a report based on its results, the spreadsheet's ease of use and ability to print results in finished form (or easily move results to a word processor) can make the total time required to solve a problem by using a spreadsheet much shorter than that with conventional programing methods.

Spreadsheets are great for

- performing the same calculations repeatedly (e.g., analyzing data from multiple experimental runs),
- working with tabular information (e.g., finding enthalpies in a steam table—once you've entered the steam table into the spreadsheet),
- producing graphs—spreadsheets provide an easy way to get a plot of your data,
- performing parametric analyses, or "what if" studies—for example, "What would happen if the flow rate were doubled?", and
- presenting results in readable form.

There was a time when spreadsheets were not the best way to handle computationally intense calculations such as iterative solutions to complex problems, but dramatic improvements in the computational speed of personal computers has eliminated a large part of this shortcoming, and improvements in the solution methods used by Excel have also helped. Excel can now handle many very large problems that just a few years ago would not have been considered suitable for implementation on a spreadsheet.

But there are still a couple of things that spreadsheets do not do well. Programs such as Mathematica[®2] and Maple[®3] are designed to handle symbolic manipulation of mathematical equations; Excel is not. Electronic spreadsheets also display only the results of calculations (just as their paper ancestors did), rather than the equations used to calculate the results. You must take special care when developing spreadsheets to indicate how the solution was found. Other computational software programs, such as Mathcad,[4] more directly show the solution process as well as the result.

2 WHAT'S NEW IN EXCEL 2010?

While Excel 2007 included a radical change from the menu system to the Ribbon (a combination of menu commands and some dialog box content), Excel 2010 has much less dramatic changes, but there are some new and improved features:

- The **Office** button, introduced with Excel 2007 and used to access file and print features, has been replaced with a **File** tab on the Ribbon.
- You can add your own tabs or groups to the Ribbon in Excel 2010.
- The Print dialog has been redesigned in Excel 2010 and now includes print preview features.

---

[2] Wolfram Research, Inc., Champaign, IL, USA.
[3] Waterloo Maple Inc., Ontario, Canada.
[4] Mathsodt Inc., Cambridge, MA, USA.

- Accessing Format dialog for chart elements (e.g., changing the appearance of an axis on a graph) has been streamlined; you can now open a Format dialog by double-clicking on a chart element. (This is possible in Excel 2003 and Excel 2010, but did not work in Excel 2007.)
- Pivot tables have been improved.
- There are now more conditional formatting options.
- Statistical functions are more accurate.
- The Solver (iterative solver) has been updated with a new interface and a new solution algorithm.
- A 64-bit version of Excel is available that allows even bigger Excel workbooks to be created (requires a 64-bit operating system).

Many of these new features will be mentioned later in the text.

2.1 Starting Excel

Excel can be purchased by itself, but it is usually installed as part of the Microsoft Office® family of products. During installation, an Excel option is added to the Start menu. To start Excel use the following menu options, as illustrated in Figure 2.

Figure 2
Start Excel using menu options: **Start/All Programs/Microsoft Office/Microsoft Excel 2010.**

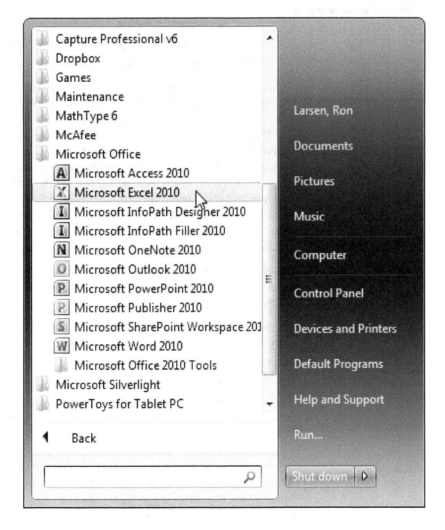

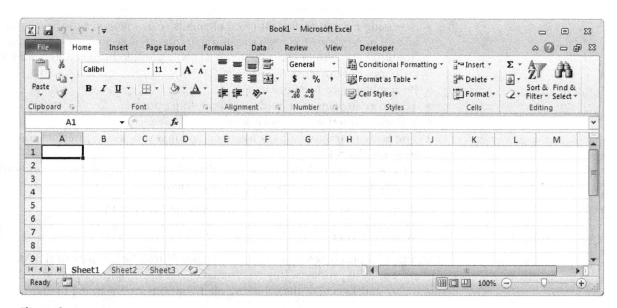

Figure 3
The Excel screen at start-up.

Excel 2010: **Start/All Programs/Microsoft Office/Microsoft Excel 2010**

Excel 2007: **Start/All Programs/Microsoft Office/Microsoft Office Excel 2007**

Recently used programs are listed on the left panel of the start menu in Windows XP. If the Excel icon appears on the start menu (as in Figure 2), then you can simply click the icon to start Excel.

When Excel starts, the Excel window should look a lot like Figure 3. Excel can be configured to suit individual preferences, so your installation of Excel could look a little different. Also, the number of buttons and boxes displayed at the top of the window changes depending on the width of the window; if you use a wide window you will see more information presented.

When you start Excel, a blank workbook is presented that contains, by default, three worksheets named Sheet1, Sheet2, and Sheet3. You can change the default number of sheets; this is covered in Section 3.7.

Note: The terms *worksheet* and *spreadsheet* can be interchanged, but Excel's help system uses the term worksheet and that term will be used in this text. A *workbook* is a collection of worksheets.

Since Excel runs within a Windows® environment, let's first review how to work with Windows.

3 A LITTLE WINDOWS®

The look of the windows depends on the version of Windows® that you are running. Images in this text are from Excel 2010 running in Windows 7. Other versions of Windows will not change the appearance greatly, but versions of Excel before 2007 will look quite different from the images shown here.

In Figure 3, the Excel workbook (called Book1 until it is saved with a different name) is shown maximized in the Excel Window. You can have multiple workbooks open at one time, and they may be easier to access if you do not maximize the workbooks, as illustrated in Figure 4.

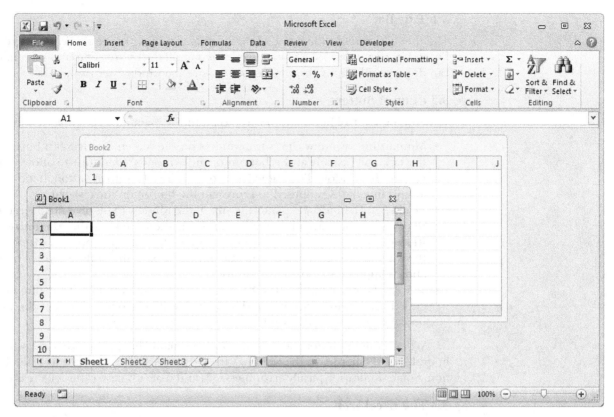

Figure 4
The Excel screen with two workbooks displayed.

Notice that the workbook names (Book1 and Book2 in Figure 4) are displayed at the top of the individual workbook rather than at the top of the Excel window as when the workbooks are not maximized.

There is a lot of command and control information at the top of an Excel window. Prominent features of Excel are indicated in Figure 5.

The top line of the Excel window contains the title bar (labeled 1 in Figure 5), the window control buttons (2), the Microsoft Excel Icon (3), the Quick Access toolbar (4), and the Ribbon (5). Each of these items is described in more detail below.

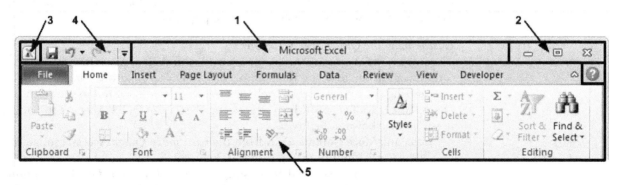

Figure 5
Command and control features of the Excel window.

3.1 Title Bar

The title bar contains the name of the program running in the window—Microsoft Excel. If the window has not been maximized to fill the entire computer screen, you can drag the title bar with your mouse to move the window across the screen.

3.2 Control Buttons

The window control buttons allow you to minimize, maximize, or close the window.

- Minimizing a window closes the window on the screen, but leaves a button on the task bar (usually at the bottom of the Windows® desktop) to allow you to reopen the window. The **Minimize** button is the left control button; it looks like a short line but is supposed to represent the button on the task bar.
- Maximizing a window expands the size of the window to fill the entire screen. If the window has already been maximized, then clicking the **Maximize** (or **Restore**) button will cause the window to shrink back to the original size, before the window was maximized. The **Maximize** button is the middle control button and is supposed to look like a window.
- The right control button (the **X**) is used to **Close** the window. If you attempt to close Excel without saving a workbook, you will be prompted to save the workbook before closing the window.

When a window is not maximized, you can usually change the size of the window by grabbing the border of the window with the mouse and dragging it to a new location. Some windows, typically error messages and dialog boxes, cannot be resized.

3.3 The Excel Icon

Microsoft Office 2007 had a very important button in the top-left corner of all Office products, the **Microsoft Office Button**. In Excel 2010, the functionality of that button has been replaced with the **File** tab on the Ribbon, and there is simply an Excel icon in the top-left corner of the Excel window. The only purpose of the Excel icon is to indicate that you are using Excel.

The usage of the File tab will be described later in the chapter, after the Ribbon is introduced.

3.4 The Quick Access Toolbar

All of the Office 2010 products feature a *Quick Access Toolbar* which is usually located at the left side of the title bar (see item 4 in Figure 5). It can also be located just below the ribbon to provide more space for buttons, if needed. To change the location of the Quick Access Toolbar, right-click on the toolbar and select **Show Quick Access Toolbar Below the Ribbon** from the pop-up menu.

Customizing the Quick Access Toolbar

The purpose of the Quick Access Toolbar is to provide a place for you to put buttons that allow you to access the features that you use frequently. You add buttons by customizing the Quick Access Toolbar. The down arrow symbol to the right of the Quick Access Toolbar provides access to the Customize Quick Access Toolbar drop-down menu, shown in Figure 6.

Selecting **More Commands...** from the Customize Quick Access Toolbar menu opens the Excel Options dialog shown in Figure 7.

You can also access this dialog using the Office button as **File Tab/Options** to open this dialog, then selecting the **Quick Access Toolbar** option on the dialog. [Excel 2007: Office/Excel Options]

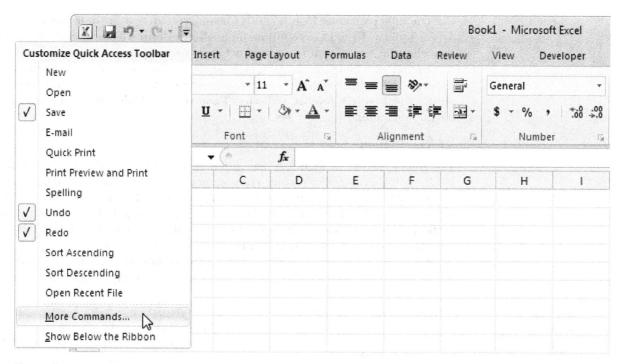

Figure 6
Customizing the Quick Access Toolbar.

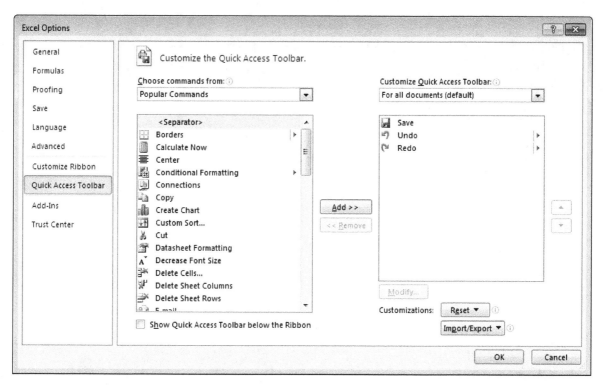

Figure 7
The Quick Access Toolbar panel on the Excel Options dialog is used to customize the Quick Access Toolbar.

The right panel (see Figure 7) lists the buttons currently included on the Quick Access Toolbar. To add a new button, highlight the desired feature on the left panel then click the **Add** >> button located between the two panels.

To remove a button from the Quick Access Toolbar, select the item in the right panel and click the <<**Remove** button. Alternatively, you can right-click any button on the Quick Access Toolbar and select **Remove from Quick Access Toolbar** from the pop-up menu.

3.5 The Ribbon

The *Ribbon*, shown in Figure 8, was a new feature in the 2007 Microsoft Office Products. It is intended to provide convenient access to commonly used features.

The Ribbon has a number of *tabs* across the top. Clicking each tab displays a collection of related *groups* of buttons. (Groups are labeled at the bottom of the Ribbon.) The *Home tab*, shown in Figure 8, provides access to the clipboard operations (cut, copy, and paste) and a variety of formatting features.

The Ribbon is context sensitive, and additional tabs appear when needed. For example, if you are working with a graph, such as the example shown in Figure 9,

Figure 8
The Ribbon, showing the contents of the **Home** tab.

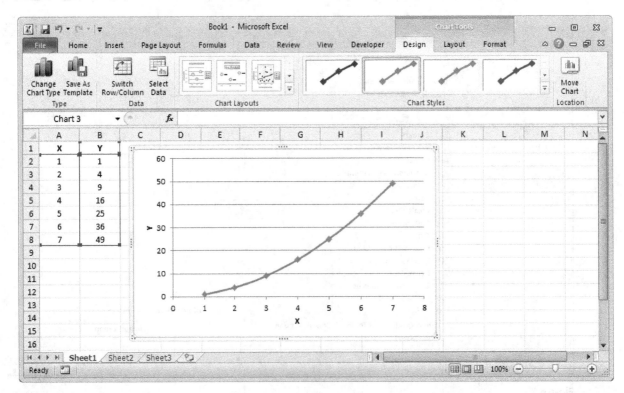

Figure 9
The Ribbon showing **Chart Tools** tabs appropriate for modifying a graph.

Design, Layout, and **Format** tabs appear on the Ribbon to allow you to customize the graph. The title **Chart Tools** appears on the title bar to let you know that these tabs are used to modify the appearance of the graph. If you click outside of the graph (somewhere on the worksheet grid), the **Chart Tools** tabs will disappear and the standard Ribbon will be displayed. To gain access to the **Chart Tools** tabs, simply click on the graph to select it.

Minimizing the Ribbon

The Ribbon is very useful, but takes up quite a bit of space in the Excel window. When necessary, you can minimize the Ribbon to show only the major tabs (**Home, Insert,** etc.). To minimize the Ribbon, right-click on the Ribbon's tab bar and select **Minimize the Ribbon** from the pop-up menu. When the Ribbon is minimized, clicking on any tab causes the groups for that tab to be displayed as a pop-up just below the tab line.

To display the full Ribbon again, right-click on the Ribbon's tab bar and click **Minimize the Ribbon** from the pop-up menu to de-select (i.e., uncheck) the **Minimize** option.

> **Note:** In Excel 2010, there is a **Minimize Ribbon Toggle** button just to the left of the **Help** button (i.e., to the left of the question mark).

3.6 Name Box and Formula Bar

Just below the Ribbon are the *Name box* and *Formula bar,* as illustrated in Figure 10. The Name box identifies the currently active cell (B3 in Figure 10) and the Formula bar displays the contents of the cell (text or formula). Equations can get quite long and a nice feature in Excel is the ability to quickly expand the size of the Formula bar by clicking on the down arrow symbol at the right side of the Formula bar (indicated in Figure 10).

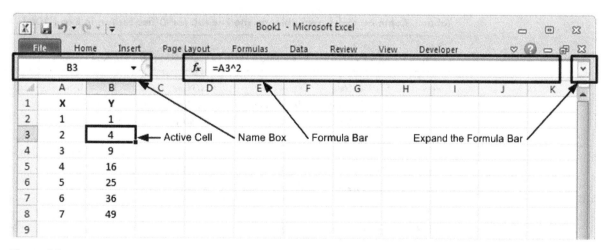

Figure 10
The Name box and Formula bar.

The Formula bar is displayed by default, but it can be turned off using the **View** tab on the Ribbon (Figure 11.) There is a **Formula Bar** checkbox on the **View** tab to activate or deactivate the display of the Formula bar (and Name box).

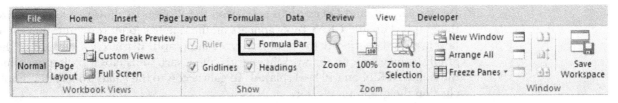

Figure 11
Use the **Formula Bar** checkbox on the **View** tab to activate and deactivate the display of the Formula bar.

3.7 The File tab

In Excel 2007, many of the tasks common to most programs (e.g., opening and closing files, printing) were collected in a menu under a new feature called the **Office** button, shown in the right panel in Figure 12. The **Office** button is gone in Excel 2010, replaced by the **File** tab on the Ribbon.

Figure 12
Excel 2007's **Office** button (right panel) has been replaced by the **File** tab in Excel 2010 (left panel).

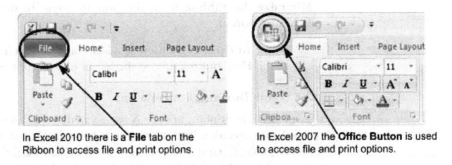

In Excel 2010 there is a **File** tab on the Ribbon to access file and print options.

In Excel 2007 the **Office Button** is used to access file and print options.

The new **File** tab contains many of the features that used to be on the **File** menu versions of Excel prior to 2007. Table 1 summarizes the features available through the **File** tab.

Table 1 Common tasks available via the File tab (or Office button in Excel 2007)

Menu Item	Excel 2010	Excel 2007	Excel 2003	Description
New	File tab/New	Office/New	File/New	Open a new, blank workbook
Open	File tab/Open	Office/Open	File/Open	Open an existing workbook
Save	File tab/Save	Office/Save	File/Save	Save the current workbook
Save As	File tab/ Save As...	Office/Save As...	File/Save As...	Save the current workbook with a different name or file format
Print	File tab/Print	Office/Print...	File/Print...	Open the print dialog
Exit	File tab/Exit	Office/Exit Excel	File/Exit	Exit the Excel program

3.7b Changing Excel Options

You can change the default options for Excel using the Excel Options dialog. The method for accessing the dialog varies depending on the version of Excel that you are using:

- Excel 2010: **File tab/Options**
- Excel 2007: **Office/Excel Options**
- Excel 2003: **File/Options**

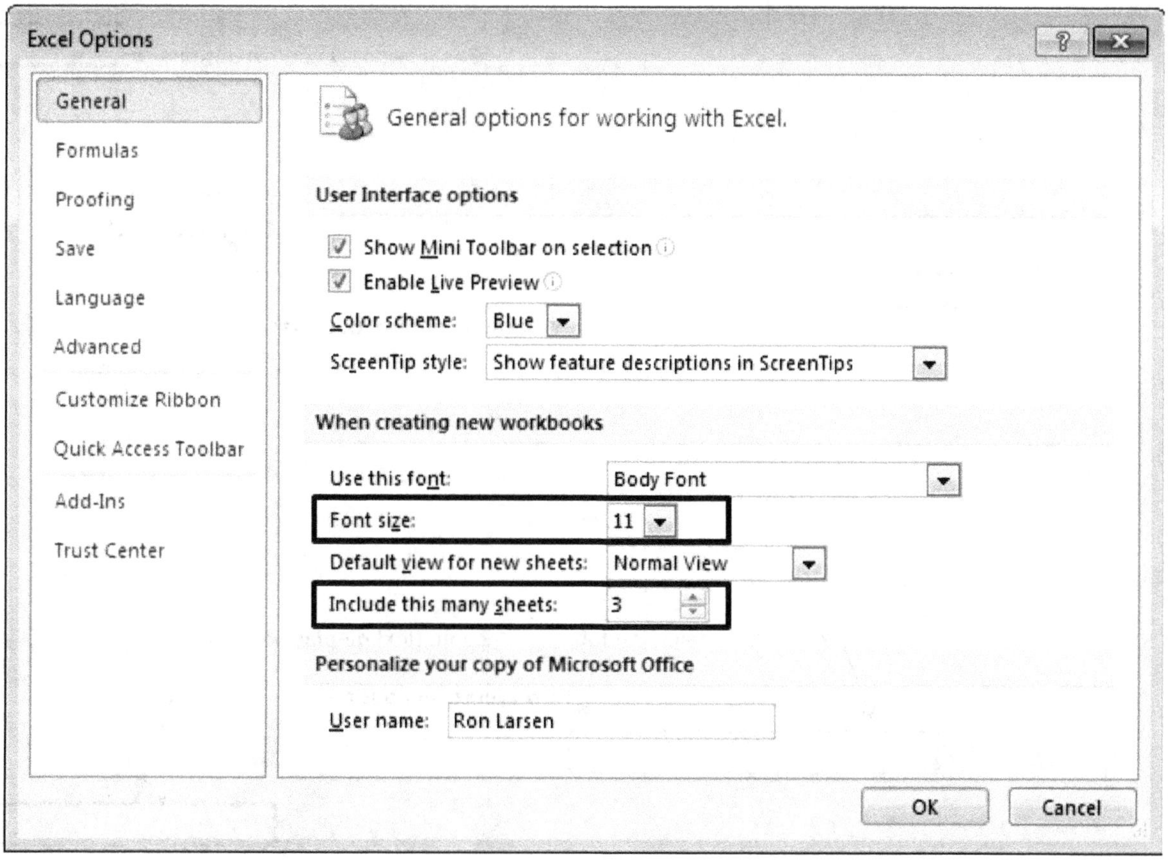

Figure 13
The Excel Options dialog, **General** panel.

In Excel 2010, the **File** tab displays a menu of commonly used features, but near the bottom of the menu is a button labeled **Options**. Click the **Options** button to open the Excel Options dialog (Figure 13).

The Excel Options dialog allows you to customize your installation of Excel to better fit your needs. There are nine panels in the Excel Options dialog to provide access to various features. The **General** panel (shown in Figure 11) (called the **Popular** panel in Excel 2007) shows some commonly changed Excel options. For example, the default font size can be increased to make the spreadsheet easier to read on the screen or decreased to display more information. Also, the default number of worksheets to include in a new workbook can be changed from the default value of 3.

3.8 Workbooks and Worksheets

By default, when a new workbook is opened it contains three worksheets, as shown in Figure 14.

When the workbook is not maximized (as in Figure 14), the workbook control buttons are at the top-right corner of the workbook window, and the worksheet selection tabs are at the bottom-left corner of the worksheet window. The right-most worksheet selection tab is actually a button that is used to create a new worksheet in the workbook.

When the workbook is maximized (as in Figure 15), the workbook control buttons appear just below the Excel window control buttons.

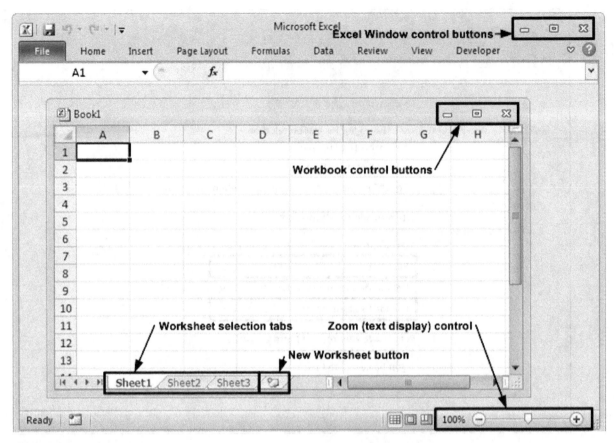

Figure 14
A (nonmaximized) workbook.

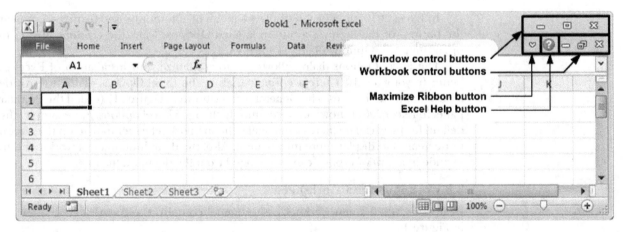

Figure 15
A maximized workbook.

While most small problems are solved using only a single worksheet, the option of using multiple worksheets is very helpful in organizing complex solutions. For example (see Figure 16), you might keep raw data on one worksheet, calculations on a second, and present results on a third.

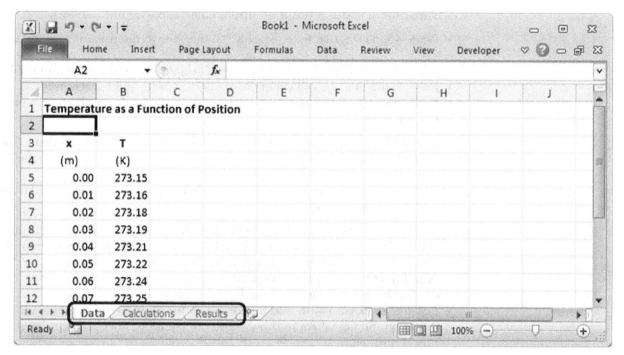

Figure 16
Using worksheets to organize a workbook.

To change the name that is displayed on a worksheet's tab, either double-click the tab or right-click on the tab and select **Rename** from the pop-up menu. The tab's pop-up menu can also be used to insert a new worksheet into the workbook, move a worksheet to a different location in the workbook, or create a copy of a worksheet in the workbook.

3.9 Customizing the Status Bar

The *Status bar* resides at bottom of the Excel window, as shown in Figure 17.

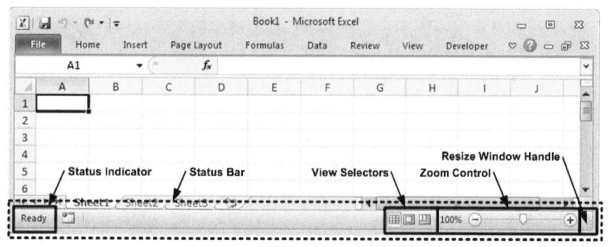

Figure 17
The Status bar.

The status indicator reveals the current mode of operation, as follows:

- **Ready**— indicates that Excel is ready (waiting) for you to type information into a cell.
- **Enter**—Excel goes into *enter mode* when you begin typing information into a cell.
- **Edit**—indicates that a cell's contents are being edited, and Excel is in *edit mode*.
- **Point**—when you use the mouse to point to a cell while entering a formula, Excel jumps to *point mode*.

By default, the right side of the status bar includes a slide control that allows you to quickly zoom in on the active cell. Drag the slide indicator or click on the [+] or [–] buttons to change the zoom level.

The view selectors provide an easy way to change between normal, page layout, and page break preview views.

- **Normal View**—the standard view of the worksheet grid that maximizes the number of cells that can be displayed in the Excel window, but provides no information on how the worksheet will appear when printed.
- **Page Layout View**—this view shows the page margins and any headers or footers. It also includes rulers that can be used to adjust margins.
- **Page Break Preview**—no margins or rulers are shown, but page breaks are shown on the worksheet to show where the breaks will occur when the worksheet is printed.

4 EXCEL BASICS

4.1 The Active Cell

When you start Excel, you see an empty grid on the screen. Each rectangle of the grid is called a *cell*, and you can enter information into any cell in the grid. Each cell is identified by its *cell address*, made up of a column letter and a row number. For example, the cell in the second column from the left and the third row from the top would be called cell B3 (see Figure 18).

When you select a cell, either by clicking with the mouse or by moving the active cell indicator (the cell border shown on cell B3 in Figure 18) using the arrow keys on the keyboard, the selected cell becomes the *active cell*.

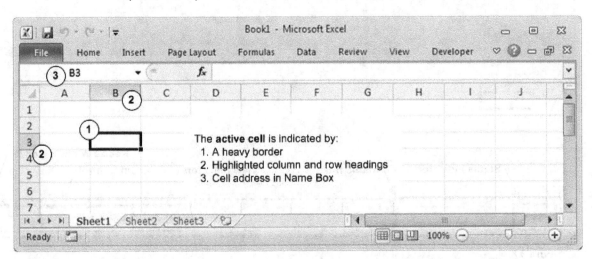

Figure 18
The active cell (B3) is indicated in several ways.

The active cell is indicated in several ways:

1. The active cell is surrounded by a heavy border.
2. The row and column headings of the active cell are highlighted.
3. The cell address of the active cell is shown in the Name box at the left side of the Formula bar.

You always type into the active cell, so any time you want to enter information into Excel, you first select a cell (to make it the active cell) and then enter the information.

4.2 Labels, Numbers, Formulas

A cell can contain one of three things:

- *Label*—one or more text characters or words.
- *Value*—a number.
- *Formula*—an equation.

Excel attempts to classify the cell contents as you type.

- If you enter a number, Excel treats the cell contents as a value, and the numeric value appears in the cell.
- If the first character you type is an equal sign, Excel will try to interpret the cell's contents as a formula (equation).
- If the first character is not a number or an equal sign, Excel will treat the cell contents as a label. You can also use a single quote ['] as the first character to tell Excel to treat the cell contents as a label.

Notes on entering formulas:

1. While you are entering a formula the characters that you type in are displayed (Excel is in entry mode). But, as soon as you press [Enter] to complete the entry, Excel returns to ready mode and displays the result of the calculation in the cell, not the equation.

    Example:

    If you enter the characters = 2 + 4, the formula = 2 + 4 would be stored as the contents of the active cell; however the result, 6, would be displayed. This is illustrated in Figure 19.

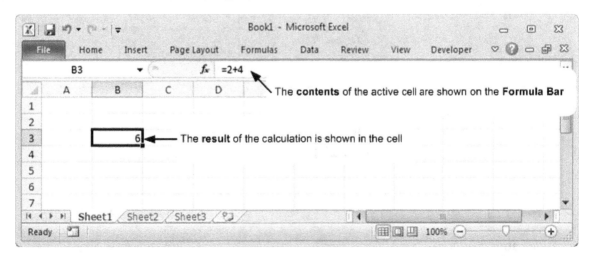

Figure 19
Only the results of a calculation appear in the cell, but the contents of the active cell are displayed in the Formula bar.

2. The formula you entered is still stored in the cell and can be edited. Double-click the cell or press [F2] to edit the contents of the active cell.

3. To inspect a formula in a cell, select the cell to make it the active cell. The contents of the active cell are displayed on the Formula bar.

Formulas are an essential part of using Excel to solve engineering problems. What makes formulas especially useful is the ability to use cell addresses (e.g., B3) as variables in formulas. The following example uses a worksheet to compute a velocity from a distance and a time interval.

EXAMPLE 1

A car drives 90 miles in 1.5 hours. What is the average velocity in miles per hour?

This is a pretty trivial example and illustrates another consideration in the use of an Excel worksheet: single, simple calculations are what calculators are for. A spreadsheet program like Excel is overkill for this example, but we'll use it as the starting point for a more detailed problem.

1. Enter labels as follows:
   • "Distance" in cell B3 and the units "miles" in cell B4.
   • "Time" in cell C3 and the units "hours" in cell C4.
   • "Velocity" in cell D3, with units "mph" in cell D4.
2. Enter values as follows:
   • 90 in cell B5 (i.e., in the Distance column (column B)).
   • 1.5 in cell C5 (i.e., in the Time column (column C)).
3. Enter the formula =B5/C5 in cell D5.

Note that cell D5 in Figure 20:

   • contains a formula =B5/C5, as indicated on the formula bar, but
   • displays the result of the formula (60 miles per hour).

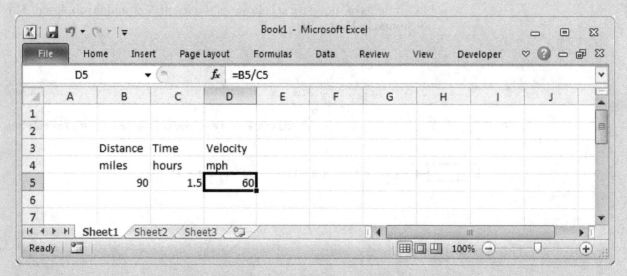

Figure 20
Using cell addresses as variables in a formula.

Note: The formula bar will be included in many screen images in this text to show the contents of the active cell.

4.3 Using the Mouse to Select Cells While Entering Formulas

Typically, when entering formulas you wouldn't actually type cell addresses like the B5 and C5 in the last example. Instead, while you are entering the formula you would enter the equal sign and then click the mouse to tell Excel which cell contents to use in the formula. Specifically, the formula =B5/C5 in cell D5 would be entered as:

1. Make cell D5 the active cell by clicking on it, or moving the active cell indicator to D5 using the keyboard arrow keys.
2. Enter the equal sign [=].
3. Use the mouse and click on cell B5. Excel will show B5 in the formula and, at this point, the formula will read =B5, as shown in Figure 21. Notice that the mouse pointer looks like a large plus sign when you are in Point mode.
4. Type the division operator [/].
5. Use the mouse and click on cell C5. Excel will show C5 in the formula. At this point, the formula will read =B5/C5, as shown in Figure 22.
6. Press [Enter] to complete the formula.

Notes:

1. Pressing an operator such as the [/] key tells Excel that you are done pointing at B5, so you can then use the mouse or arrow keys to point at cell C5. Technically, typing the operator jumps Excel out of Point mode back into Enter mode.
2. While you are entering or editing a formula, Excel shows the cells being used in the formula in color-coded boxes (see Figure 22). This visual indication of the cells that are being used in a calculation is very helpful when checking your worksheet for errors.

Figure 21

Using the mouse to point at cell B5 when needed in a formula.

Figure 22

Using the mouse to point at cell C5 when needed in a formula.

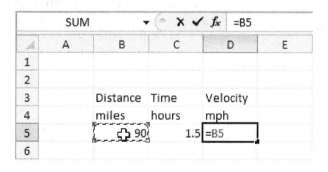

4.4 Copying Cell Ranges to Perform Repetitive Calculations

It is common to perform the same calculation for each value in a column or row of data. Fortunately, Excel makes it easy to perform this type of repetitive calculation; you do not have to type the equation over and over again. Instead, simply copy the formula you typed (in cell D5 in Example 1) to all of the cells that need to calculate a velocity.

EXAMPLE 2

If you have a column of distances (cells B5 through B9) and another column of times (cells C5 through C9) as shown in Figure 23, simply copy the formula in cell D5 to cells D6 through D9.

In Excel, a group of adjacent cells, such as D6 through D9, is called a *cell range* and written as D6:D9.

The procedure for copying the contents of cell D5 to D6:D9 is as follows:

1. Select the cell (or cells, if more than one) containing the formula(s) to be copied. In this example, we simply need to select cell D5.
2. Copy the contents of cell D5 to the Windows clipboard in either of the following ways:
   - Using the copy button on the Ribbon: **Home/Clipboard/Copy**.
   - Using the keyboard shortcut [Ctrl-c]
     Excel uses a dashed border to show the cell that has been copied to the clipboard, as shown in Figure 24.
3. Select the beginning cell of the destination range, cell D6, by clicking on cell D6 or using the down arrow key.
4. Select the entire destination range by dragging the mouse to cell D9 (or, hold the [Shift] key and click on cell D9 or hold the [Shift] key and use the down arrow key to move to cell D9). Excel uses a heavy border to show the selected range of cells, as shown in Figure 25.
5. Paste the information stored on the Windows clipboard (the contents of cell D5, from step 1) into the destination cells (D6:D9) by:

Figure 23
Preparing to copy the velocity formula in cell D5 to cells D6:D9.

	D5	▼	f_x	=B5/C5	
	A	B	C	D	E
1					
2					
3		Distance	Time	Velocity	
4		miles	hours	mph	
5		90	1.5	60	
6		120	6		
7		75	3		
8		80	2		
9		135	9		
10					

Figure 24
A cell that has been copied to the clipboard is shown with a dashed border.

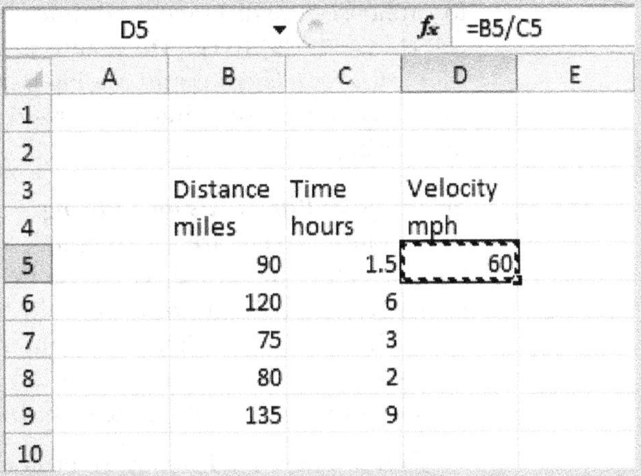

	D5			f_x	=B5/C5
	A	B	C	D	E
1					
2					
3		Distance	Time	Velocity	
4		miles	hours	mph	
5		90	1.5	60	
6		120	6		
7		75	3		
8		80	2		
9		135	9		
10					

Figure 25
A heavy border is used to indicate a selected range of cells.

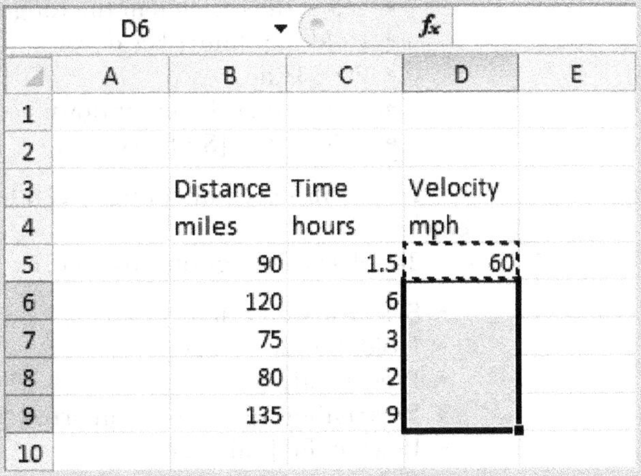

	D6			f_x	
	A	B	C	D	E
1					
2					
3		Distance	Time	Velocity	
4		miles	hours	mph	
5		90	1.5	60	
6		120	6		
7		75	3		
8		80	2		
9		135	9		
10					

Figure 26
Completing the velocity calculations.

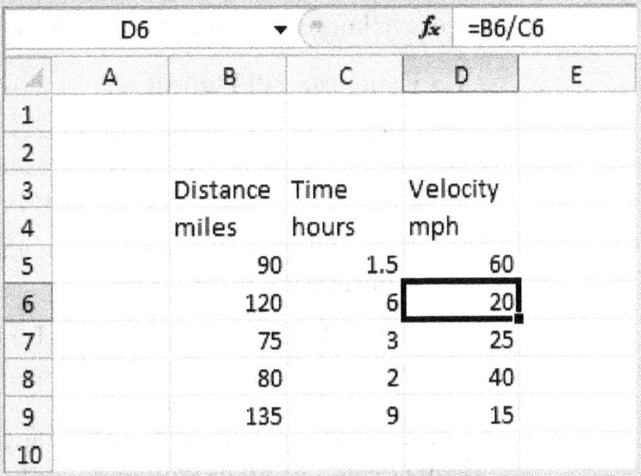

	D6			f_x	=B6/C6
	A	B	C	D	E
1					
2					
3		Distance	Time	Velocity	
4		miles	hours	mph	
5		90	1.5	60	
6		120	6	20	
7		75	3	25	
8		80	2	40	
9		135	9	15	
10					

- Using the paste button on the Ribbon: **Home/Clipboard/Paste**, or
- Using the keyboard shortcut [Ctrl-v]

The result of pasting the velocity formulas into cells D6:D9 is shown in Figure 26.

Notice in Figure 26 that the velocity formula in cell D6 is =B6/C6; that is, the formula uses the distances and times in row 6. When Excel copied the formula in cell D5 (=B5/C5) to cell D6, it automatically incremented the row numbers. This is called *relative addressing* and is a big part of why electronic spreadsheets are so easy to use. Relative addressing is discussed further in Section 4.6, but first a little more on copying and pasting.

Selecting Multiple Cells for Copying

When multiple cells are to be copied, select the source range of cells by clicking on the first cell in the range. Then use the mouse to drag the cursor to the other end of the range (or hold down the shift key while using the mouse or arrow keys to select the cell at the other end of the range). Do not click on the little box at the lower-right corner of a cell. This is the *fill handle*, which is useful for several things, but not for selecting a range of cells. Its use will be described in Section 4.5.

Note: There is a fast way to select a column of values by using the [End] key.

- Select the first cell in the range
- Hold the [Shift] key down
- Press [End]
- Press either the up or down arrow key
- Release the [Shift] key

Excel will select all contiguous filled cells in the column, stopping at the first empty cell.

To select a contiguous row of cells:

- Select an end cell
- Hold the [Shift] key down
- Press [End]
- Press either the left or right arrow key
- Release the [Shift] key

It is pretty straightforward to copy and paste using the procedures listed in this section, but Excel provides an even easier approach; it's called the *fill handle*.

4.5 Using the Fill Handle

The small square at the bottom-right corner of the active cell border is called the *fill handle*. If the cell contains a formula and you grab and drag the fill handle, the formula will be copied to all of the cells you select in the drag operation.

Note: *Dragging the mouse* simply implies holding the left-mouse button down while moving the mouse.

After selecting the source cell (D5 in our example), grab the fill handle of the selected cell with the mouse and drag, as shown in Figure 27.

The destination range will be outlined as you drag, as shown in Figure 27. Continue dragging until the entire range (cell range D5:D9) is outlined. The mouse icon changes to a plus symbol when the fill handle is in use.

When you have selected the desired destination range, release the mouse. Excel will copy the contents of the original cell to the entire destination range. The result is shown in Figure 28.

The little square icon next to the fill handle after the copy is a link to a pop-up menu that allows you to modify how the copy process is carried out. If you click on

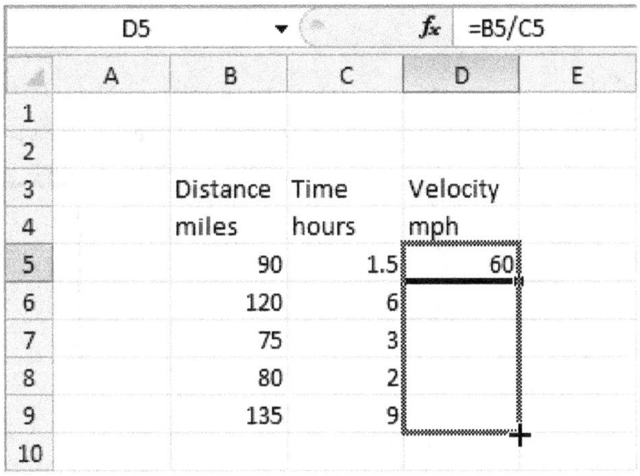

Figure 27

Using the fill handle to copy and paste in a single operation.

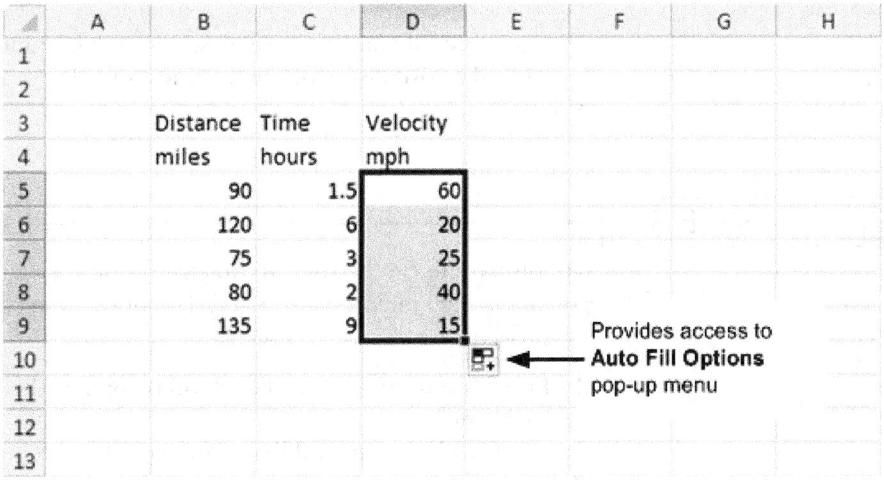

	D5	▼		f_x	=B5/C5

	A	B	C	D	E
1					
2					
3		Distance	Time	Velocity	
4		miles	hours	mph	
5		90	1.5	60	
6		120	6		
7		75	3		
8		80	2		
9		135	9		
10					

Figure 28

After using the fill handle, a pop-up menu of fill options is available.

	A	B	C	D	E	F	G	H
1								
2								
3		Distance	Time	Velocity				
4		miles	hours	mph				
5		90	1.5	60				
6		120	6	20				
7		75	3	25				
8		80	2	40				
9		135	9	15				
10								
11								
12								
13								

Provides access to **Auto Fill Options** pop-up menu

the icon, a pop-up menu will appear with some options for how the copy using the fill handle should be completed (see Figure 29).

The **Copy Cells** option (default) copies both the contents and the formatting of the source cell. Other options allow you to copy only the contents or only the formatting.

The fill handle can be used for other purposes as well:

- To fill a range with a series of values incremented by one, place the first value (not formula) in a cell and then drag the fill handle with the left-mouse button to create the range of values.
- If you want a range of values with an increment other than one, enter the first two values of the series in adjacent cells, select both cells as the source, and drag the fill handle with the left-mouse button.
- If you want a nonlinear fill, enter the first two values of the series in adjacent cells, select both cells as the source, and drag the fill handle by using the right-mouse button. When you release the mouse, a menu will be displayed giving a variety of fill options.

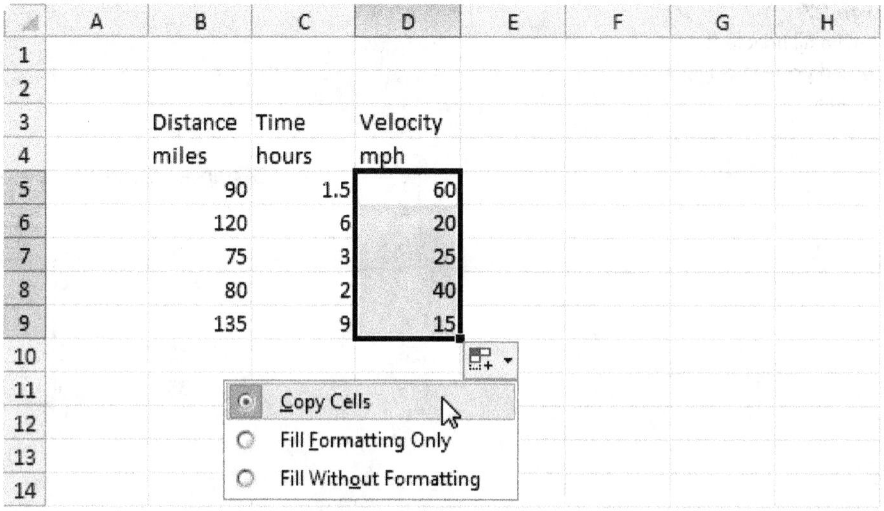

Figure 29
The Auto Fill Options pop-up menu after using the fill handle to copy and paste.

◢	A	B	C	D	E	F	G	H
1								
2								
3		Distance	Time	Velocity				
4		miles	hours	mph				
5		90	1.5	60				
6		120	6	20				
7		75	3	25				
8		80	2	40				
9		135	9	15				
10								
11			⦿ Copy Cells					
12			○ Fill Formatting Only					
13			○ Fill Without Formatting					
14								

Using the fill handle to create series of data values is very handy, but the operations listed above also work with times and dates, as Illustrated in the following example.

EXAMPLE 3

The fill handle can be used to quickly set up a class schedule showing hours from 8:00 am to 4:00 pm on the left and days of the week across the top.

Procedure:

1. Enter "8 am" in cell B3. (Excel will recognize that the entry is a time and display "8:00 am.")
2. Use the fill handle and drag from cell B3 to cell B11.
3. Enter "Monday" in cell C2.
4. Use the fill handle and drag from cell C2 to cell G2.

The result is shown in Figure 30.

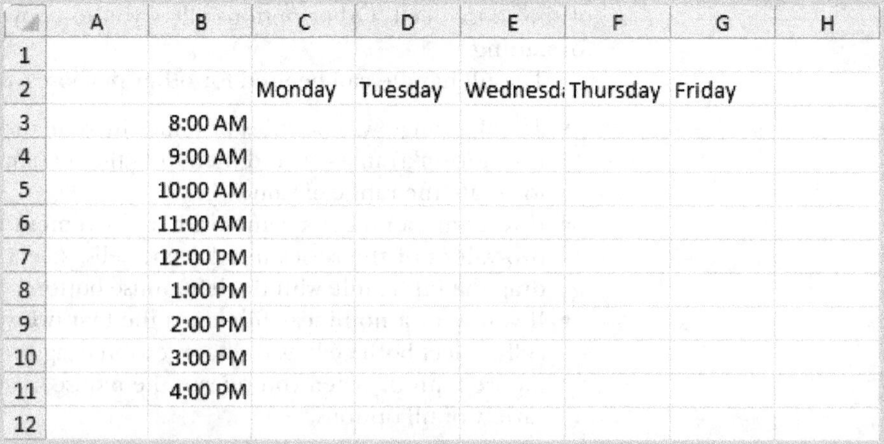

Figure 30
Using the fill handle to create a class schedule.

◢	A	B	C	D	E	F	G	H
1								
2			Monday	Tuesday	Wednesd:	Thursday	Friday	
3		8:00 AM						
4		9:00 AM						
5		10:00 AM						
6		11:00 AM						
7		12:00 PM						
8		1:00 PM						
9		2:00 PM						
10		3:00 PM						
11		4:00 PM						
12								

The next step would be to enter your classes in the appropriate cells, and some formatting is needed to display all of "Wednesday."

4.6 Relative and Absolute Addressing

Returning to the velocity calculation example (Example 2), we used the fill handle to copy the formula entered in cell D5 to cells D6:D9. The result is shown in Figure 31.

At this point, the contents of cell D5 have been copied, with significant modifications, to cells D6:D9. As you can see in the formula bar in Figure 31, cell D6 contains the formula =B6/C6.

As the formula =B5/C5 in cell D5 was copied from row 5 to row 6, the row numbers in the formula were incremented by one, so the formula in cell D6 is =B6/C6. Similarly, as the formula was copied from row 5 to row 7, the row numbers in the formula were incremented by two and the formula =B7/C7 was stored in cell D7. So, the velocity calculated in cell D7 uses the distance and time values from row 7, as desired. This automatic incrementing of cell addresses during the copy process is called *relative cell addressing* and is an important feature of electronic spreadsheets.

Note: If you had copied the formula in D5 across to cell E5, the column letters would have been incremented. If you had copied the formula in D5 diagonally to cell E9, both the row numbers and column letters would have been incremented.

- Copying down increments row numbers
- Copying across increments column letters
- Copying diagonally increments both row numbers and column letters

Sometimes you don't want relative addressing; you want the cell address to be copied unchanged. This is called *absolute cell addressing*.

You can make any address absolute in a formula by including dollar signs in the address, as $B$5. The nomenclature $B$5 tells Excel not to automatically increment either the B or the 5 while copying. Similarly, $B5 tells Excel it is OK to increment the 5, but not the B during a copy, and B$5 tells Excel it is OK to increment the B, but not the 5. During a copy, any row or column designation preceded by a $ is left alone. One common use of absolute addressing is building a constant into your calculations, as illustrated in Example 4.

Figure 31

The result of copying the velocity formula in cell D5 to cells D6:D9.

D6			f_x	=B6/C6	
	A	B	C	D	E
1					
2					
3		Distance	Time	Velocity	
4		miles	hours	mph	
5		90	1.5	60	
6		120	6	20	
7		75	3	25	
8		80	2	40	
9		135	9	15	
10					

EXAMPLE 4

Modify the worksheet developed for Example 2 to display the velocities in feet per second. The conversion factor between miles per hour (mph) and feet per second (fps) is 1.467 fps/mph.

First, we need to get the conversion factor onto the worksheet. To help keep things organized, I typically place constants and parameter values near the top of the worksheet, where they are easy to find. This has been done in Figure 32.

Figure 32
Adding the conversion factor to the worksheet.

	D5				f_x	=B5/C5	
	A	B	C	D	E		
1	Factor:		1.467	fps/mph			
2							
3		Distance	Time		Velocity		
4		miles	hours		mph		
5		90	1.5		60		
6		120	6		20		
7		75	3		25		
8		80	2		40		
9		135	9		15		
10							

Notice that the label (cell A1), value (cell B1), and units (cell C1) are in three different cells. The value must be in a cell by itself so that Excel treats it as a value (a number) rather than as a label.

Next, we use the conversion factor in the formulas in column D. We change (edit or reenter) one formula to include the conversion factor (and change the units on velocity in cell D4).

Notice (Figure 33) that an absolute address has been used for the conversion factor in the formula in cell D5. The $B$1 will not be changed when this formula is copied.

Finally, use the fill handle to copy the formula to cells D6:D9. The result is shown in Figure 34. Notice that after copying the formula in cell D5 to cell D6, the new formula still references the conversion factor in cell B1. The dollar signs on $B$1 told Excel not to increment the cell address when the formula was copied.

Figure 33
Editing the velocity formula to include the conversion factor.

	D5				f_x	=B5/C5*$B$1	
	A	B	C	D	E		
1	Factor:		1.467	fps/mph			
2							
3		Distance	Time		Velocity		
4		miles	hours		fps		
5		90	1.5		88.0		
6		120	6				
7		75	3				
8		80	2				
9		135	9				
10							

Figure 34
The resulting velocities, in feet per second.

	D6				f_x	=B6/C6*$B$1
	A	B	C	D	E	
1	Factor:	1.467	fps/mph			
2						
3		Distance	Time	Velocity		
4		miles	hours	fps		
5		90	1.5	88.0		
6		120	6	29.3		
7		75	3	36.7		
8		80	2	58.7		
9		135	9	22.0		
10						

FLUID STATICS

The pressure at the bottom of a column of fluid is caused by the mass of the fluid, m, being acted on by the acceleration due to gravity, $g = 9.8$ m/s^2. The resulting force is called the weight of the fluid, F_W and can be calculated as

$$F_W = mg \tag{1}$$

which is a specific version of Newton's law when the acceleration is due to the earth's gravity. The pressure at the bottom of the column is the force divided by the area of the bottom of the column, A:

$$P = \frac{F_W}{A} = \frac{mg}{A} \tag{2}$$

The mass of the fluid can be calculated as the density, ρ, times the fluid volume, V.

$$P = \frac{F_W}{A} = \frac{mg}{A} = \frac{\rho V g}{A} \tag{3}$$

The fluid volume is calculated as area of the column, A, times its height, h.

$$P = \frac{F_W}{A} = \frac{mg}{A} = \frac{\rho V g}{A} = \frac{\rho A h g}{A} = \rho h g \tag{4}$$

Determine the pressure at the bottom of a column of mercury 760 mm high. The specific gravity of mercury is 13.6, meaning that mercury is 13.6 times as dense as water.

Do not consider any imposed pressure (e.g., air pressure) on the top of the column in this problem.

The solution is shown in Figure 35.

The equations in cells C9 through C12 are as follows:

```
C9:      =C5/1000
C10:     =C6*1000
C11:     =C10*C9*C4   or,  ρ·h·g
C12:     =C11/101300; the conversion factor between pascals
         and atmospheres is 101300 Pa/atm
```

APPLICATIONS

27

Figure 35
Determining the pressure at the bottom of a column of fluid.

	C11		▼	f_x	=C10*C9*C4	
	A	B	C	D	E	
1	**Pressure at the Bottom of a Column of Fluid**					
2						
3	**Information from Problem Statement**					
4	Grav. Acceleration:		9.8	m/s^2		
5	Column Height:		760	mm		
6	Specific Gravity:		13.6			
7						
8	**Calculated Values**					
9	Column Height (SI):		0.76	m		
10	Density:		13600	kg/m^3		
11	Pressure:		101293	Pa, or N/m^2		
12	Pressure:		1.00	atm		
13						

Create the worksheet shown in Figure 35 and use it to determine the pressure at the bottom of the columns of fluid specified below. [Do not consider any imposed pressure (e.g., air pressure) on the top of the column.]

a. A column of water 10 m high (SG$_{water}$ = 1.0) [Answer: 0.97 atm]
b. A column of seawater 11,000 m high. This is the depth of the Marianas Trench, the deepest spot known in the earth's oceans (SG$_{seawater}$ = 1.03) (ignore the variation in water density with pressure). [Answer: 1090 atm]

Letting Excel Add the Dollar Signs

You don't actually have to enter the dollar signs used to indicate absolute cell addresses by hand. If you enter cell address B1 and then press the [F4] key, Excel will automatically enter the dollar signs for you. Pressing [F4] once converts B1 to $B$1. Pressing the [F4] key multiple times changes the number and arrangement of the dollar signs, as follows:

- Press [F4] once $B$1
- Press [F4] a second time   B$1
- Press [F4] a third time $B1
- Press [F4] a fourth time   B1

In practice, you simply press [F4] until you get the dollar signs where you want them.

If you use the mouse to point to a cell in a formula, you must press [F4] right after you click on the cell. You can also use [F4] while editing a formula; just move the edit cursor to the cell address that needs the dollar signs and then press [F4].

Using Named Cells

Excel supports *named cells*, allowing you to assign descriptive names to individual cells or ranges of cells. Then you can use the names, rather than the cell addresses, in formulas. For example, the cell containing the conversion factor in the Example 4 (cell B1 in Figure 34) might be given the name, **ConvFactor**. This name could then be used in the velocity formulas instead of $B$1.

To give a single cell a name, click on the cell (cell B1 in this example) and enter the name in the Name box at the left side of the formula bar, as illustrated in Figure 36.

The name can then be used in place of the cell address in the velocity formulas, as in the formula in cell D5 in Figure 37.

Figure 36

Cell B1 has been assigned the name, ConvFactor.

	A	B	C	D	E
	ConvFactor			f_x	1.467
1	Factor:	1.467	fps/mph		
2					
3		Distance	Time	Velocity	
4		miles	hours	fps	
5		90	1.5	88.0	
6		120	6	29.3	
7		75	3	36.7	
8		80	2	58.7	
9		135	9	22.0	
10					

Figure 37

Using a named cell in a formula.

	A	B	C	D	E	F
	D5			f_x	=B5/C5*ConvFactor	
1	Factor:	1.467	fps/mph			
2						
3		Distance	Time	Velocity		
4		miles	hours	fps		
5		90	1.5	88.0		
6		120	6			
7		75	3			
8		80	2			
9		135	9			
10						

Using named cells in your formulas can make them easier to comprehend.

When the formula in cell D5 is copied to cells D6 through D9, the cell name is included in the formulas, as shown in cell D6 in Figure 38.

Notice that ConvFactor copied in the same way that $B$1 had copied previously. A cell name acts as an absolute cell address and is not modified when a formula is copied.

Naming Cell Ranges

It is also possible to assign names to cell ranges, such as the columns of distance values. To assign a name to a cell range, first select the range and then enter the name in the name box as shown in Figure 39.

Figure 38
Named cells act as absolute cell addresses when copied.

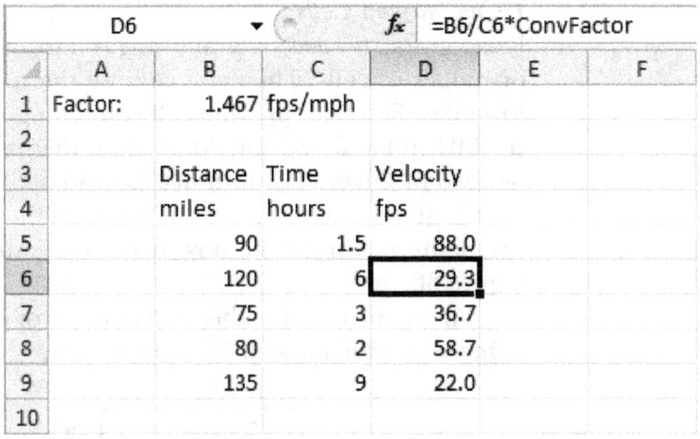

	D6		▼	f_x	=B6/C6*ConvFactor	
	A	B	C	D	E	F
1	Factor:	1.467	fps/mph			
2						
3		Distance	Time	Velocity		
4		miles	hours	fps		
5		90	1.5	88.0		
6		120	6	29.3		
7		75	3	36.7		
8		80	2	58.7		
9		135	9	22.0		
10						

Figure 39
Naming a cell range. Here, cell range B5:B9 has been named "Distance."

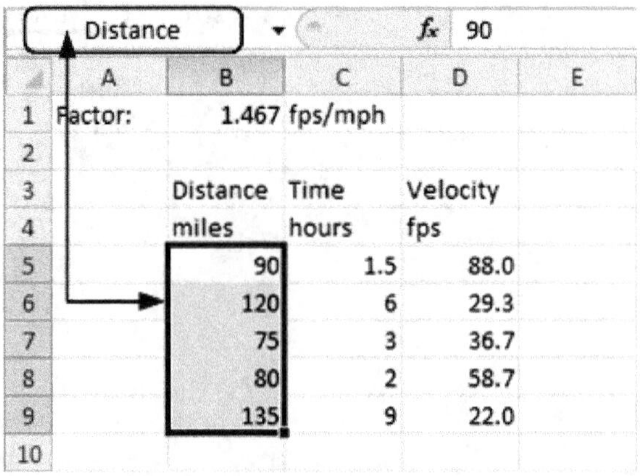

	Distance		▼	f_x	90	
	A	B	C	D	E
1	Factor:	1.467	fps/mph		
2					
3		Distance	Time	Velocity	
4		miles	hours	fps	
5		90	1.5	88.0	
6		120	6	29.3	
7		75	3	36.7	
8		80	2	58.7	
9		135	9	22.0	
10					

Figure 40
Using a cell range name in a function.

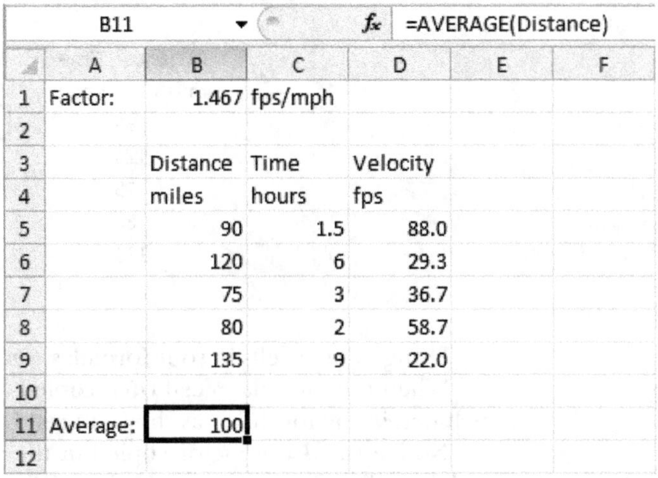

	B11		▼	f_x	=AVERAGE(Distance)	
	A	B	C	D	E	F
1	Factor:	1.467	fps/mph			
2						
3		Distance	Time	Velocity		
4		miles	hours	fps		
5		90	1.5	88.0		
6		120	6	29.3		
7		75	3	36.7		
8		80	2	58.7		
9		135	9	22.0		
10						
11	Average:	100				
12						

The name can then be used in place of the cell range, as in the =AVERAGE(Distance) formula in cell B11 in Figure 40. (**AVERAGE** is Excel's built-in function for calculating the arithmetic average of a set of values.)

If you have assigned a name and decide to remove it, use Ribbon commands **Formulas/Name Manager** to see a list of the defined names in the worksheet. [Excel 2003: Insert/Name/Define.]

Figure 41
The Name Manager
dialog.

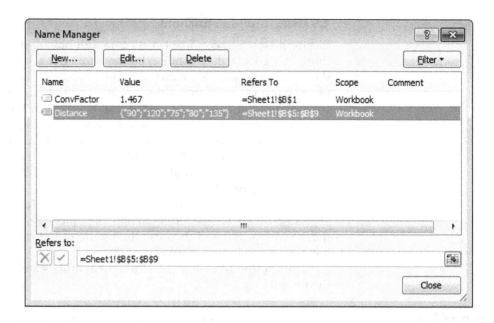

Select the name to remove, and then click the Delete button. Any formula that was using the deleted name will show the error message, **#NAME**?, since the name in the formula will no longer be recognized.

Notice in Figure 41 that both the named cell (ConvFactor) and the named cell range (Distance) show "Workbook" as their *scope*. This means that the name will be recognized throughout the workbook; that is, you can use these names in any worksheet in the workbook. By default, any name you create using the Name Box will have a workbook scope.

4.8 Editing the Active Cell

You can enter *edit mode* to change the contents of the active cell either by double-clicking the cell or by selecting the cell and then pressing [F2]. Be sure to press [Enter] when you are done editing the cell contents, or your next mouse click will change your formula.

> **Note:** Changing a formula that was previously copied to another range of cells does not cause the contents of the other cells to be similarly modified. If the change should be made to each cell in the range, edit one cell, then re-copy the cell range.

You can edit either on the Formula bar or right in the active cell if this option is activated. (Excel's default is to allow editing in cells.) The editing process is the same whether you edit directly in the cell or use the Formula bar. About the only time it makes a difference is when you want to edit a long formula in a cell near the right edge of the Excel window; then the extra space in the Formula bar is useful.

Excel's defaults are to show the Formula bar and allow editing directly in cells. However, if you are using a shared computer, someone could have turned these features off.

* To activate or deactivate editing in the active cell, use the **File** tab (Office button in Excel 2007) and select **Options/Advanced** panel and use the checkbox labeled **Allow editing directly in cells**.
* To show or hide the Formula bar, use Ribbon options **View/[Show/Hide]** and use the **Formula Bar** checkbox.

4.9 Using Built-In Functions

Electronic spreadsheets like Excel come with built-in functions to do lots of handy things. Originally, they handled business functions, but newer versions of spreadsheet programs also have many additional functions useful to engineers. For example, you can compute the arithmetic average and standard deviation of a column (or row) of values using Excel's **AVERAGE** and **STDEV** functions. These functions work on a range of values, so we'll have to tell the spreadsheet which values to include in the computation of the average and standard deviation.

In the last example (Figure 40), we calculated the average distance. Without using cell names, the formula could be written as =AVERAGE(B5:B9) as shown in cell B11 in Figure 42.

Again, you don't normally enter the entire formula from the keyboard. Typically, you would type the equal sign, the function name, and the opening parenthesis =AVERAGE(, and then use the mouse to indicate the range of values to be included in the formula (see Figure 43).

Then you would enter the closing parenthesis and press [Enter] to complete the formula.

Figure 42
Using the **AVERAGE** function.

	A	B	C	D	E	F
		B11		f_x =AVERAGE(B5:B9)		
1	Factor:	1.467	fps/mph			
2						
3		Distance	Time	Velocity		
4		miles	hours	fps		
5		90	1.5	88.0		
6		120	6	29.3		
7		75	3	36.7		
8		80	2	58.7		
9		135	9	22.0		
10						
11	Average:	100				
12						

Figure 43
Using the mouse to select the cell range for the **AVERAGE** function.

	A	B	C	D	E	F
		SUM		× ✓ f_x =AVERAGE(B5:B9		
1	Factor:	1.467	fps/mph			
2						
3		Distance	Time	Velocity		
4		miles	hours	fps		
5		90	1.5	88.0		
6		120	6	29.3		
7		75	3	36.7		
8		80	2	58.7		
9		135	9	22.0		
10						
11	Average:	=AVERAGE(B5:B9				
12		AVERAGE(**number1**, [number2], ...)				
13						

Figure 44
Using the **STDEV** function.

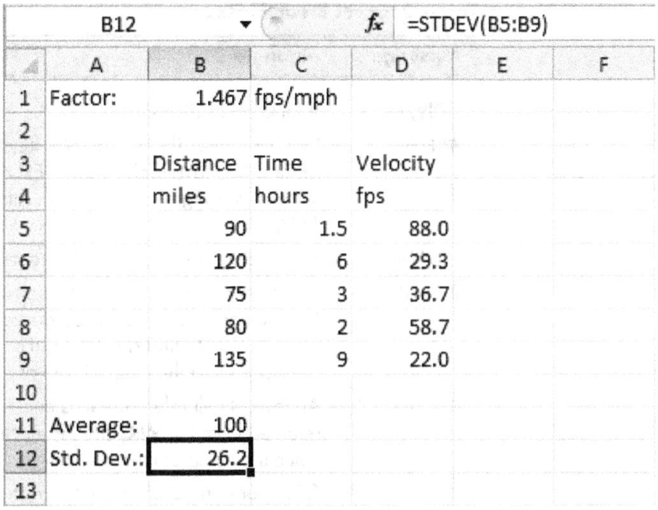

	B12	▾	f_x	=STDEV(B5:B9)		
	A	B	C	D	E	F
1	Factor:	1.467	fps/mph			
2						
3		Distance	Time	Velocity		
4		miles	hours	fps		
5		90	1.5	88.0		
6		120	6	29.3		
7		75	3	36.7		
8		80	2	58.7		
9		135	9	22.0		
10						
11	Average:	100				
12	Std. Dev.:	26.2				
13						

Figure 45
Copying cells B11:B12
to columns C and D.

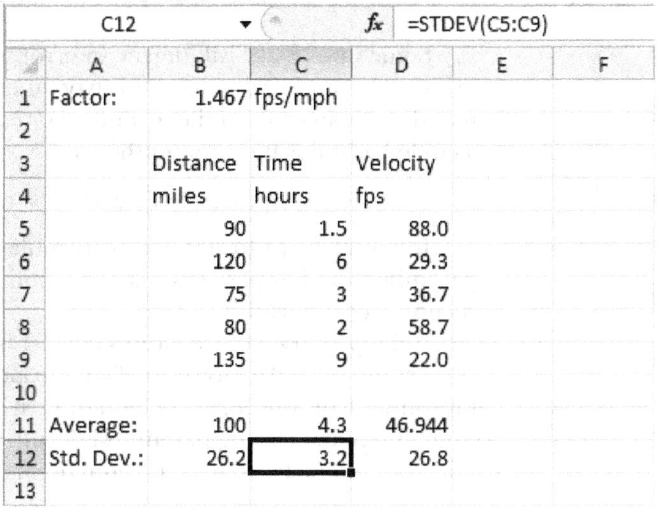

	C12	▾	f_x	=STDEV(C5:C9)		
	A	B	C	D	E	F
1	Factor:	1.467	fps/mph			
2						
3		Distance	Time	Velocity		
4		miles	hours	fps		
5		90	1.5	88.0		
6		120	6	29.3		
7		75	3	36.7		
8		80	2	58.7		
9		135	9	22.0		
10						
11	Average:	100	4.3	46.944		
12	Std. Dev.:	26.2	3.2	26.8		
13						

To compute the standard deviation of the distance values, use the same process with Excel's **STDEV** function, as shown in Figure 44.

To compute the averages and standard deviations of the Time and Velocity columns, simply copy the source range, B11:B12, to the destination range C11:D11. (Yes, D11, not D12—you tell Excel where to copy the top-left corner of the source range, not the entire source range.) The final worksheet is shown in Figure 45; cell C12 has been selected to show the contents.

4.10 Error Messages in Excel

Sometimes Excel cannot recognize the function you are trying to use (e.g., when the function name is misspelled) or cannot perform the requested math operation (e.g., because of a divide by zero). When this happens, Excel puts a brief error message in the cell to let you know that something went wrong. Some common error messages are listed in Table 2.

When these error messages are displayed, they indicate that Excel detected an error in the formula contained in the cell. The solution involves fixing the formula or the values in the other cells that the formula references.

Table 2 Excel Error Messages

Message	Meaning
#DIV/0	Attempted to divide by zero.
#N/A	Not available. There is an **NA** function in Excel that returns #N/A, meaning that the result is "not available." Some Excel functions return #N/A for certain errors, such as failures in using a lookup table. Attempts to do math with #N/A values also return #N/A.
#NAME?	Excel could not recognize the name of the function, cell, or cell range you tried to use.
#NUM!	Not a valid number. A function or math operation returned an invalid numeric value (e.g., a value too large to be displayed). This error message is also displayed if a function fails to find a solution. (For example, the **IRR** function uses an iterative solution to find the internal rate of return and may fail.)
#REF!	An invalid cell reference was encountered. For example, this error message is returned from the **VLOOKUP** function if the column index number (offset) points at a column outside of the table range.
#VALUE!	This error can occur when the wrong type of argument is passed to a function, or when you try to use math operators on something other than a value (such as a text string).

Sometimes Excel will detect an error when you press [Enter] to save a formula in a cell. When Excel detects this type of error, it pops up a message box indicating that there is an error in the formula. For example, the following formula for area of a circle has unbalanced parentheses:

$$\texttt{=PI()*(B3/2\^{}2}\quad\text{should be}\quad\texttt{=PI()*(B3/2)\^{}2}$$

If you attempt to enter this formula in a cell, Excel will detect the missing parenthesis and display a message box indicating the problem and proposing a correction (see Figure 46).

If the proposed correction is correct, simply click the **Yes** button and let Excel correct the formula. However, if the proposed solution is not correct, click the **No** button and fix the formula by hand. In this example, the proposed correction would place the closing parenthesis in the wrong place, so the formula must be corrected by hand. The corrected equation is shown in Figure 47.

Figure 46
Excel will (often) propose corrections when errors are detected in your formulas.

Figure 47
The corrected formula for the area of a circle.

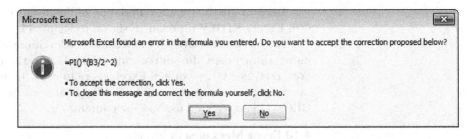

5 ORGANIZING YOUR WORKSHEETS

Computer programs, including Excel worksheets, typically contain the following standard elements:

- **Titles**: including a problem description and identifying the author(s)
- **Input Values**: values entered by the user when the worksheet is used
- **Formulas**: the equations that calculate results based on the input values
- **Results**: the computed values

Your worksheets will be easier to create and use if you group these elements together (when possible) and develop a standard placement of these items on your worksheets. These elements can be placed anywhere, but, for small problems, a common placement puts titles at the top followed by input values further down the page. Formulas and results are placed even further down the page. This layout is illustrated in Figure 48.

One feature of this approach is that the information flows down the page, making the worksheet easier to read. One drawback of this approach is that the results are separated from the input values, making it harder to prepare a report showing the input values and the calculated results together.

The layout shown in Figure 49 puts the input values next to the results, but can be harder to read, because the information flow is not simply from top to bottom.

The layout illustrated in Figure 50 is often used when the input values include columns of data values.

Figure 48

A common worksheet layout for small problems.

	A	B	C	D	E	F	G	H
1								
2		Title, Author, Date						
3								
4								
5		Input Values (usually from the problem statement)						
6								
7								
8		Formulas (calculated values)						
9								
10								
11		Results						
12								
13								

Figure 49

A modified layout that keeps the results near the input values.

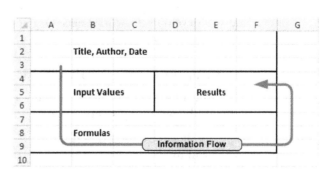

Figure 50

A worksheet layout suitable for working with columns of data values.

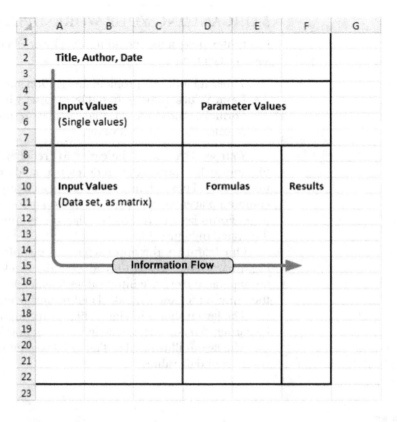

Figure 51

Large problems can be organized by using multiple worksheets.

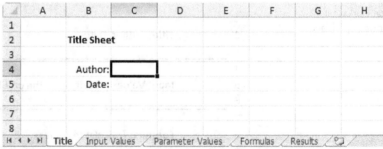

When the problem requires a lot of space on the worksheet (several screens), it can be convenient to put the input values, formulas, and results on different worksheets within the same workbook, as illustrated in Figure 51.

There is no single layout that works for all problems, but taking time to organize your worksheets and being consistent with your layouts will make your life easier as you develop your worksheets. Organized worksheets are also easier for others to understand and use.

6 PRINTING THE WORKSHEET

Printing an Excel worksheet is usually a two- or three-step process. For small worksheets, the two-step process includes:

1. Set the area to be printed
2. Print the worksheet

For larger worksheets, or when you want to modify print options, include an additional step:

1. Set the area to be printed
2. Set print options using the Print dialog (Excel 2007: Print Preview screen)
3. Print the worksheet

6.1 Setting the Print Area

By default, Excel will print the rectangular region of the currently selected worksheet that includes all nonempty cells. If you want all of the cells that you have used to print, then you can skip the "set print area" step.

To specify exactly which cells to print, use the mouse to select the region of the spreadsheet that should be printed (see Figure 52). Then use Ribbon options **Page Layout/Page Setup/Print Area/Set Print Area** [Excel 2003: File/Print Area/Set Print Area].

Figure 52
Setting the print area.

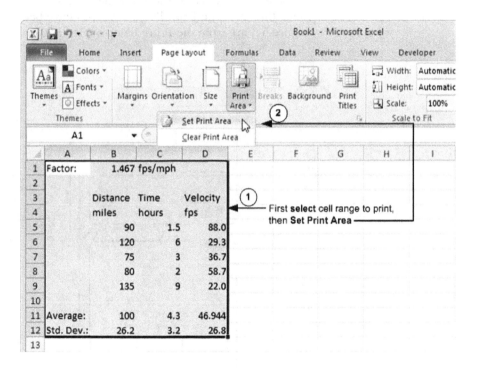

Once a print area has been set, Excel shows the region that will be printed with dashed lines, as shown in Figure 53. If multiple pages are to be printed, Excel also shows the page breaks with dashed lines.

6.2 Printing Using Current Options

Once the desired print area has been set, you can print the worksheet as follows:

- Excel 2010: **File tab/Print**
- Excel 2007: **Office/Print**
- Excel 2003: **File/Print**

Figure 53
Once a print area has been set, dashed lines show the print area.

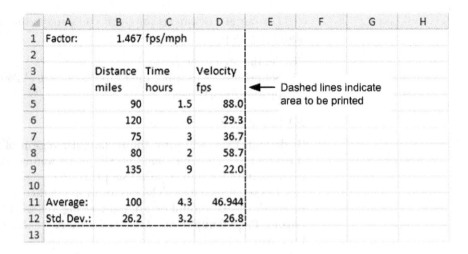

The appearance of the Print dialog has changed significantly in Excel 2010, since the Print and Print Preview dialogs have been combined. Images here (e.g., Figure 54) are from the Print dialog in Excel 2010.

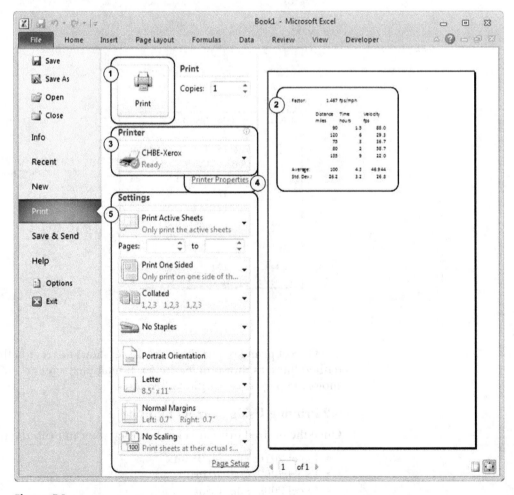

Figure 54
The Print dialog (the appearance of this dialog may vary depending on the features available on your printer).

The following items are indicated in Figure 54:

1. The **Print** button—click this button to send the data to your printer.
2. The Print Preview area—a preview of your printout is displayed at the right side of the Print dialog.
3. The Printer that will be used—use the drop-down list to select another printer.
4. **Printer Properties** link—click this link to access the printer's control dialog.
5. Printer **Settings**—common printer settings are available directly from the Print dialog in Excel 2010. In previous versions, these were accessed via the printer's control dialog or from the Ribbon's Page Layout tab. These options are still available in Excel 2010.

> **Note:** You can customize the Quick Access Toolbar to include a **Quick Print** button. If you use the Quick Print button, the currently selected area of the current worksheet will print without displaying the Print dialog.

6.3 Changing Printing Options

There are several ways to change printing options with Excel; here we focus on using the Ribbon's **Page Layout** tab (Figure 55) to control how the worksheet will print.

Expand Button
Opens the **Page Setup** dialog

Figure 55
The Ribbon's Page Layout tab.

Page Layout Tab/Page Setup Group
The **Page Setup** group allows you to set or modify the following print features:

- *Margins:* Choose predefined or custom margins for the printed pages.
- *Orientation:* Select portrait or landscape printing.
- *Size:* Choose the desired paper size.
- *Print Area:* First select the desired cell region, then use the Print Area button to set the print area.
- *Breaks:* Insert page breaks; Excel will insert them automatically when needed.
- *Background:* Choose a background image for your worksheet.
- *Print Titles:* Select cells that contain titles that should be included on every printed page.

One of the few features that is not directly accessible from the Page Layout tab is the ability to add a header and/or footer to a printed worksheet. Headers and footers are text lines that appear in the margins of the printout that are used to provide information about the worksheet, like file name, page number, and print date.

To add a header or footer, click the **Expand** button at the bottom-right corner of the **Page Setup** group to open the Page Setup dialog shown in Figure 56.

You can use the drop-down lists to select from standard headers and footers, or you can click the **Custom Header ...** or **Custom Footer ...** buttons to create your own. Clicking the **Custom Header ...** button opens the Header dialog shown in Figure 57.

Figure 56
The Page Setup dialog,
Header/Footer Tab.

Figure 57
The Header dialog.

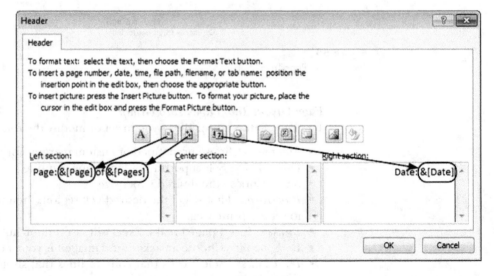

You can type into any of the sections (left, center, or right) to include text in the header. But the buttons just above the entry fields provide an easy way to include:

- Current page number (set while printing)
- Number of pages
- Current date (while printing)
- Current time (at start of printing)
- File path (drive and folder(s))
- File name
- Worksheet name

Using a header and/or footer is an easy way to add page numbers to your printed worksheets. In Figure 57, the header has been set to indicate the current page number (e.g., Page: 1 of 4) on the left and the date on which the worksheet was printed on the right.

Page Layout Tab/Scale to Fit Group

A handy printing feature is the ability to scale your worksheet to fit to a limited number of pages. There are many times when it is convenient to force a worksheet to print on a single sheet or paper. To do so, use the Ribbon's **Page Layout** tab and **Scale to Fit** group. Set the **Width** and **Height** options (see Figure 58) to "1 page" to force the printed worksheet to fit onto a single sheet of paper.

Figure 58

Set the Width and Height options to "1 page" to force the printed worksheet to fit onto a single sheet of paper.

Page Layout Tab/Sheet Options Group

When the reader needs to understand the formulas used in a worksheet, it is very helpful to print the worksheet showing the gridlines and (column and row) headings. To instruct Excel to include gridlines and headings on the printout, use the **Print** checkboxes in the **Sheet Options** group, as shown in Figure 59.

Figure 59

Use the **Print** checkboxes for **Gridlines** and **Headings** (cell labels) when you want them to appear on the printout.

Changing Print Options for Multiple Worksheets

When you use Ribbon options to set print options, you are setting the print options only for the currently selected worksheet. If you need to print multiple worksheets in a workbook and want them to have the same margins (and other print options), first select all of the worksheets to be printed before setting the print options. The print options that you select will then apply to all selected worksheets.

To select multiple worksheets, hold the [Ctrl] key down while you click on each worksheet's tab (near the bottom of the Excel window).

CAUTION: Be sure to de-select multiple worksheets before editing any cells because any cell changes will also be applied to all selected worksheets.

7 SAVING AND OPENING WORKBOOKS, EXITING EXCEL

7.1 Saving the Workbook

To save the workbook as a file, press the **Save** button (looks like a diskette) on the Quick Access toolbar or use:

- Excel 2010: **File tab/Save**
- Excel 2007: **Office/Save**
- Excel 2003: **File/Save**

If the workbook has not been saved before, you will be asked to enter a file name in the Save As dialog box.

Notes:

1. In Windows, it is generally preferable not to add an extension to the file name. Excel will allow you to add an extension, but the file name will not appear in any future selection box unless Excel's default extension is used. If you do not include a file name extension, Excel will add its default extension, .xlsx.

2. Prior to Excel 2007, Excel's default file extension was .xls. The new file extension with Excel 2007 indicates that the latest version of Excel is saving files in a new file format. Files saved with the new file format and with the new .xlsx extension cannot be read by earlier versions of Excel. If you need to maintain compatibility with a previous version of Excel, use **Save As** and select **Excel 97-2003 Workbook** as the type of file format to use. This causes Excel to use the old file format and the old .xls extension.

7.2 Opening a Previously Saved Workbook

To open an existing Excel workbook:

- Excel 2010: **File tab/Open**
- Excel 2007: **Office/Open**
- Excel 2003: **File/Open**

Then select the workbook file you wish to use from the Open File dialog box.

7.3 Setting AutoRecover Options

By default, Excel saves a backup, called an *AutoRecover file*, of any workbook you are editing. This is done every 10 minutes. When you successfully save your work and exit Excel, the AutoRecover file is deleted. But, if something goes wrong (e.g., power failure) and you don't exit Excel cleanly, the next time you start Excel you will have a chance to recover most of your lost work via the AutoRecover file.

To verify or modify the AutoRecover settings, use the Excel Options dialog available using the **Options** button on the **File** tab [Excel 2007, use **Office/Excel Options**]. The AutoRecover settings can be modified using the **Save** panel on the Excel Options dialog.

7.4 Exiting Excel

Use the Close button (Figure 60) or

- Excel 2010: **File tab/Exit**
- Excel 2007: **Office/Exit Excel**
- Excel 2003: **File/Exit**

Figure 60

Use the Close button to exit Excel.

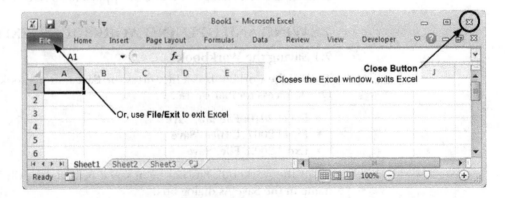

If there are open unsaved workbooks, Excel will ask if you want to save your changes before exiting.

FLUID STATICS

Manometers are tubes of fluid connected to two different locations (see Figure 61) that can be used to measure pressure differences between the two locations.

A general equation for manometers can be written as:

$$P_L + \rho_L g h_L = P_R + \rho_R g h_R + \rho_M g R$$

In this equation,

P_L is the pressure at the top of the left arm of the manometer,
P_R is the pressure at the top of the right arm of the manometer,
g   is the acceleration due to gravity,
ρ_L is the density of the fluid in the upper portion of the left manometer arm,
ρ_R is the density of the fluid in the upper portion of the right manometer arm,
ρ_M is the density of the manometer fluid in the lower portion of the manometer,
h_L is the height of the column of fluid in the upper portion of the left manometer arm,
h_R is the height of the column of fluid in the upper portion of the right manometer arm,
R is the manometer reading, the height difference between the left and right columns of manometer fluid.

There are three commonly used types of manometers, and each has a particular purpose.

Sealed-End Manometer

A *sealed-end manometer* is used to determine an absolute pressure. The sealed-end manometer in Figure 62 can be used to determine the absolute pressure at the location marked P_L.

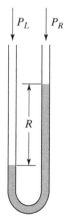

Figure 61
A manometer to measure the pressure difference between P_L and P_R.

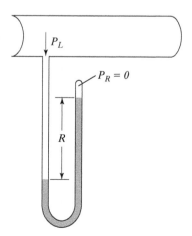

Figure 62
Sealed-end manometer.

To determine the absolute pressure, the space above the manometer fluid on the right side is evacuated, so the density of the vacuum is $\rho_R = 0$ and the pressure on the right is $P_R = 0$.

The general manometer equation can be simplified to

$$P_L = \rho_M g R - \rho_L g h_L$$

for a sealed-end manometer.

Problem: Water $(\rho_L = 1{,}000\,\text{kg/m}^3)$ flows in the pipe connected to a sealed-end manometer. The height of the water column on the left side is $h_L = 35\,\text{cm}$. The manometer reading is 30 cm of mercury $(\rho_M = 13{,}600\,\text{kg/m}^3)$. What is the absolute pressure, P_L?

The solution to this problem is shown in Figure 63.

Figure 63
The solution to a sealed-end manometer problem.

◢	A	B	C	D	E	F
1	**Sealed-End Manometer**					
2						
3		ρ_L	1000	kg/m³		
4		ρ_M	13600	kg/m³		
5		g	9.8	m/s²		
6		h_L	0.35	m		
7		R	0.3	m		
8						
9		P_L	36554	kg/m s² = N/m² = Pa		
10		P_L	0.3608	atm		
11						
12	**Formulas Used**					
13			C9: =C4*C5*C7-C3*C5*C6			
14			C10: =C9/101325			
15						

Open-End Manometer

A *gauge pressure* is a pressure measured relative to the current barometric pressure instead of perfect vacuum. An open-end manometer (Figure 64) is used to determine a

Figure 64
Gauge pressure manometer.

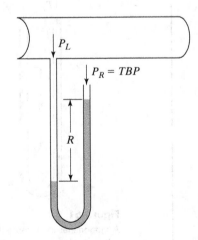

gauge pressure; it is very similar to the sealed-end manometer except that the right side is left open to the atmosphere.

The open-end manometer shown in Figure 64 measures the pressure at the location marked P_L relative to the atmospheric pressure at P_R. (*TBP* stands for "today's barometric pressure.")

Assigning "today's barometric pressure" a value of zero $(P_R = 0)$ causes the calculated pressure at P_L to be a gauge pressure. (The pressure due to the column of air on the right side is neglected.)

The general manometer equation again simplifies to

$$P_L = \rho_M gR - \rho_L gh_L$$

for an open-end manometer, with the understanding that P_L is now a gauge pressure, not absolute.

Problem: Air $(\rho_L \approx 0)$ flows in the pipe connected to an open-ended manometer. The manometer reading is 12 cm of mercury $(\rho_M = 13{,}600\,\text{kg/m}^3)$. The barometric pressure when the manometer was read was 740 mm Hg. What is the gauge pressure, P_L?

The solution to this problem is shown in Figure 65.

Note that the barometric pressure (740 mm Hg) was not used in the problem. This value would be used to convert the calculated gauge pressure to an absolute pressure, as shown in Figure 66.

Figure 65
The solution to an open-end manometer problem.

	A	B	C	D	E	F
1	Open-End Manometer					
2						
3		ρ_M	13600 kg/m^3			
4		g	9.8 m/s^2			
5		R	0.12 m			
6						
7		P_L	15994 kg/m s^2 = N/m^2 = Pa			
8		P_L	0.1578 atm (gauge)			
9						
10	Formulas Used					
11			C7: =C3*C4*C5			
12			C8: =C9/101325			
13						

Differential Manometer

A differential manometer is used to determine the pressure difference between two locations, as illustrated in Figure 67.

For a differential manometer, the difference in column heights on the left and right sides is related to the manometer reading $(h_L - h_R = R)$, and the general manometer equation simplifies to

$$P_L - P_R = R_g(\rho_M - \rho_F)$$

where ρ_F is the density of the fluid in the left and right arms of the manometer $(\rho_F = \rho_L = \rho_R)$ (assumed equal).

Figure 66
Converting a gauge pressure to absolute pressure.

	A	B	C	D	E	F
1	**Open-End Manometer**					
2						
3		ρ_M	13600 kg/m³			
4		g	9.8 m/s²			
5		R	0.12 m			
6						
7		P_L	15994 kg/m s² = N/m² = Pa			
8		P_L	0.1578 atm (gauge)			
9						
10		P_{TBP}	740 mm Hg			
11		P_{TBP}	0.9737 atm			
12						
13		P_L	1.1315 atm (abs.)			
14						
15	**Formulas Used**					
16			C7: =C3*C4*C5			
17			C8: =C7/101325			
18			C11: =C10/760			
19			C13: =C8+C11			
20						

Problem: Water $(\rho_L = \rho_R = 1000\,\text{kg/m}^3)$ flows in a pipe connected to a differential manometer. The manometer reading is 30 cm of mercury $(\rho_M = 13{,}600\,\text{kg/m}^3)$. What is the pressure difference, $P_L - P_R$?

The solution to this problem is shown in Figure 68.

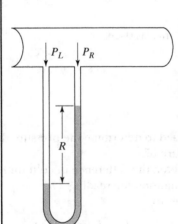

Figure 67
Differential manometer.

	A	B	C	D	E	F
1	**Differential Manometer**					
2						
3		ρ_F	1000 kg/m³			
4		ρ_M	13600 kg/m³			
5		g	9.8 m/s²			
6		R	0.3 m			
7						
8		P_L-P_L	37044 kg/m s² = N/m² = Pa			
9		P_L-P_L	0.3656 atm			
10						
11	**Formulas Used**					
12			C8: =C6*C5*(C4-C3)			
13			C9: =C8/101325			
14						

Figure 68
The solution to a differential manometer problem.

KEY TERMS

Absolute cell addressing	Edit mode	Range of cells
Active cell	Electronic spreadsheet	Relative cell addressing
Automatic recalculation	Fill handle	Spreadsheet
AutoRecover file	Formula	Status bar
Built-in functions	Formula bar	Title bar
Cell address	Label	Value
Cell cursor	Name box	Workbook
Cells	Named cells	

SUMMARY

Cell Contents

Cells can contain labels (text), numbers, and equations (formulas).

Excel interprets what you type into a cell as follows:

- If the entry begins with an equal sign (or a plus sign followed by something other than a number), it is considered a formula.
- If the entry begins with a number, a currency symbol followed by a number, or a minus sign, Excel assumes that you are entering a value.
- If your entry cannot be interpreted as a formula or a value, Excel treats it as a label.

Cell References: Relative and Absolute Addressing

In formulas, cells are identified by using the cell's address, such as G18. Dollar signs are used to prevent the row index (18) and the column index (G) from incrementing if the formula is copied to other cells.

For example:

=$G18+2   Here, the column index G will not change if the formula is copied. If the formula is copied down the column, the 18 will automatically be incremented as the formula is entered into each new cell.

=G$18+2   In this case, the row index 18 will not change if the formula is copied. If the formula is copied across the row, the G will automatically be incremented as the formula is entered into each new cell.

=$G$18+2   In this case, neither the column index G nor the row index 18 will change if the formula is copied.

Selecting Cell Ranges

- To select a single cell, simply click on the cell, or use the arrow keys to locate the cell. The selected cell becomes the active cell.
- To select multiple cells in a rectangular region, click on a corner cell and move the mouse cursor to the opposite corner of the rectangular region. Or use the

arrow keys to select the first corner cell and hold the [Shift] key down while moving the cell cursor to the opposite corner of the rectangular region.

Copying Cell Ranges by Using the Clipboard

1. Select the source cell or range of cells.
2. Copy the contents of the source cell(s) to the clipboard by selecting **Edit/Copy**.
3. Select the destination cell or range of cells.
4. Paste the clipboard contents into the destination cell(s) by selecting **Edit/Paste**.

Copying Cell Ranges by Using the Fill Handle

1. Select the source cell or range of cells.
2. Click the fill handle with the mouse and drag it to copy the selected cell contents to the desired range.

Editing a Cell's Contents

Double-click the cell or select the cell and press [F2].

Printing a Spreadsheet

1. Select the area to be printed and then use Ribbon options: **Page Layout/Page Setup/Set Print Area** [Excel 2003: **File/Print Area/Set Print Area**].
2. Use the Print dialog, as
   - Excel 2010: **File tab/Print**
   - Excel 2007: **Office/Print**
   - Excel 2003: **File/Print**

Setting Print Options

Use Ribbon options: **Page Layout/Page Setup, Page Layout/Scale to Fit**, and **Page Layout/Sheet Options** to set print options.

Adding a Header or Footer to Printed Documents

1. Use the Expand button at the bottom-right corner of the **Page Layout/Page Setup** group to open the Page Setup dialog.
2. Choose the **Header/Footer** tab.
3. Click the **Custom Header ...** or **Custom Footer ...** button.
4. Create the desired header or footer.
5. Click **OK** to exit the dialog.

Saving a Workbook

Press the [Save] button (looks like a diskette) on the Quick Access toolbar, or use:

- Excel 2010: **File tab/Save**
- Excel 2007: **Office/Save**
- Excel 2003: **File/Save**

Opening a Previously Saved Workbook

Use the Open button as:

- Excel 2010: **File tab/Open**
- Excel 2007: **Office/Open**
- Excel 2003: **File/Open**

Exiting Excel

Click the Close button at the top-right corner of the Excel window, or:

- Excel 2010: **File tab/Exit**
- Excel 2007: **Office/Exit Excel**
- Excel 2003: **File/Exit**

PROBLEMS

1 Calculating an Average

In Section 4.7 Excel's **AVERAGE** function was introduced. Create an Excel worksheet similar to the one shown in Figure 69 to calculate the arithmetic average of the five values listed below.

$$3.6; 3.8; 3.5; 3.7; 3.6$$

First, calculate the average the long way, by summing the values and dividing by five.

$$\bar{x} = \frac{(x_1 + x_2 + x_3 + x_4 + x_5)}{5}$$

Then calculate the average using Excel's **AVERAGE** function by entering the following formula in a cell:

```
=AVERAGE(cell range)
```

Replace "cell range" by the actual addresses of the range of cells holding the five values (e.g., the cell range is B4:B8 in Figure 69).

Figure 69
Checking Excel's **AVERAGE** function.

⊿	A	B	C	D	E	F	G
1	Checking Excel's AVERAGE() Function						
2							
3		Values					
4		3.6					
5		3.8					
6		3.5					
7		3.7					
8		3.6					
9							
10	AVG₁:		<< computed by summing and dividing				
11	AVG₂:		<< computed using AVERAGE(B4:B8)				
12							

2 Determining Velocities (in mph and kph)

Some friends at the University of Calgary are coming south for Spring Break. Help them avoid a speeding ticket by completing a velocity conversion worksheet like the one shown in Figure 70. A conversion factor you might need is 0.62 mile/km.

Figure 70
Vehicles speeds in two-unit systems.

	A	B	C	D	E	F	G
1	Vehicle Speed Conversion Chart						
2							
3		Conversion Factor:		0.62	miles per kilometer		
4							
5		Canadian to US			US to Canadian		
6		Speed (KPH)	Speed (MPH)		Speed (MPH)	Speed (KPH)	
7		10			10		
8		20			15		
9		30			20		
10		40			25		
11		50			30		
12		60			35		
13		70			40		
14		80			45		
15		90			50		
16		100			55		
17		110			60		
18		120			65		
19		130			70		
20		140			75		
21							

3 Temperature Increase due to Incandescent Lighting

When energy is added to a fluid, the temperature of the fluid increases. An equation describing this phenomenon is

$$Q = M C_p \Delta T$$

where Q is the amount of energy added (joules)
M is the mass of the fluid (kg)
C_p is the heat capacity of the fluid (joules/kg K)
ΔT is the change in temperature (K, or °C)

A garage (24 ft × 24 ft × 10 ft) is illuminated by six 60-W incandescent bulbs. It is estimated that 90% of the energy to an incandescent bulb is dissipated as heat. If the bulbs are on for 3 hours, how much would the temperature in the garage increase because of the light bulbs (assuming no energy losses). Complete an Excel worksheet like the one illustrated in Figure 71 to answer this question.
Potentially useful information:

- Air density (approximate): 1.2 kg/m^3
- Air heat capacity (approximate): 1000 joules/kg K
- 3.28 ft = 1 m

Figure 71

Garage temperature change calculation.

	A	B	C	D	E	F	G
1	**Temperature Change in a Garage When Lights Left On**						
2							
3	**Specified Information**						
4		Number of Bulbs:		6			
5		Bulb Power:		60	W		
6	Bulb Percent Power Loss as Heat:			90%			
7		Bulbs on Time:		3	hrs		
8		Garage Air Volume:		5760	ft^3		
9		Air Density:		1.2	kg/m^3		
10		Air Heat Capacity:		1000	joules/kg K		
11							
12	**Calculated Information**						
13		Total Bulb Power:			W		
14		Total Bulb Power Lost as Heat:			W		
15		Total Bulb Power Lost as Heat:			joules/second		
16		Total Bulb Energy Lost as Heat:			joules		
17		Garage Air Volume:			m^3		
18		Garage Air Mass:			kg		
19		Temperature Change:			K		
20							

4 Savings from Using CFL Bulbs

Compact fluorescent light (CFL) bulbs have been available for years; they are very efficient, but a little pricey. A CFL bulb that puts out as much light as a 60-W incandescent bulb might cost $10, compared to about $1 for the incandescent bulb. But CFL bulbs are expected to last (on average) 15,000 hours, compared to about 1000 hours for an incandescent bulb. So it is easy to see that you would need 15 incandescent bulbs (total cost $15) to last the 15,000 hours that you would get from one ($10) CFL bulb; you save $5 and a lot of climbing ladders to replace all those incandescent bulbs.

But there's more. A CFL bulb that puts out as much light as a 60-W incandescent bulb will use about 13 W or power. According to the US Energy Information Administration (www.eia.doe.gov), residential electricity costs average about $0.10 per kilowatt/hour (1 kW/h = 3600 kW/s = 3600 kJ). Over the 15,000 hours that one CFL bulb is expected to last, how much will you save on power if you replace an incandescent bulb in your home with a CFL bulb?

Develop an Excel worksheet something like the one shown in Figure 72 to find the answer.

Figure 72

Savings by replacing one incandescent bulb with a CFL bulb.

	A	B	C	D	E	F	G
1	**Savings from One CFL Bulb**						
2				**CFL Bulb**	**Incand. Bulb**		
3		Power Consumption:		13	60	W	
4		On Time:		15000	15000	hours	
5		Cost of Electricity:	$	0.10	$ 0.10	per kw·hr	
6		Total Energy Cost:				(dollars)	
7							
8		Savings:			(dollars)		
9							

5 Comparing Cell Phone Services

Anna is thinking of changing her cell phone service, and she is comparing three plans:

1. Plan 1 has a $20/month access fee, unlimited nights and weekends, 300 anytime minutes plus $0.29/minute for minutes over 300, text messages cost $0.10 each, and roaming costs $0.39/minute whenever she leaves the state.

2. Plan 2 has a $40/month access fee, unlimited nights and weekends, 750 anytime minutes plus $0.29/minute for minutes over 750, text messages cost $0.05 each, and roaming costs $0.39/minute whenever she leaves the state.

3. Plan 3 has a $60/month access fee, unlimited nights and weekends, 1500 anytime minutes plus $0.19/minute for minutes over 1500, text messages are included in the anytime minutes (1 minute per message), and roaming is free.

Her primary concern is during the summer when she is away from college, out of the cell phone company's state, and spending a lot of time communicating with her friends. Looking at her bills from last summer, and trying to predict what will likely happen this summer, she anticipates the following monthly cell phone usage during the summer months:

- 400 minutes nights and weekends
- 500 anytime minutes
- 370 text messages
- 150 roaming minutes

Develop an Excel worksheet something like the one shown in Figure 73 to determine which plan is the best for Anna.

Figure 73

Comparing the expected costs of cell phone plans.

	A	B	C	D	E	F	G	H	I
1	Comparing Cell Phone Services								
2			Anna's	Allowed					
3			Expectation	Free	Paid	Cost each	Total Cost		
4	PLAN 1								
5	Night and Weekend Minutes:		400	UNLIMITED	0	$ -	$ -		
6	Anytime Minutes:		500	300	200	$ 0.29	$ 58.00		
7	Text Messages:		370	0	370	$ 0.10	$ 37.00		
8	Roaming Minutes:		150	0	150	$ 0.39	$ 58.50		
9	Access Fee:						$ 20.00		
10						PLAN 1 TOTAL COST:	$ 173.50	per month	
11									
12	PLAN 2								
13	Night and Weekend Minutes:								
14	Anytime Minutes:								
15	Text Messages:								
16	Roaming Minutes:								
17	Access Fee:								
18						PLAN 2 TOTAL COST:		per month	
19									
20	PLAN 3								
21	Night and Weekend Minutes:								
22	Anytime Minutes:								
23	Text Messages:								
24	Roaming Minutes:								
25	Access Fee:								
26						PLAN 3 TOTAL COST:		per month	
27									
28	It looks like Plan 3 is the best one for Anna right now.								
29									

Using Excel's Ribbon

Objectives

By the end of this chapter, you will be able to

- Use the Ribbon to access Excel features
- Cut and paste within a worksheet
- Change the appearance of characters displayed in a cell by controlling
  - font style, size, and color
  - cell borders and background colors
  - text alignment
  - special numeric formats (currency, percentage, thousand separators)
  - displayed precision (number of decimal places)
- Use the format painter to copy an existing format to a new cell range
- Change the width of a column or the height of a row
- Hide columns or rows
- Use predefined styles to change the appearance of cells
- Use conditional formatting to highlight cells containing values that meet specified criteria
- Define a range of cells as a table
- Use formatting to make your worksheets easier to read
- Lock cells to prevent unwanted alterations to cell contents

Excel 2010 continues to use the redesigned menu system called the Microsoft Office *Ribbon* to provide easier access to features. A lot of the more accessible features are related to formatting your worksheet. In this chapter, we focus on the formatting options available in Excel 2010.

From Chapter 2 of *Engineering with Excel*, Fourth Edition. Ronald W. Larsen. Copyright © 2013 by Pearson Education, Inc. Published by Pearson Prentice Hall. All rights reserved.

1 NAVIGATING THE RIBBON

In Office 2007, Microsoft consolidated the menus, toolbars, and many of the dialog boxes used in previous editions by adding the *Ribbon* near the top of the window (see Figure 1). The Ribbon provides easy access to commonly used and advanced features through a series of *tabs*, such as the Home tab, Insert tab, and so on. Tabs provide access to related *groups* of features. The Excel features we explore in this chapter are located on the Home tab of the ribbon.

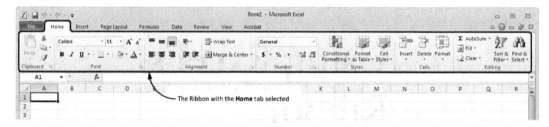

Figure 1

The Ribbon with the Home tab selected.

The Home tab of the Ribbon is divided into the following groups:

- *Clipboard*—provides quick access to the cut, copy, and paste functions as well as the format painter.
- *Font*—allows you to change the font type, size, and appearance as well as cell borders and colors.
- *Alignment*—allows you to change the way displayed text and values are aligned
- *Number*—provides quick access to the number formatting options
- *Styles*—allows you to apply a style to a range of cells, format a range of cells as a table, or apply conditional formatting to a range of cells.
- *Cells*—allows you to easily insert or delete a range of cells, hide or unhide columns or rows, and protect cell contents by locking the cells.
- *Editing*—provides access to some commonly used functions to sum, count, and average cell values, allows you to fill a range of cells with a series of values.

The groups on the Ribbon's Home tab provide a convenient way to organize the content of this chapter. We begin with the Clipboard group.

2 USING THE CLIPBOARD GROUP

The Clipboard group on the Ribbon's Home tab (Figure 2) provides access to:

- **Paste** button and **Paste Option** menu
- **Cut** button
- **Copy** button
- **Format Painter** button and **Format Painter toggle** switch

Figure 2

The Clipboard group on the Ribbon's Home tab.

The *Windows clipboard* is a temporary storage location that allows you to move or duplicate information without retyping it. When you copy the contents of a cell or a range of cells, the original cells are left unchanged, but a copy of the contents is placed on the clipboard. You can then move the cell cursor to a different location and paste the copied information from the clipboard back into an Excel worksheet.

The clipboard is a Windows feature, not just an Excel feature. This means that the content stored on the clipboard becomes available to any Windows program, not just the program in which it was created. The Windows clipboard is commonly used to move information between programs as well as within one program. In this chapter we show how to use the clipboard within an Excel workbook.

2.1 Using the Copy Button

When the **Copy** button is pressed, a copy of the currently selected information is placed on the Windows clipboard. The currently selected information is typically a cell, or a range of cells, but other information can be copied to the clipboard. You can copy a graph, for example.

The **Copy** button is accessed in Excel 2010 and Excel 2007 using Ribbon options **Home/Clipboard/Copy**. In older versions of Excel, use menu options Edit/Copy. You can also use a keyboard shortcut, [Ctrl-c], by holding down the Ctrl key while pressing the c key.

The copy process can be summarized as follows:

1. Select the information that you want copied to the clipboard.
2. Press the Copy button to copy the selected information.

Selecting Information to Be Copied

Selecting information is usually accomplished using the mouse. To select a single cell, simply click on it.

To select a cell range, click in a corner cell, and then drag (hold the left mouse button down while moving the mouse) the mouse icon to the opposite corner of the cell range. This is illustrated in Figure 3.

A selected range of cells is indicated (see Figure 3) by a heavy border; most of the selected cells have a colored background. The cell that was first clicked is shown without the colored background; that cell is still considered the active cell even though a range of cells has been selected. A cell range is indicated with a colon between the first and last cell addresses. For example, the selected cell range in Figure 3 would be described as B3:C7.

Figure 3
Selecting a cell range.

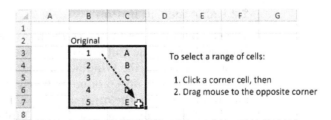

Checking the Contents of the Clipboard

In the recent versions of Excel, it is easy to see what is on the clipboard, just as the **Expand** control at the bottom-right corner of the Clipboard group (Figure 4).

Clicking the Clipboard group's **Expand** control opens the *Clipboard pane* so that you can see the contents of the clipboard. You may be surprised what you find on the clipboard because the Clipboard pane will display information copied from other programs as well, not just Excel.

Notice in Figure 4 that once a cell range (or cell) has been copied to the clipboard, the selection is indicated in the worksheet with a dashed border. That dashed border is a reminder that the information is on the clipboard and ready to be pasted back into the worksheet in another location.

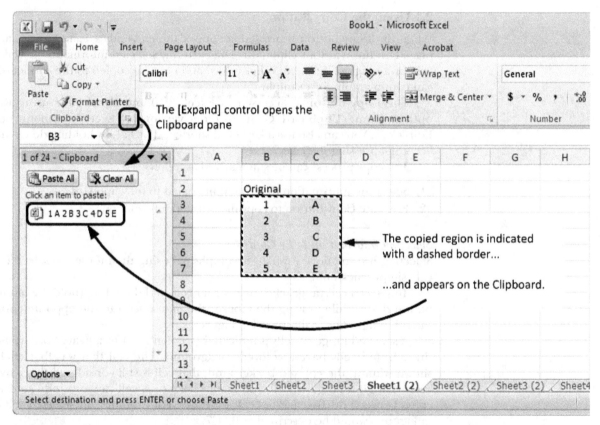

Figure 4
Using the Clipboard group's **Expand** control to open the Clipboard pane to view the Clipboard contents.

2.2 Using the Cut Button

The **Cut** button is used when you want to move (not duplicate) information to the clipboard. When the **Cut** button is pressed, a copy of the currently selected information is placed on the Windows clipboard, and the selected information is marked for deletion. Excel does not immediately delete the selection, but when you paste the cut information, the original is deleted.

The **Cut** button is accessed using Ribbon options **Home/Clipboard/Cut**. In older versions of Excel, use menu options Edit/Cut. You can also use a keyboard shortcut, [Ctrl-x].

The cut process can be summarized as follows:

1. Select the information that you want copied to the clipboard and delete (cut).
2. Press the **Cut** button to copy the selected information. The information will not be deleted until the paste operation is completed.

2.3 Using the Paste Button

The **Paste** button is used to copy information on the Windows clipboard to a selected location on an Excel worksheet.

The **Paste** button is accessed using Ribbon options **Home/Clipboard/Paste**. In older versions of Excel, use menu options Edit/Paste. You can also use a keyboard shortcut, [Ctrl-v].

The paste process (assuming information is available on the clipboard) can be summarized as follows:

1. Select the location (in a worksheet) where you want the clipboard information to be inserted.
2. Press the **Paste** button to copy the selected information from the clipboard to the worksheet.

In Figure 4, cell range B3:C7 has been copied to the clipboard. We need to tell Excel where to put the copy when we paste the information from the clipboard back into the worksheet. In Figure 5, we have selected cell E3; this tells Excel that the top-left corner of the cell range on the clipboard should go in cell E3 during the paste operation.

Note: You need to indicate just the top-left corner of the paste destination cell range, not the entire range.

Click the **Paste** button on the Ribbon's **Home** tab, or use the keyboard shortcut [Ctrl-v] to paste from the clipboard into the worksheet. The result is shown in Figure 6.

Figure 5
Indicating where the top-left corner of the copied cell range will be located.

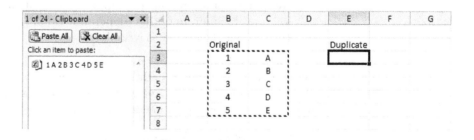

Figure 6
The result of the paste operation.

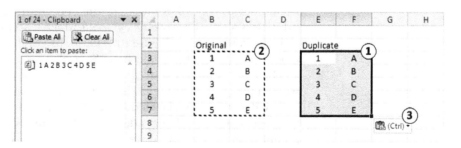

Notice that the contents of the original cell range (B3:C7) have been duplicated in cell range E3:F7; this is indicated with a label "1" in Figure 6. But the original, copied cell range is still indicated with a dashed border (label "2"); this is a reminder that the copied information is still available on the clipboard so that you can paste the same information into the worksheet multiple times, if needed.

Label "3" in Figure 6 is pointing out an icon that appears after the information is pasted into the cells. This icon gives you access to the Paste Options pop-up menu, as shown in Figure 7.

Figure 7

The Paste Options pop-up menu.

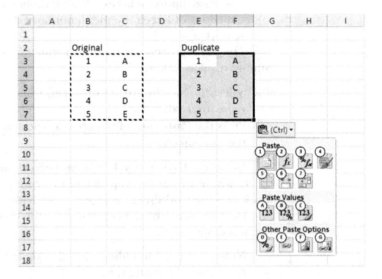

The Paste Options pop-up menu allows you to control the formatting of the pasted information. This is particularly useful when copying formulas because the pop-up menu allows you to indicate whether the copied formulas or just the numerical results (the values) should be pasted into the destination cells.

Note: The Paste Options pop-up menu is context sensitive; that is, the menu will provide different options depending on the type of information (e.g., number, formula, label) that is pasted.

There are 14 options for how to paste information into Excel cells! The option marked "1" is the default method, and that works most of the time. Option "A" is also useful when you want only values (not formulas) pasted into cells. The other options are less commonly needed. The options are listed in Table 1.

2.4 Using the Paste Options Menu

Another way to control how the information on the clipboard gets pasted into the worksheet is to use the *Paste Options menu*, which is accessed using the button directly below the **Paste** button (Figure 8). That is, use Ribbon options **Home/Clipboard/ Paste (menu)** Excel 2003: Edit/Paste Special.

The Paste Options menu, shown in Figure 9, allows you to instruct Excel how to carry out the paste operation. The various options are listed in Table 1.

The default option, labeled **Paste**, simply pastes the currently selected contents of the clipboard using Excel's defaults. The defaults are to paste formulas (not values) and apply the formatting assigned to the source cell. Selecting the **Paste** option

Table 1 Paste options

1	Paste using Excel defaults
2	Paste formulas
3	Paste formulas and number formatting
4	Paste; keeping source formatting
5	Paste with no borders
6	Paste and keep source column widths
7	Transpose values when pasting
A	Paste values only (no formulas or formatting)
B	Paste values and number formatting
C	Paste values with source formatting
D	Paste formatting only (no values or formulas)
E	Paste link
F	Paste picture
G	Paste linked picture

Note: Numbers and letters refer to annotations in Figure 7.

Figure 8
The lower **Paste** button opens the Paste Options menu.

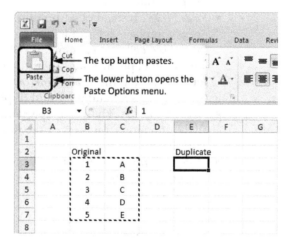

Figure 9
The Paste Options menu.

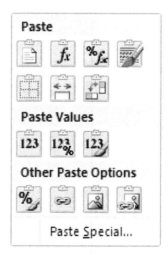

(top-left icon) from the Paste Options menu is equivalent to using the (upper) **Paste** button on the Ribbon.

The other options allow you to control how the information is pasted into a worksheet:

- *Paste:* Pastes using Excel's defaults (paste formulas and use the source cell's formatting).
- *Formulas:* If any of the copied cell contents included a formula, the formula (not the evaluated result) will be pasted into the destination cell(s).

    Note: If the copied formula contained relative cell addresses (without $), those cell addresses will be adjusted when the formula is pasted into the worksheet. Absolute addresses (with $) are not adjusted during the paste operation. This will be illustrated in Example 1.

- *Paste Values:* If any of the copied contents included a formula, the evaluated result of the formula (not the equation) will be pasted into the destination cell(s).
- *No Borders:* The copied cell contents (including formulas) and all formatting of the source cell(s) will be copied, except for borders.
- *Transpose:* If a cell range was copied to the clipboard, using the **Transpose** option will cause the rows and columns in the cell range to be switched during the paste operation.
- *Paste Link:* Instead of pasting the contents of the copied cells, the **Paste Link** operation places a formula in the destination cell(s) that points (links) back to the source cell. For example, if cell A3, containing the formula =12+2, is copied to the clipboard, and then the clipboard contents are pasted using **Paste Link** to cell C4, the **Paste Link** operation will place the formula =A3 into cell C4. Both cells A3 and C4 would display 14.
- *Paste Special...:* The **Paste Special...** option opens the Paste Special dialog to allow even more control over the way the clipboard contents are pasted into the worksheet.
- *Paste as Picture:* The **Paste as Picture** option allows you to paste the clipboard contents as an image. If a formula was copied to the clipboard, an image of the calculated result would be pasted with the **Paste as Picture** option.

Figure 10
The Paste Special dialog.

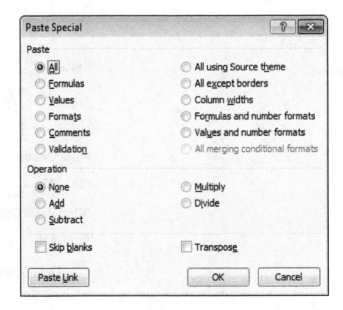

EXAMPLE 1

COPYING AND PASTING FORMULAS

In the worksheet shown in Figure 11, the formulas in cells C5 and D5 determine the surface area and volume of a sphere, using the radius in cell B5. Notice that the formula in cell C5 (shown in Figure 11) is based on the radius in cell B5,

$$=4*PI()*B5^2$$

We can tell that this formula uses relative addressing for cell B5, since there are no dollar signs on the B or the 5. The formula also uses the Excel function **PI** which tells Excel to use its built-in value of π (3.1415...).

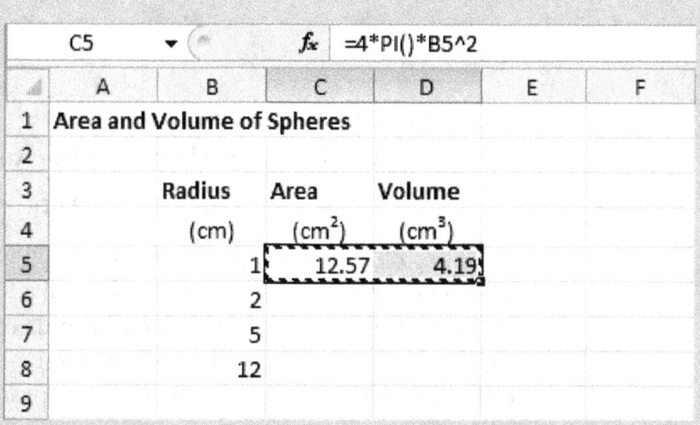

Figure 11
Copying and pasting formulas.

We want to copy and paste the formulas to rows 6 through 8 to calculate the area and volume of the other three spheres. The dashed border around cells C5:D5 in Figure 11 indicates that the cells have already been copied to the clipboard. We just need to paste the formulas into the desired rows. We will do this using three different methods just to show some possible Excel techniques.

Paste Method 1: Paste the formulas into cells C6 and D6.

A two-step process is used to select the destination and then paste.

1. Select cell C6 to indicate the paste destination (Figure 12).
2. Use Ribbon options **Home/Clipboard/Paste** or keyboard shortcut [Ctrl-v] to paste the clipboard contents into the destination cells.

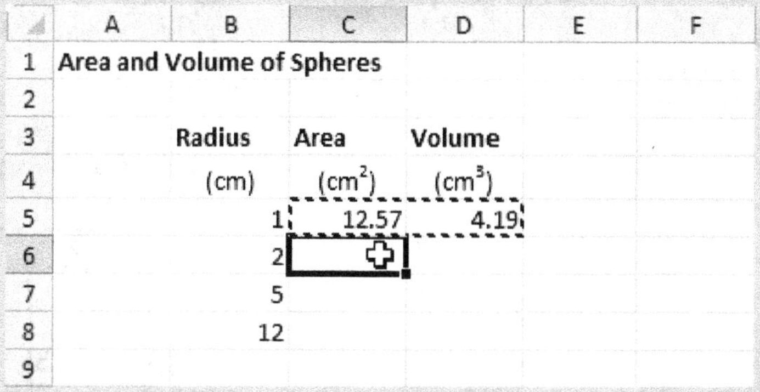

Figure 12
Selecting the destination cell (method 1).

(continued)

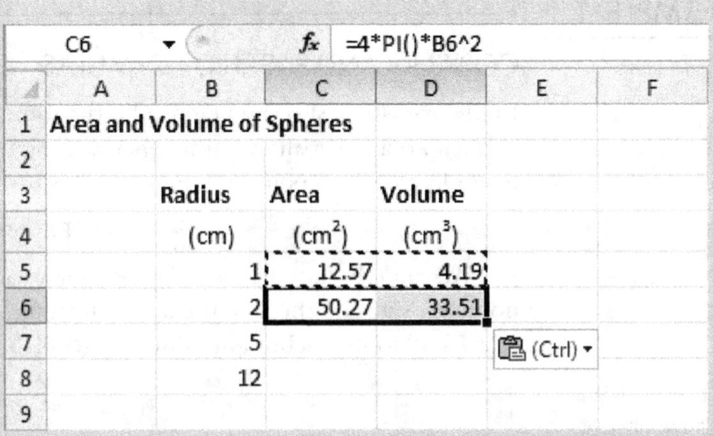

Figure 13
The result of the paste operation.

The result is shown in Figure 13.

Notice that the formula in cell C6 (shown in Figure 13) is

$$=4*PI()*B6^2$$

The "B5" in the original formula in cell C5 became "B6" when the formula was pasted below the original. The relative cell address used in the formula was adjusted in the paste process so that the new formula in cell C6 uses the radius just to the left (in the same relative position). The volume formula in cell D5 also uses a relative cell address (B5) for the radius, so the pasted volume formula also includes an adjusted cell address (B6):

D5 (original): $=(4/3)*PI()*B5^3$
D6 (duplicate): $=(4/3)*PI()*B6^3$

The dashed border around the source cells C5:D5 are a reminder that they are still available on the clipboard, so we could immediately repeat the two-step paste process to determine the area and volume of the 5 cm sphere—but there's a better way.

Paste Method 2: Paste the formulas into cells C6 through D8 (all three destination rows)

A two-step process is used to select the destination, and then paste, but we will paste the formulas into all three destination rows in the second step.

1. Select cells C6:C8 to indicate the paste destination (Figure 14).

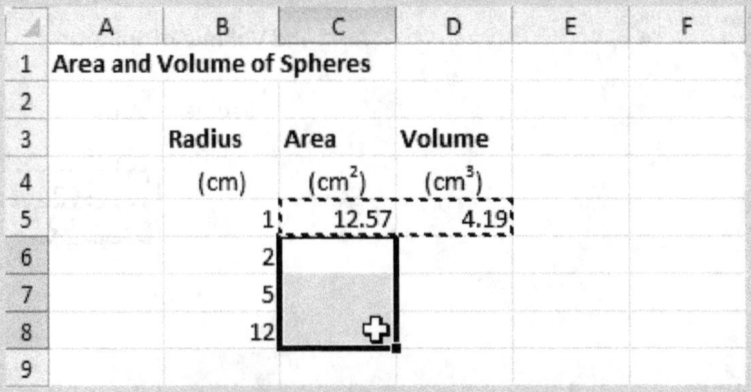

Figure 14
Select all three destination rows by selecting cells C6:C8.

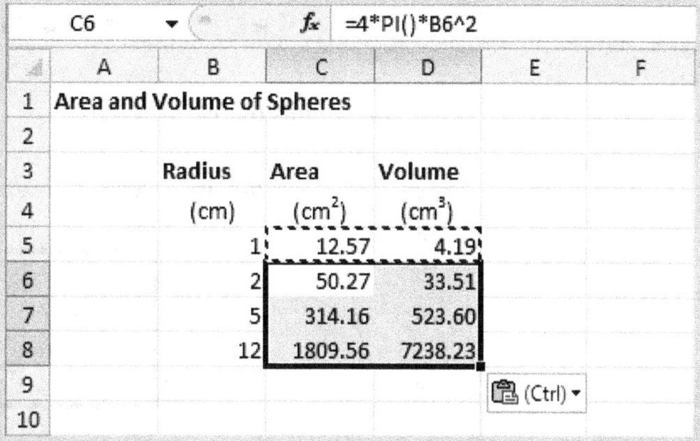

Figure 15
The result of pasting into three destination rows.

Notice that only cells in column C have been selected to indicate the left side of the destination rows. Since the source (cells C5:D5) is only one row high, by selecting three destination rows you are telling Excel to paste the clipboard contents into each destination row.

2. Paste the clipboard contents into the destination cells using Ribbon options **Home/Clipboard/Paste**, or keyboard shortcut [Ctrl-v].

The result is shown in Figure 15.

Again, the paste operation has adjusted the relative cell address so that each formula uses the radius value on the correct row:

Original	C5:	`=4*PI()*B5^2`	D5:	`=(4/3)*PI()*B5^3`
Duplicates	C6:	`=4*PI()*B6^2`	D6:	`=(4/3)*PI()*B6^3`
	C7:	`=4*PI()*B7^2`	D7:	`=(4/3)*PI()*B7^3`
	C8:	`=4*PI()*B8^2`	D5:	`=(4/3)*PI()*B8^3`

In the distant past, this method was the usual way that formulas were copied in Excel, but the Fill Handle provides an even easier way to copy and paste formulas.

Paste Method 3: Duplicating formulas using the Fill Handle

The *Fill Handle* is the little black square in the bottom-right corner of the heavy border that shows a selected cell or cell range. In Figure 16, the original area and volume formulas have been selected (but not copied to the clipboard).

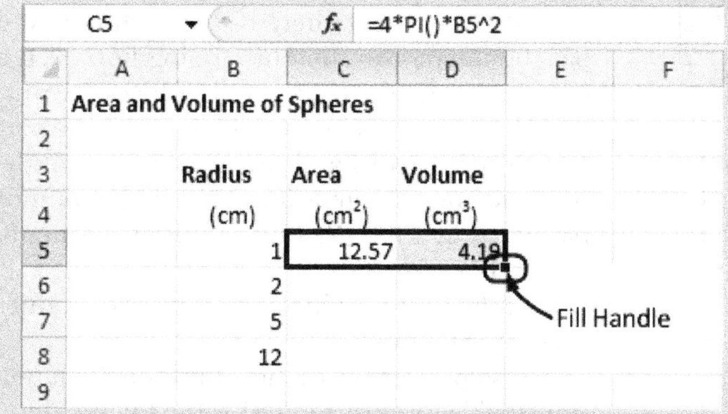

Figure 16
Selecting the cells to be duplicated.

(*continued*)

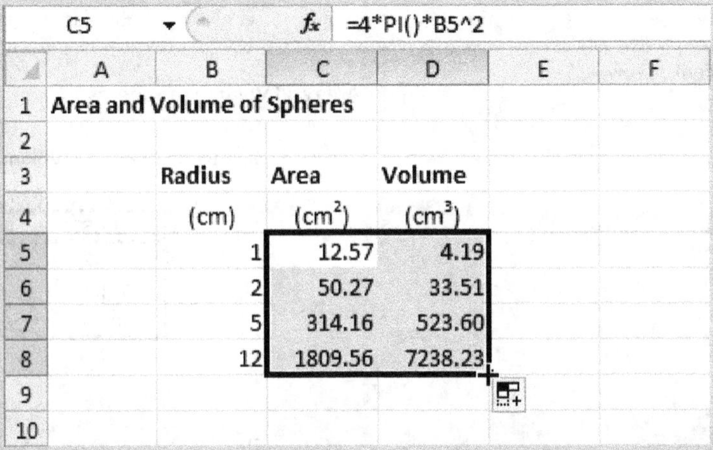

Figure 17
The result of duplicating the formulas using the Fill Handle.

To copy the formulas down the worksheet, just grab the Fill Handle with the mouse and drag it down three more rows. The formulas will be copied to the destination cells without ever using the clipboard.

There is yet another option when using the Fill Handle! Since the radius values were already entered into a column adjacent to the destination cells, you can select the original two formulas (C5:D5) and then double-click on the Fill Handle. Excel will automatically generate formulas for each radius value. The ability to double-click the Fill Handle to have Excel automatically complete a table can be very handy when you have many rows to fill with formulas.

LOAN AMORTIZATION TABLE

When you borrow money to buy a vehicle or a home, the bank may provide you with a *loan amortization table* showing how much you still owe each month. In this application, we'll show you how to create your own amortization table.

Consider a $25,000 loan to buy a new pickup. The loan has an annual percentage rate (APR) of 6%, and you will be making payments for 5 years. Create an amortization table showing how much is left to be paid after each payment.

The basic theory here is that each time you make a payment, you first have to pay the interest on the outstanding borrowed amount (called the *principal*); whatever doesn't go toward interest reduces the principal before the next payment.

The amount of interest depends on the length of the period between payments (typically 1 month) and the periodic (monthly) interest rate. In this example, the periodic interest rate is 6%/12 = 0.5% per month. The loan requires $5 \times 12 = 60$ payments of $483.32. The required payment amount can be determined using Excel's **PMT** function.

We begin by giving the worksheet a title and entering the basic loan data (Figure 18).

In step 2, we create headings for the amortization table and indicate that the principal before payment #1 is the full amount borrowed. Note that the formula in cell B14 is simply a link to the amount borrowed that was indicated in cell D3. That is, cell B14 contains the formula =D3 as shown in Figure 19.

APPLICATION

D5	▼	f_x	=D4/12		
	A	B	C	D	E	F

	A	B	C	D	E	F
1	Loan Amortization Table					
2						
3		Amount Borrowed:			25000 dollars	
4		APR:		6.0%		
5		Periodic Interest Rate:		0.5%		
6		Term:		5 years		
7		Payments/Year:		12		
8		Payments:		60		
9		Payment Amount:		483.32 dollars		
10						

Figure 18

Loan amortization table, step 1.

B14	▼	f_x	=D3		

	A	B	C	D	E	F
1	Loan Amortization Table					
2						
3		Amount Borrowed:			25000 dollars	
4		APR:		6.0%		
5		Periodic Interest Rate:		0.5%		
6		Term:		5 years		
7		Payments/Year:		12		
8		Payments:		60		
9		Payment Amount:		483.32 dollars		
10						
11		Principal			Principal	
12		Before	Interest	Paid on	After	
13	Payment	Payment	Payment	Principal	Payment	
14	1	25000				
15						

Figure 19

Step 2, creating table headings and identifying the initial principal.

For step 3, we calculate the interest on that principal by multiplying the "principal before payment" by the "periodic interest rate", or

C14: =B14*$D$5

Note: The address of the periodic interest rate was made absolute in the formula above by using dollar signs as $D$5. By using absolute addresses whenever any of the input values in rows 3 through 9 is used in the table, the cell addresses for those input values will not change when the formula is copied down the table.

The calculation of interest payments based on periodic interest rates and remaining principal is termed *simple interest*. There are other ways to calculate interest payments, but simple interest is typically used for automobile and home loans.

C14		fx	=B14*$D$5		

	A	B	C	D	E	F
1	Loan Amortization Table					
2						
3			Amount Borrowed:	25000	dollars	
4			APR:	6.0%		
5			Periodic Interest Rate:	0.5%		
6			Term:	5	years	
7			Payments/Year:	12		
8			Payments:	60		
9			Payment Amount:	483.32	dollars	
10						
11		Principal			Principal	
12		Before	Interest	Paid on	After	
13	Payment	Payment	Payment	Principal	Payment	
14	1	25000	125			
15						

Figure 20
Step 3, calculating the interest in the first month.

Next (step 4), we subtract the interest payment from the total payment amount to determine how much was paid on principal in the first month.

D14: =$D$9-C14 (again, an absolute address was used for the payment amount)

D14		fx	=$D$9-C14		

	A	B	C	D	E	F
1	Loan Amortization Table					
2						
3			Amount Borrowed:	25000	dollars	
4			APR:	6.0%		
5			Periodic Interest Rate:	0.5%		
6			Term:	5	years	
7			Payments/Year:	12		
8			Payments:	60		
9			Payment Amount:	483.32	dollars	
10						
11		Principal			Principal	
12		Before	Interest	Paid on	After	
13	Payment	Payment	Payment	Principal	Payment	
14	1	25000	125	358.32		
15						

Figure 21
Step 4, determining how much was paid on principal with the first payment.

E14	▼	f_x	=B14-D14		

	A	B	C	D	E	F
1	Loan Amortization Table					
2						
3		Amount Borrowed:		25000	dollars	
4		APR:		6.0%		
5		Periodic Interest Rate:		0.5%		
6		Term:		5	years	
7		Payments/Year:		12		
8		Payments:		60		
9		Payment Amount:		483.32	dollars	
10						
11		Principal			Principal	
12		Before	Interest	Paid on	After	
13	Payment	Payment	Payment	Principal	Payment	
14	1	25000	125	358.32	24641.68	
15						

Figure 22
Step 5, determining the principal after the first payment.

In step 5, the principal after the payment is determined as $25,000 − $358.32 = $24,641.68, or

E14: `=B14-D14`

For step 6, we start the calculations for the second payment by increasing the payment number by one and using the payment #1 "principal after payment" as the "before payment" principal for payment #2.

A15: `=A14+1`
B15: `=E14`

Step 7. The last three calculations for payment #2 can be completed simply by copying the formulas in cells C14:E14 down to row 15. The results are shown in Figure 24.

Notice that the interest payment has decreased slightly for payment #2 because it was calculated using a slightly smaller principal.

Step 8. Copy the formula in cell A15 down another 58 rows to handle all 60 payments. The result is shown in Figure 25 with many rows (19 through 71) hidden. (How to hide rows is the topic of Section 7.6.)

Step 9. To complete the table, select the formulas in cells B15:E15 (as shown in Figure 25) and double-click on the Fill Handle. Excel will copy the formulas in row 15 (payment #2) down to all 58 remaining rows. The first five payments and last two payments are shown in Figure 26.

This example was included at this point in this chapter to illustrate how handy the Fill Handle is for completing tables (step 9). The appearance and readability of the amortization table could certainly be improved with some formatting, such as bolding the title and column headings, including dollar signs on currency values, and always presenting currency values to two decimal places (cents). These formatting topics are covered in the rest of this chapter.

	A15	▼	f_x	=A14+1	
	A	B	C	D	E	F

	A	B	C	D	E	F
1	Loan Amortization Table					
2						
3		Amount Borrowed:		25000	dollars	
4		APR:		6.0%		
5		Periodic Interest Rate:		0.5%		
6		Term:		5	years	
7		Payments/Year:		12		
8		Payments:		60		
9		Payment Amount:		483.32	dollars	
10						
11		Principal			Principal	
12		Before	Interest	Paid on	After	
13	Payment	Payment	Payment	Principal	Payment	
14	1	25000	125	358.32	24641.68	
15	2	24641.68				
16						

Figure 23
Step 6, starting the calculations for the second payment.

	C15	▼	f_x	=B15*$D$5	
	A	B	C	D	E	F

	A	B	C	D	E	F
1	Loan Amortization Table					
2						
3		Amount Borrowed:		25000	dollars	
4		APR:		6.0%		
5		Periodic Interest Rate:		0.5%		
6		Term:		5	years	
7		Payments/Year:		12		
8		Payments:		60		
9		Payment Amount:		483.32	dollars	
10						
11		Principal			Principal	
12		Before	Interest	Paid on	After	
13	Payment	Payment	Payment	Principal	Payment	
14	1	25000	125	358.32	24641.68	
15	2	24641.68	123.21	360.11	24281.57	
16						

Figure 24
Step 7, copy the formulas in cells C14:E14 down to row 15 to complete the calculations for payment #2.

	A	B	C	D	E	F
1	Loan Amortization Table					
2						
3		Amount Borrowed:		25000	dollars	
4		APR:		6.0%		
5		Periodic Interest Rate:		0.5%		
6		Term:		5	years	
7		Payments/Year:		12		
8		Payments:		60		
9		Payment Amount:		483.32	dollars	
10						
11		Principal			Principal	
12		Before	Interest	Paid on	After	
13	Payment	Payment	Payment	Principal	Payment	
14	1	25000	125	358.32	24641.68	
15	2	24641.68	123.21	360.11	24281.57	
16	3					
17	4					
18	5			Hidden Rows		
72	59					
73	60					
74						

Figure 25
Step 8, establishing the number of payments.

	A	B	C	D	E	F
1	Loan Amortization Table					
2						
3		Amount Borrowed:		25000	dollars	
4		APR:		6.0%		
5		Periodic Interest Rate:		0.5%		
6		Term:		5	years	
7		Payments/Year:		12		
8		Payments:		60		
9		Payment Amount:		483.32	dollars	
10						
11		Principal			Principal	
12		Before	Interest	Paid on	After	
13	Payment	Payment	Payment	Principal	Payment	
14	1	25000	125	358.32	24641.68	
15	2	24641.68	123.21	360.11	24281.57	
16	3	24281.57	121.41	361.91	23919.66	
17	4	23919.66	119.60	363.72	23555.93	
18	5	23555.93	117.78 *Hidden Rows*	365.54	23190.39	
72	59	959.44	4.80	478.52	480.92	
73	60	480.92	2.40	480.92	0.00	
74						

Figure 26
The completed amortization table (only 10 of 60 payments shown).

2.5 Using the Format Painter

The Microsoft Office programs include a handy feature called the *Format Painter*. In Excel 2010, it is part of the Clipboard Group on the Ribbon's **Home** tab, as shown in Figure 27.

Figure 27
The Format Painter button.

The **Format Painter** is used to copy the format used in one cell to another cell or cell range, and nothing else (no values or formulas). This allows you to apply any number of formatting attributes to one cell and then apply all of those attributes to other cells at one time. For example, if you have a portion of your worksheet looking just the way you want it to look and have specified the following attributes:

- Numeric format
- Font type
- Font size
- Font color
- Fill color
- Border style
- Border thickness
- Border color

You do not have to set all of those attributes again in another portion of the worksheet; just use the Format Painter to copy the format from the previous portion of the worksheet and apply it to the new portion.

The **Format Painter** can be used in two ways:

- Single format application
- Multiple format application

Single Format Application

If you need to format one cell or one cell range to look just like an existing cell, then:

1. Click the cell with the desired formatting, to select it.
2. Click the **Format Painter** button.
3. Click the cell (or select the cell range) that is to be formatted.

The formatting of the first cell will be applied to the new cell or cell range.

Multiple Format Application

If you need to format multiple (noncontiguous) cells or multiple cell ranges to look just like an existing cell, then:

1. Click the cell with the desired formatting, to select it.
2. Double-click the **Format Painter** button to activate continuous format painting.
3. Click each cell (or select each cell range) that is to be formatted.
4. Click the **Format Painter** button to deactivate continuous format painting.

The formatting of the first cell will be applied to the each new cell or cell range.

3 USING THE FONT GROUP

The *Font group* on the Ribbon's Home tab (Figure 28) provides access to:

- Font typeface and point size selectors
- Font increase and decrease size buttons
- Bold, underline, and italics attribute toggle buttons
- Border application button and drop-down selection list
- Cell background color application and selection button
- Font color application and selection button
- Font group **Expand** button to open the Format Cells dialog

Figure 28
The font group on the Ribbon's **Home** tab.

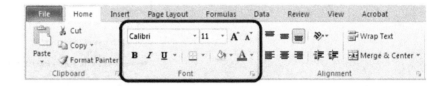

Many of the formatting options available through the Font group are very familiar to word processor users and will only be presented briefly here.

3.1 Font Typeface and Point Size

The default font in the last two versions of Microsoft Office is called Calibri (see Figure 28). The Calibri font is a simple font that is easy to read. In older versions of Excel, the Arial font was the default typeface. You can change the font type or size, either for a selected cell or range of cells, or for the entire workbook.

Changing the Default Typeface or Size Used for New Workbooks
Use the Excel Options dialog to change the default typeface and size. Access the Excel Options dialog as,

- Excel 2010: **File tab/Options**
- Excel 2007: **Office/Excel Options**
- Excel 2003: File/Options

Once the Excel Options dialog is open, select the **Popular** panel, and then change the font listed as **Use this font:** (to create new workbooks). This is illustrated in Figure 29.

The default typeface may appear as "Body Font" on the Excel Options dialog. Body font is simply the typeface used for the body of a document—the basic (default) font on your computer system.

Changing the Default Typeface or Size Used for a Currently Open Workbook
By default, text in a workbook is displayed using the *Normal style*. A *style* is a collection of attributes such as typeface and color, font size, attributes like bold and italics, cell background color, and many others. Any change you make to the Normal Style will automatically show up in the appearance of every cell that uses the Normal style, which is all cells when you first open the workbook. Changing the Normal style is covered in the next section of this chapter.

Figure 29

Changing the default typeface and/or font size for new workbooks.

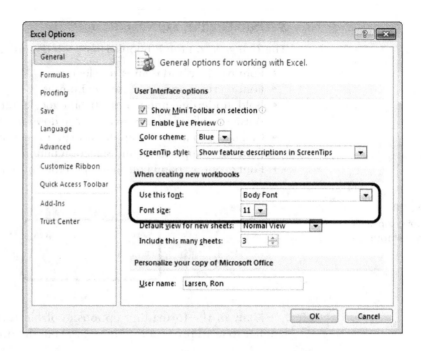

Changing the Typeface or Font Size for a Selected Cell or Range of Cells

The **Font** (style) and **Font Size** drop-down selectors (Figure 30) are used to change the typeface or font size of a selected cell or group of cells.

If we use the worksheet developed in Example 1 again, the readability could be improved by increasing the size of font used for the title. To do so:

1. Select the cell containing the title (cell A1 in Figure 31).
2. Choose a larger font size from the Font Size drop-down selection list.

In Figure 31, the title font size has been changed to 20 points; notice that the row height automatically adjusts when the font size is increased.

Figure 30

The Font and Font Size drop-down selection lists, with Font Size list displayed.

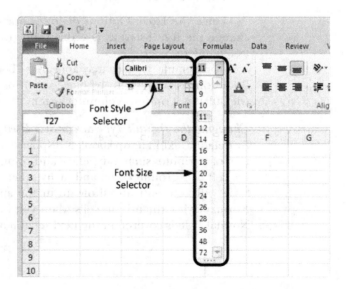

Figure 31
Increasing the size of the
worksheet title.

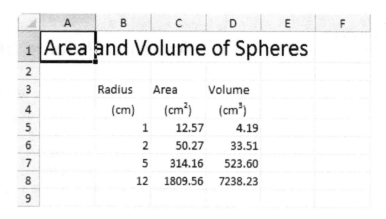

3.2 Font Increase and Decrease Size Buttons

There are many instances when you might not care what point size is used for your fonts, you just want them to "look right" on the screen or printout. For these situations, the **Font Increase** and **Font Decrease** buttons (indicated in Figure 32) are very handy, simply keep clicking the buttons until the font is the size you want.

To increase the text size for the column headings in our example:

1. Select the column headings in cells B3:D3.
2. Click the **Font Increase** button a few times.

The result is shown in Figure 32.

Figure 32
The **Font Increase** and
Font Decrease buttons.

3.3 Bold, Underline, and Italics Attribute Toggle Buttons

The **Bold**, **Underline**, and **Italics** toggle buttons, indicated in Figure 33, allow you to apply or remove these font attributes to the text displayed in a selected cell or range of cells.

Figure 33
The Bold, Underline, and
Italics toggle buttons.

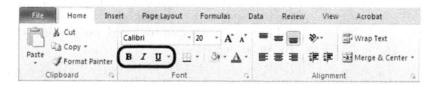

Figure 34

After adding the bold attribute to the title in cell A1.

	A	B	C	D	E	F
1	**Area and Volume of Spheres**					
2						
3		Radius	Area	Volume		
4		(cm)	(cm^2)	(cm^3)		
5		1	12.57	4.19		
6		2	50.27	33.51		
7		5	314.16	523.60		
8		12	1809.56	7238.23		
9						

To activate the bold font attribute for the title in our example worksheet:

1. Select cell A1.
2. Click the **Bold** toggle button.

The result is shown in Figure 34.

The **Bold**, **Underline**, and **Italics** buttons are called *toggle* buttons because they toggle or switch back and forth between two states. Clicking the **Bold** button once, for example, activates the bold attribute for the text in the selected cell, and clicking it a second time deactivates the bold attribute. The **Underline**, and **Italics** toggle buttons work in the same manner to activate and deactivate their respective font attributes.

In Figure 35, you can see a small down-pointing arrow to the right of the **Underline** toggle button. Those down-arrows indicate that there is an option menu available. In this case, clicking on the down-arrow to the right of the **Underline** button gives you the option of using a single underline (the default) or a double underline (see Figure 35).

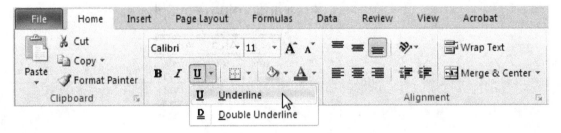

Figure 35

Underline options.

3.4 Cell Border

The **Border** button also has a companion menu, as shown in Figure 36.

When you click the **Border** button, the currently selected border style and location is applied to the selected cell or cell range. If the currently selected border style and location is not what you need, use the drop-down menu to choose the desired type of border.

Figure 36

The border selection list.

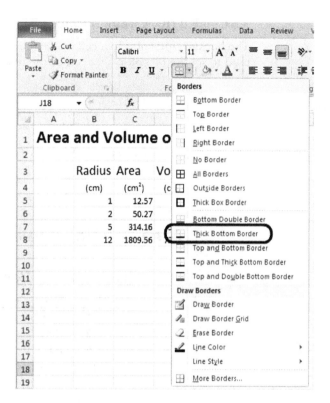

To add a thick border below the units in cells B4:D4 (to separate the column headings from the numeric values):

1. Select cells B4:D4 to select all of the cells displaying units.
2. Use the drop-down border selection list and choose **Thick Bottom Border** from the list of options.

The result is shown in Figure 37. Notice that the **Border** button now shows the **Thick Bottom Border** icon; the most recently used border style is always used when the **Border** button is used without the drop-down menu.

Figure 37

The example worksheet after adding a border below the column headings.

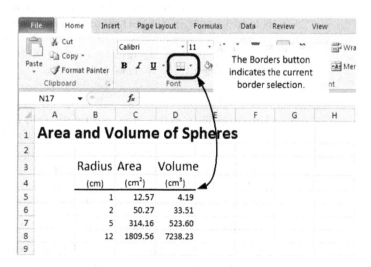

3.5 Cell Fill (Background) Color

The background color in a cell is called the *fill* color. The button and color selector used to set the fill color for a cell or range of cells is shown in Figure 38.

Figure 38

The button and color selector used to set the fill color for a cell or range of cells.

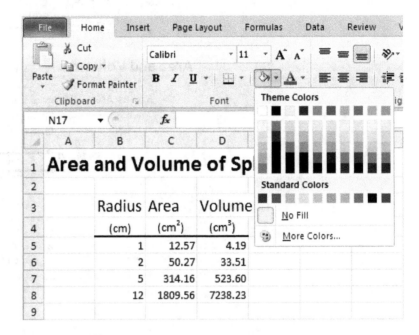

There are three ways to choose colors on the drop-down menu.

1. Near the top are the theme colors; every workbook has a theme that includes a color scheme. If you change the theme applied to the workbook, the choice of theme colors on the menu will change as well. Use Ribbon options **Page Layout/Themes (group)/Themes (button)** to change the applied theme.
2. Below the theme colors are some standard, common computer colors.
3. The **More Colors...** button opens the Colors dialog to allow you to select from a wide range of colors.

An important button on the colors drop-down menu is the **No Fill** button which is used to remove the background color from cells if you decide you don't want a colored background. (An alternative is to reapply the **Normal** style to a cell to remove the cell's background color. Use Ribbon options **Home/Styles/Cell Styles/Normal** to apply the **Normal** style.)

3.6 Font (Text) Color

The drop-down menu for choosing the font color (Figure 39) is very similar to the menu for choosing the cell fill color and provides the same three ways to choose a color: Theme Colors, Standard Colors, and opening the Colors dialog using the **More Colors...** button. A difference is that the font color is typically set to **Automatic** which generally means black. You can override automatic color selection by choosing a color. If you decide to remove color, you normally set the font color back to **Automatic**.

3.7 Format Cells Dialog

The small arrow button, called the **Expand** button at the bottom-right corner of the Font group (see Figure 40), can be used to open the Format Cells Dialog to the Font panel, as shown in Figure 41.

Figure 39
The button and color selector used to set the font (text) color for a cell or range of cells.

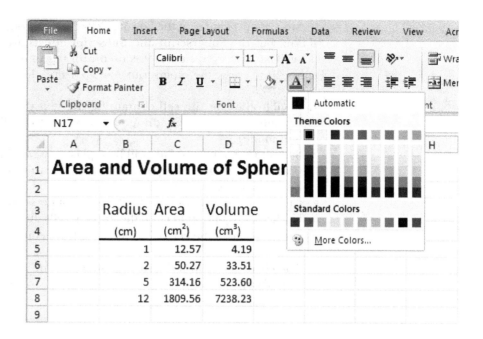

Figure 40
The Font group Expand button.

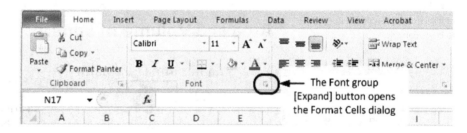

Figure 41
The Format Cells Dialog, **Font** panel.

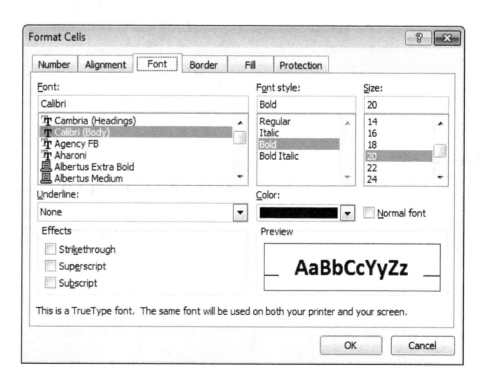

Most of the features of the Format Cells Dialog's **Font** panel are available on the Ribbon, but the **Superscript** and **Subscript** effects are only available from this dialog. The **Superscript** effect was used with the units in our example (shown in Figure 39) to create the superscript 2 and 3. Here's how:

1. Double-click on the cell containing the text that will have the superscript (or subscript) to enter edit mode (or select the cell and press [F2] to enter edit mode).
2. Select the character(s) that will be superscripts, as illustrated in Figure 42.
3. Click the Font group **Expand** button to open the Format Cells dialog to the **Font** panel (Figure 41).
4. Check the **Superscript** box to tell Excel to superscript the selected character(s).
5. Click the **OK** button to close the Format Cells dialog.
6. Click outside of the cell being edited to leave edit mode.

The character(s) with the superscript effect are raised and reduced in size, as shown in Figure 43.

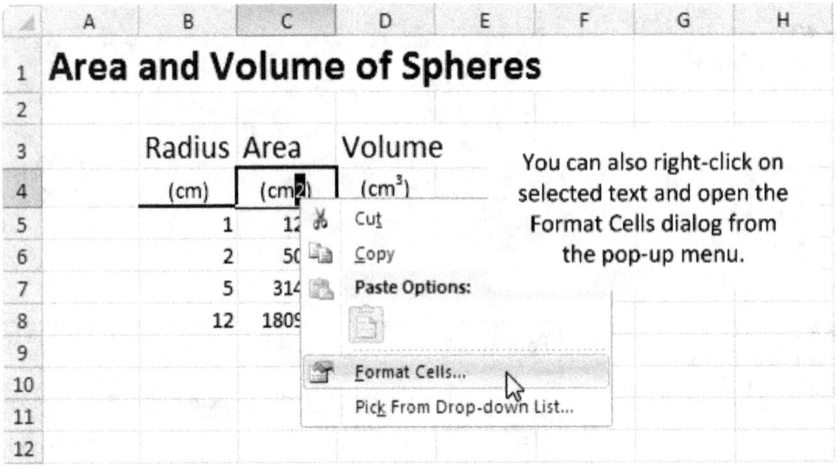

Figure 42
Select the character(s) that are to be superscripts.

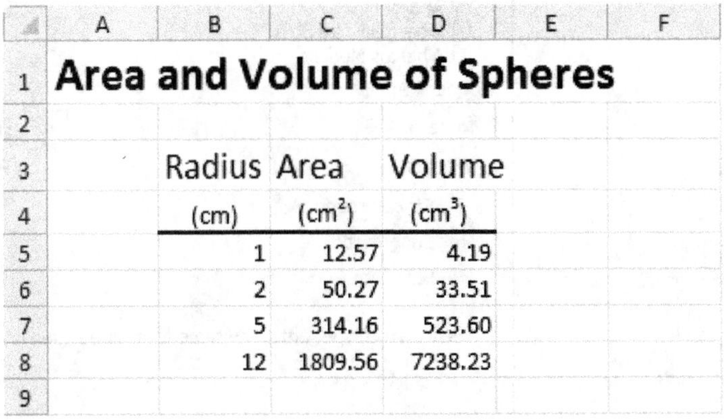

Figure 43
The result of superscripting the "2" in cm^2 (cell C4).

4 USING THE ALIGNMENT GROUP

The Alignment group on the Ribbon's **Home** tab (Figure 44) provides access to:

- Horizontal alignment buttons
- Vertical alignment buttons
- **Wrap Text** toggle button
- **Merge & Center** toggle button

Figure 44
The Alignment group on the Ribbon's **Home** tab.

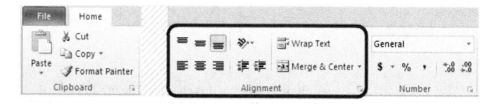

4.1 Horizontal Alignment Buttons

The *horizontal alignment* buttons in the Alignment group are indicated in Figure 45. These buttons allow you to left-, center-, or right-justify the displayed contents of a cell or range of cells. By default, Excel left-justifies text (labels) and right-justifies displayed values, but you can use the horizontal alignment buttons to override the default when desired.

Figure 45
The horizontal alignment buttons in the Alignment group.

Note: Alignment is part of the Normal style; modify the Normal style if you want to change the default alignment.

As an example of using these horizontal alignment buttons, we will remove the centering of the column headings in the worksheet used in Example 1. The process is:

1. Select the cells containing the headings to be centered (cells B3:D4).
2. Click on the **Left Align** button (the left horizontal alignment button).

The result is shown in Figure 46. The difference in the heading labels between Figures 43 and 46 is not pronounced since the labels in row 3 nearly fill the cells anyway, but it is apparent that the units in row 4 are no longer centered beneath the labels.

4.2 Wrapping Text in Cells

When a label is too long to fit within a cell, Excel goes ahead and shows the entire label, as long as it doesn't interfere with the contents of another cell. An example of this is the worksheet title in Figure 46. The label, "Area and Volume of Spheres," is much longer than the space assigned to cell A1, but there is nothing else on row 1, so Excel shows the entire title.

When long labels do interfere, only the portion that fits in the cell is displayed. As an example of this, consider a modified version of the loan amortization table

Figure 46
The worksheet after left aligning the column headings in cells B3:D4.

	A	B	C	D	E	F
1	**Area and Volume of Spheres**					
2						
3		Radius	Area	Volume		
4		(cm)	(cm^2)	(cm^3)		
5		1	12.57	4.19		
6		2	50.27	33.51		
7		5	314.16	523.60		
8		12	1809.56	7238.23		
9						

developed earlier in this chapter. The modified version, shown in Figure 47, has the column headings in individual cells—and they don't fit. This makes the column headings hard to read. We can fix this by wrapping the text in the cells containing these column headings (cells A11:E11).

The difference between this version and the table presented in Figure 26 is the column headings. The column headings in cells B11 through D11 are:

A11: Payment

B11: Principal Before Payment

C11: Interest Payment

D11: Paid on Principal

E11: Principal After Payment

In the earlier example (Figure 26), we got around this problem by using three cells for each heading. This time we will use *text wrapping,* which means the text to be displayed on multiple text rows within the cells. To allow text wrapping in the column headings,

1. Select the column headings that will be set to allow text wrapping (cells A11:E11).
2. Click the **Wrap Text** button in the Alignment group.

This process is indicated in Figure 48, with the result illustrated in Figure 49.

Figure 47
The loan amortization table, with long column headings in row 11.

	A	B	C	D	E	F	G
1	**Loan Amortization Table**						
2							
3			**Amount Borrowed:**	25000	dollars		
4			**APR:**	6.0%			
5			**Periodic Interest Rate:**	0.5%			
6			**Term:**	5	years		
7			**Payments/Year:**	12			
8			**Payments:**	60			
9			**Payment Amount:**	483.32	dollars		
10							
11	Payment	Principal Bef	Interest P	Paid on Princ	Principal After Payment		
12	1	25000	125	358.32	24641.68		
13	2	24641.68	123.21	360.11	24281.57		
14	3	24281.57	121.41	361.91	23919.66		

Figure 48

The process used to allow text wrapping in selected cells.

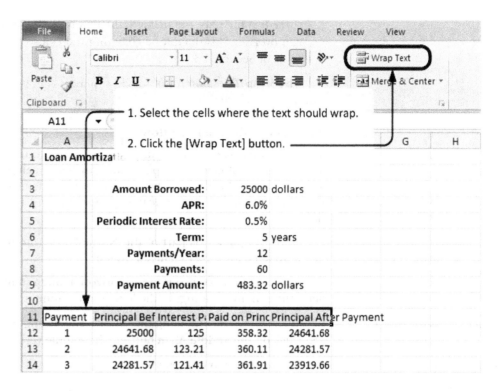

Text wrapping is used to allow long labels to be displayed in a cell by allowing multiple text lines in the cell. In Figure 49, you can see two features of Excel's method of text wrapping:

1. The height of row 11 was automatically increased to accommodate the headings. When text wrapping is requested, the row height will be increased to show all of the wrapped text.

2. By default, the vertical alignment of wrapped text is at the bottom of the cell. You can see this with the short headings, like the "Payment" in cell A11. When

Figure 49

The column headings after allowing text wrapping in cells A11:E11.

three text lines are not needed, the text is placed at the bottom of the cell. You can override this default by changing the cell's vertical alignment. This is the topic of Section 4.3.

The **Wrap Text** switch is a toggle switch; it can also be used to deactivate text wrapping in selected cells.

4.3 Vertical Alignment Buttons

The *vertical alignment* buttons in the Alignment group are indicated in Figure 50. These buttons allow you to top-, middle-, or bottom-align the displayed contents of a cell or range of cells. By default, Excel bottom-aligns the contents displayed in a cell, but you can use the vertical alignment buttons to override the default when desired.

Note: Alignment is part of the Normal style; modify the Normal style if you want to change the default alignment.

As an example of using these horizontal alignment buttons, we will middle-align the column headings in the loan amortization worksheet. The process is:

1. Select the cells containing the headings to be aligned (cells A11:E11).
2. Click on the **Middle Align** button (the middle vertical alignment button).

The result is shown in Figure 51.

Figure 50
The vertical alignment buttons in the Alignment group.

Figure 51
After middle-aligning the headings in cells A11:E11.

	A	B	C	D	E	F
1	Loan Amortization Table					
2						
3		Amount Borrowed:		25000	dollars	
4		APR:		6.0%		
5		Periodic Interest Rate:		0.5%		
6		Term:		5	years	
7		Payments/Year:		12		
8		Payments:		60		
9		Payment Amount:		483.32	dollars	
10						
11	Payment	Principal Before Payment	Interest Payment	Paid on Principal	Principal After Payment	
12	1	25000	125	358.32	24641.68	
13	2	24641.68	123.21	360.11	24281.57	
14	3	24281.57	121.41	361.91	23919.66	

4.4 Centering Labels in Merged Cells

Excel allows multiple cells to be merged. Once the cells are merged, the *merged cells* are treated as a single cell for calculations. When you merge cells, no more than one cell should have any content. If you try to merge two or more cells that each have content, Excel will display a warning that some content will be lost during the merge.

One common use of a merged cell is to create a common heading for several columns in a table. For example, a data set might contain temperature readings from five digital thermometers (T1 through T5), each of which is sampled each second. The data set might look like Figure 52.

Since the data in columns C through H are all temperatures, a single "Temperatures (K)" heading over all six columns makes sense. The process for adding the common heading is:

1. Enter the text "Temperatures (K)" in (any) one of the cells C3 through H3.
2. Select cell range C3:H3.
3. Click the **Merge & Center** button in the Alignment group.

The process is illustrated in Figure 53, with the result shown in Figure 54.

In Figure 54, a border was added around the new heading to better illustrate the merged cells.

The **Merge & Center** button acts as a toggle button; if you select a previously merged cell and then click the **Merge & Center** button, the cells will be unmerged.

The **Merge & Center** button also has an associated drop-down menu. When the drop-down menu is opened, the following menu options are available:

- *Merge & Center:* Same as the **Merge & Center** button; selected cells are merged and the cell contents are displayed in the center (left to right) and using the currently selected vertical alignment (typically bottom-aligned).

	A	B	C	D	E	F	G	H	I
1	Temperature Data								
2									
3									
4	Sample #	Time (sec.)	T1	T2	T3	T4	T5	T avg	
5	1	0	243.2	246.8	241.2	242.2	244.1		
6	2	1	243.3	246.9	242.0	242.6	244.5		
7	3	2	243.4	247.0	242.8	243.0	244.9		
8	4	3	243.5	247.2	243.6	243.4	245.3		
9	5	4	243.6	247.3	244.4	243.8	245.7		
10	6	5	243.7	247.4	245.2	244.2	246.1		
11	7	6	243.8	247.5	246.0	244.6	246.5		
12	8	7	243.9	247.6	246.9	245.0	246.9		
13	9	8	244.0	247.8	247.7	245.4	247.3		
14	10	9	244.1	247.9	248.5	245.8	247.7		
15	11	10	244.2	248.0	249.3	246.2	248.1		
16									

Figure 52
Temperature data, before merging and cells.

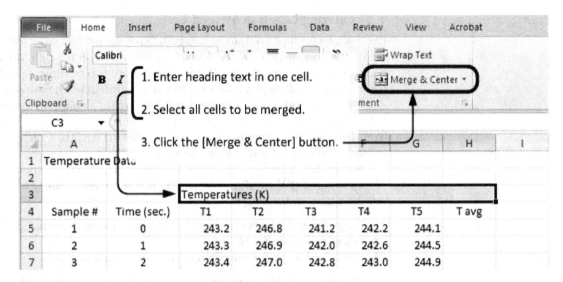

Figure 53
The process used to create a centered heading.

	A	B	C	D	E	F	G	H	I
1	Temperature Data								
2									
3			Temperatures (K)						
4	Sample #	Time (sec.)	T1	T2	T3	T4	T5	T avg	
5	1	0	243.2	246.8	241.2	242.2	244.1		
6	2	1	243.3	246.9	242.0	242.6	244.5		
7	3	2	243.4	247.0	242.8	243.0	244.9		
8	4	3	243.5	247.2	243.6	243.4	245.3		
9	5	4	243.6	247.3	244.4	243.8	245.7		
10	6	5	243.7	247.4	245.2	244.2	246.1		
11	7	6	243.8	247.5	246.0	244.6	246.5		
12	8	7	243.9	247.6	246.9	245.0	246.9		
13	9	8	244.0	247.8	247.7	245.4	247.3		
14	10	9	244.1	247.9	248.5	245.8	247.7		
15	11	10	244.2	248.0	249.3	246.2	248.1		
16									

Figure 54
The temperature data, with a centered heading over the temperature columns.

- *Merge Across:* Merges across selected columns, but does not merge rows. Cell content display is aligned according to the horizontal and vertical alignments currently selected for the merged cell.
- *Merge Cells:* Merges selected cells. Cell content display is aligned according to the horizontal and vertical alignments currently selected for the merged cell.
- *Unmerge Cells:* Separates previously merged cells. The cell content will be placed in the top-left cell of the unmerged cell range.

5 FORMATTING NUMBERS

The *Number group* on the Ribbon's **Home** tab (Figure 55) provides access numeric formats, including:

- Increase and Decrease Decimal buttons
- Currency and Accounting button and drop-down menu
- Percentage button
- Thousand Separator (Comma) button
- Named formats
  - General
  - Number
  - Currency
  - Accounting
  - Short Date
  - Long Date
  - Time
  - Percentage
  - Fraction
  - Scientific
  - Text
- Number group **Expand** button

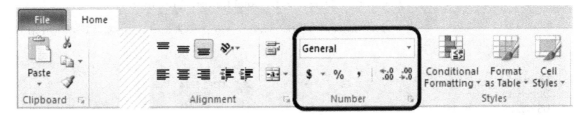

Figure 55
The Number group on the Ribbon's **Home** tab.

By default, the contents of the cells in a worksheet are displayed using the *General format*. The General format is a very flexible format that tries to display numbers in a readable form. Numbers around zero are presented in their entirety, but scientific notation is used when values are very large or very small.

Note: The General format is the default because it is specified as part of the Normal style; modify the Normal style if you want to change the default format used in cells.

Excel provides a number of predefined, named formats, but many of the best features of the named formats are now available directly on the Ribbon's **Home** tab and Number group. In older versions of Excel, these named formats are accessed using menu options **Format/Cells**. The number formatting options available directly from the Ribbon will be presented first.

5.1 Changing the Number of Displayed Decimal Places

One of the most common formatting needs for engineers is the ability to control the number of decimal places displayed on a calculated result. By default, Excel does not show trailing zeros, but if a calculated value is inexact, Excel will show as many decimal places as will fit into the cell. Leaving these extra digits makes it harder to read your worksheet and can make people think your results are far more accurate than they really are.

EXAMPLE 2

US CROSS-COUNTRY DRIVING DISTANCES

As an example of how a lot of decimal places can be displayed on inaccurate numbers, consider the driving distances between some US cities shown in Figure 56.

The values listed in miles are approximations from values listed at various Internet sites, and they are not very accurate. For example, the reported distance between New York and Los Angeles ranges from 2400 to 3000 miles and probably depends a lot on the route you take (and if there is a detour to Orlando, en route).

The values listed in kilometers were calculated from the values in miles by using the conversion factor 0.6214 miles per kilometer. One of the calculations is shown in the Formula bar in Figure 56. Excel displayed the calculated results with three decimal places, and someone might see those values and think those are highly precise values; but they were calculated using highly imprecise and inaccurate mileage values. We need to get rid of those extra decimal places to eliminate some of the confusion. Here's the process:

1. Select the cells containing values to be reformatted with fewer decimal places (F3:F5).
2. Click the **Decrease Decimal** button three times.

The process is illustrated in Figure 57, and the result is shown in Figure 58.

Figure 56
Distances between
US cities.

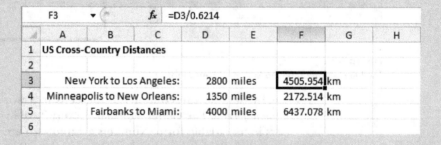

Figure 57
The process used to change
the number of displayed
decimal points.

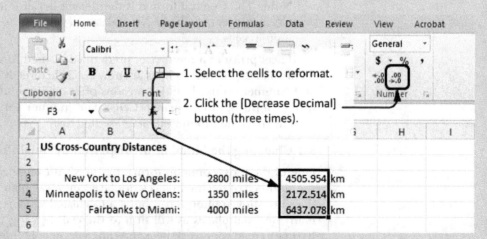

◢	A	B	C	D	E	F	G	H
1	US Cross-Country Distances							
2								
3	New York to Los Angeles:			2800	miles	4506	km	
4	Minneapolis to New Orleans:			1350	miles	2173	km	
5	Fairbanks to Miami:			4000	miles	6437	km	
6								

Figure 58
The result of changing the number of displayed decimal points in cells F3:F5.

While the kilometer values still suggest they are accurate to one kilometer, that's the best we can do using the **Decrease Decimal** button in the Number group on the Ribbon, and the new values are at least an improvement over the extreme number of decimal places initially presented.

There is a way to reduce the number of displayed digits even further, but it requires the use of an Excel function. We'll present the **ROUND** function here to fix this table. If you have never used a function before, you may want to skip the next two paragraphs.

Excel's **ROUND** function takes two arguments: the number to be rounded and the number of decimal places desired. It then returns the rounded number for display in the cell. For example, =ROUND(4505.954, 2) would return the distance from New York to Los Angeles rounded to 2 decimal places, or 4505.95 km. That's too many decimal places for this example; we want to round into the digits on the left side of the decimal point. To do that, we request a negative number of decimal points in the function call. The formula =ROUND(4505.954, -2) will return 4500 km. But we don't want to type the distances into the **ROUND** function, so instead we build the **ROUND** function into the calculation of the distances in kilometers, as illustrated in Figure 59.

The results shown in column F now more accurately reflect the low level of precision in these distances.

F3	▼		f_x	=ROUND(D3/0.6214,-2)				
◢	A	B	C	D	E	F	G	H
1	US Cross-Country Distances							
2								
3	New York to Los Angeles:			2800	miles	4500	km	
4	Minneapolis to New Orleans:			1350	miles	2200	km	
5	Fairbanks to Miami:			4000	miles	6400	km	
6								

Figure 59
The result after rounding two digits left of the decimal point.

5.2 Adding Currency Symbols

Working with monetary values is a common practice in engineering, and Excel makes it easy to include currency symbols in calculations. The Number group on the **Home** tab of the Ribbon provides an **Accounting Number Format** button and a drop-down menu for additional currency and accounting formatting options.

The **Accounting Number Format** button is indicated in Figure 60.

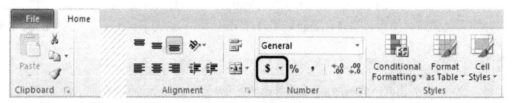

Figure 60
The **Accounting Number Format** button.

Excel provides two named formats for monetary values: *Accounting format* and *Currency format*. The difference is in the way the currency symbols are displayed. This is illustrated in Figure 61.

Figure 61
Contrasting the currency symbol location with the Accounting and Currency formats.

	A	B	C	D	E	F
1						
2	Accounting Format			Currency Format		
3	$	12.32			$12.32	
4	$	15.48			$15.48	
5	$	125.21			$125.21	
6	$1,157.32				$1,157.32	
7						

The Accounting format aligns all of the currency symbols, which makes them easier to see and the values easier to read. Because of this, the Accounting format is more commonly used.

As an example of applying the Accounting format, let's return to the loan amortization table which could benefit from some improved formatting, especially for the monetary values. As a reminder, the mostly unformatted table is shown in Figure 62, with the monetary values indicated.

The simplest way to apply the Accounting format to monetary values is to:

1. Select the cell or range of cells that represents a monetary value.
2. Click the **Accounting Number Format** button to (at least in the US) add the dollar sign and display two decimal places (cents).

The result of applying this process is shown in Figure 63.

After applying the Accounting format to all of the monetary values in the loan amortization table, all of the monetary values are shown with a dollar sign, with a comma as a thousand separator, and shown with two decimal places.

Showing these values to two decimal places is appropriate in this case because loan values would be tracked to the penny. However, cents are not used in many high-value engineering situations. When you use the **Accounting Number Format**

Figure 62

Loan amortization table (truncated at 5 of 60 payments) with dollar values indicated.

	A	B	C	D	E	F
1	**Loan Amortization Table**					
2						
3		**Amount Borrowed:**		25000	dollars	
4			APR:	6.0%		
5		**Periodic Interest Rate:**		0.5%		
6			Term:	5 years		
7		**Payments/Year:**		12		
8			Payments:	60		
9		**Payment Amount:**		483.32	dollars	
10						
11	Payment	Principal Before Payment	Interest Payment	Paid on Principal	Principal After Payment	
12	1	25000	125	358.32	24641.68	
13	2	24641.68	123.21	360.11	24281.57	
14	3	24281.57	121.41	361.91	23919.66	
15	4	23919.66	119.60	363.72	23555.93	
16	5	23555.93	117.78	365.54	23190.39	

	A	B	C	D	E	F
1	**Loan Amortization Table**					
2						
3		**Amount Borrowed:**		$ 25,000.00		
4			APR:	6.0%		
5		**Periodic Interest Rate:**		0.5%		
6			Term:	5 years		
7		**Payments/Year:**		12		
8			Payments:	60		
9		**Payment Amount:**		$ 483.32		
10						
11	Payment	Principal Before Payment	Interest Payment	Paid on Principal	Principal After Payment	
12	1	$ 25,000.00	$ 125.00	$ 358.32	$ 24,641.68	
13	2	$ 24,641.68	$ 123.21	$ 360.11	$ 24,281.57	
14	3	$ 24,281.57	$ 121.41	$ 361.91	$ 23,919.66	
15	4	$ 23,919.66	$ 119.60	$ 363.72	$ 23,555.93	
16	5	$ 23,555.93	$ 117.78	$ 365.54	$ 23,190.39	

Figure 63

Loan amortization table with dollar values reformatted.

button, the values will always be shown with two decimal places, but you can then use the **Decrease Decimal** button to eliminate the extra decimal places.

5.3 Working with Percentages

The *Percentage format* has already been used in the loan amortization table, in cells D4 and D5. The value entered into cell D4 was 6%; Excel recognized the percent symbol and automatically applied the Percentage format to the cell and displayed the value with the percent symbol.

The APR value in cell D4 was used to calculate the periodic interest rate in cell D5, as

$$D5: \ =D4/12$$

Since this is also a percentage, the **Percent** button was used to cause Excel to display the calculated result as a percentage, with the percent symbol. The **Percent** button is indicated in Figure 64.

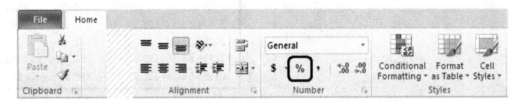

Figure 64
The **Percent** format button.

When you use the percent symbol, remember that it means "per *cent*" as in *cent*ury, or 100. Using the percent symbol is equivalent to dividing the value in front of the percent symbol by 100. So the 6% that appears in cell D4 of the loan amortization table in Figure 63 is numerically equivalent to 6/100 = 0.06. If you remove the **Percentage** formatting on cell D4, and return to **General** formatting, the value will be shown as 0.06 and the rest of the calculations will be unaffected. To Excel, 6% and 0.06 are equivalent.

5.4 Using Commas as Thousand Separators

The **Accounting** format automatically included commas as thousand separators, as seen in Figure 63. Placing a comma every third digit can make large numbers easier to read. If you want to use commas as thousand separators on nonmonetary values, you can use the **Comma** style button indicated in Figure 65.

When you use the **Comma** style button, you are actually applying the **Accounting** format without a currency symbol. Most of the time, this works fine, but you could have problems if your worksheet includes either very large or very small values because the **Accounting** format will not switch over to scientific notation for

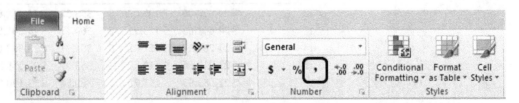

Figure 65
The **Comma** style button.

extreme values. Stick with **General** format or **Scientific** format for very large or very small values.

Note: In some parts of the world, people use commas as decimal points and periods as thousand separators. By default, Excel uses your computer system's definitions for decimal points and thousand separators. You can override the default using the Excel Options dialog, **Advanced** panel, **Editing Options** section.

5.5 Using Named Formats

We have already presented several named formats:

- **General** format (Section 5)
- **Accounting** and **Currency** formats (Section 5.2)
- **Percentage** format (Section 5.3)

These and other named formats are available via a drop-down list of formats in the Number group of the Ribbon's **Home** tab. The location of the drop-down list of named formats is indicated in Figure 66.

Figure 66

The drop-down list of named formats.

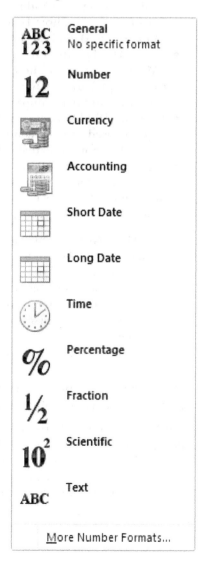

The named formats that have not been presented here include:

- *Number:* Similar to the General format, but with a specified number of decimal places displayed. When you use the **Increase Decimal** or **Decrease Decimal** buttons, you automatically switch the cell's formatting to Number format.
- *Scientific:* Numbers are presented as a mantissa and an exponent. For example, the values 20,000 could be written as a mantissa of 2 with an exponent of 4, or 2 × 104. In Excel, like most computer programs, the exponent is indicated by an E, so 20,000 written in Excel's scientific notation becomes "2.00 E +04."
- *Short Date:* Excel provides good support for working with dates in the last century. By representing dates and times as serial date/time codes, it is easy to do math with dates and times. The Short Date format causes a date to be displayed as **Month/Day/Year** (US default), **Day/Month/Year**, or **Year/Month/Day**, depending on where you live. The order of the day, month, and year is determined by the Region settings in Windows; it is not an Excel option. It can be modified using the Windows Control Panel. Example: 12/25/2010.
- *Long Date:* The Short Date format causes a date to be displayed as **Day of Week, Month Date, Year**. Example: Saturday, December 25, 2010.
- *Time:* Displays the time portion of a date/time code as **HH:MM:SS AM/PM**. You can change the type of display (to 13:00:00 instead of 1:00:00 PM for example) by clicking the Number group **Expand** button (bottom-right corner of Number group) while a Time formatted cell is selected.
- *Fraction:* Displays a numeric value as a fraction. You can change the number of digits allowed in the fraction by clicking the Number group **Expand** button while a Fraction formatted cell is selected.
- *Text:* The contents of cells formatted as Text are treated as text, even if the cell contains a numeric value or a formula. Formulas in cells formatted as Text are not evaluated. Numbers in cells formatted as Text can be used in formulas in other cells (the other cell must not be formatted as Text).

The **More Number Formats** option at the bottom of the drop-down list of named formats (see Figure 66) opens the Format Cells dialog's **Number** panel, as shown in Figure 67.

The only categories (named numeric formats) that have not been presented are the **Special** and **Custom** formats. The **Special** format is locale dependent, but provides some useful formats for regionally specific values (such as formats for Zip Codes in the US).

The **Custom** format allows you to define your own special formats.

5.6 Using the Number Group's Expand Button to Open the Format Cells Dialog

The Number group's **Expand** button (see Figure 68) also opens the Format Cells dialog's **Number** panel, as shown in Figure 67.

The Format Cells dialog provides more formatting options than are available on the Ribbon's Number group (**Home** tab), but the Ribbon is a handier way to access the more commonly used formatting features.

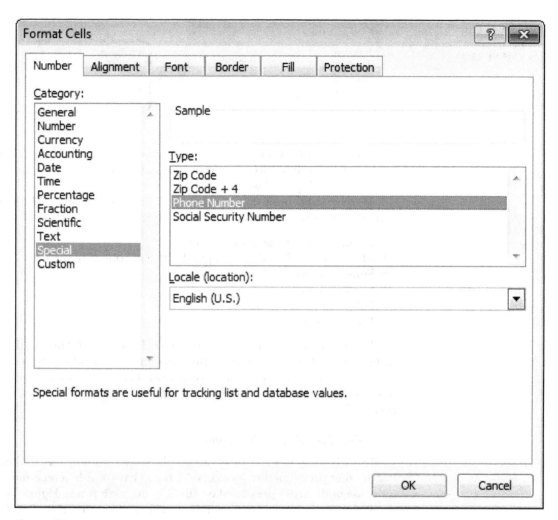

Figure 67
The Format Cells dialog, **Number** panel.

Figure 68
The Number group's **Expand** button.

6 USING THE STYLES GROUP

The *Styles group* on the Ribbon's Home tab (Figure 69) can be used to:

- Apply predefined styles to cells or cell ranges
- Create and modify styles
- Create a table within a worksheet
- Use conditional formatting to highlight parts of a data set

Figure 69

The Styles group on the Ribbon's **Home** tab.

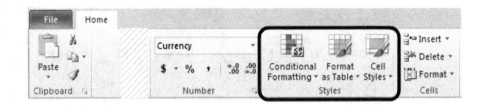

A *style* is a collection of attributes that can be applied to cells. They are usually used to create a "look" for certain portions of a worksheet. By default, all cells in a worksheet are displayed with the Normal style.

More specifically, a style defines the following attributes. The information in parentheses indicates how the Normal style is defined, by default.

- Numbers format (general format)
- Alignment (cell content is aligned with the bottom of the cell)
- Font (11 point Calibri)
- Border (none)
- Fill (none)
- Protection (locked)

It may surprise you that by default, the cells are *locked*. The fact that the cells are locked will not be noticed until the worksheet is *protected*, which is not done by default. If you choose to protect your worksheet, then the locked cells begin to function and prevent unauthorized editing. Protecting worksheets is presented in Section 7.

6.1 Using Predefined Cell Styles

While the **Normal** style, as the default, is the most commonly used, there are a number of other predefined styles available. If you have a wide-screen monitor, you may see some of the styles presented on the Ribbon, as shown in Figure 70.

If there is no room on the Ribbon to show the styles, then Excel shows a **Cell Styles** button, as shown in Figure 69. Click the **Cell Styles** button to open a selection box showing numerous styles (Figure 71).

By default, Excel 2010 and 2007 will show you what each style looks like on the currently selected cells as you move the mouse over the style selectors; this is called *Live Preview* and is activated by default. Live Preview is fairly resource intensive, and on slower computers you might want to turn it off. You can change the Live Preview default using the Excel Options dialog as follows:

- Excel 2010: **File tab/Options/General panel/Enable Live Preview**
- Excel 2007: **Office/Excel Options/Popular panel/Enable Live Preview**

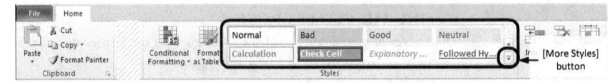

Figure 70

Styles available on the Ribbon (wide-screen monitors only).

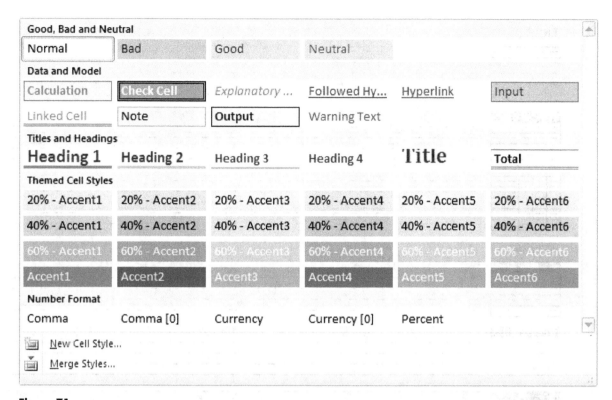

Figure 71
Predefined styles.

The process to apply a predefined style to one or more cells is:

1. Select the cells that are to be formatted using the predefined style.
2. Open the style selector using Ribbon options **Home/Styles/Cell Styles**.
3. Click on the style you wish to apply.

If you right-click on any of the predefined styles, you can modify them. You can also use the **New Cell Style...** button at the bottom of the style selector (Figure 71) to create your own style.

6.2 Defining a Table in a Worksheet

Clicking the **Format as Table** button opens a selector for predefined table styles, as shown in Figure 72. By default, Live Preview will show you what your table (selected cells) will look like as you move your mouse over the table style options.

While the **Format as Table** button in the Styles group does allow you to apply a table style to a selected range of cells, it does quite a bit more than just changing the appearance of the selected cells; it defines the selected cells as an *Excel table*.

An Excel table is a set of rows and columns containing related information (a data set) that Excel treats as separate from the rest of the worksheet. The key feature that is gained by defining a table is that you can sort and filter the data within the table without changing the rest of the worksheet. This can be very handy at times.

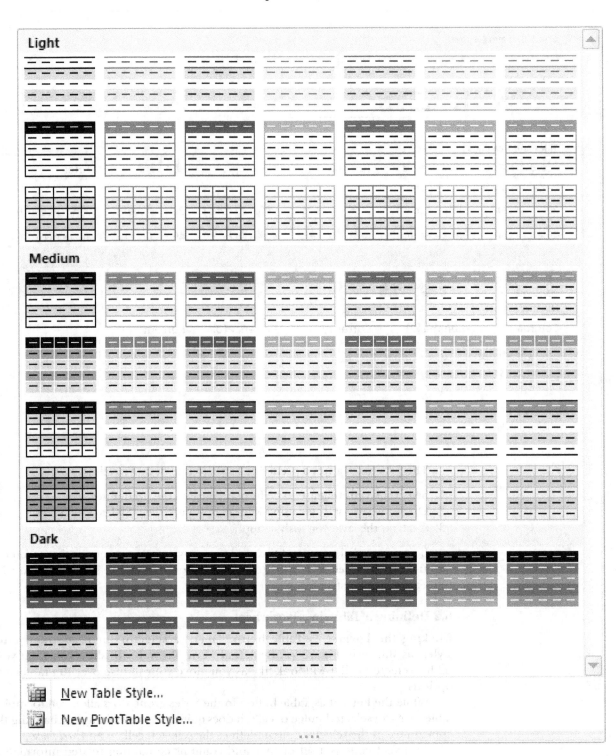

Figure 72
Predefined table styles.

A defined Excel table:

- Is kept largely separate from the rest of the worksheet.
- Has sorting and filtering enabled.
- Can have a *total row* automatically inserted that can do a lot more than just display the column totals. While it may be called a total row, you are not limited to just column totals. For any column, the total row can automatically display:
  - Average value
  - The number (count) of items in the column
  - The maximum value
  - The minimum value
  - The sum (total) of the values in the column
  - The sample standard deviation of the values in the column
  - The sample variance of the values in the column

Defining an Excel Table

As an example of working with an Excel table, consider the temperature data used in Section 4.4, shown again in Figure 73.

In Figure 73, cells A4:H15 have been selected; this cell range will become the Excel table. The Check column will be left outside of the table.

An Excel table can be defined in two ways:

Method 1: Using Ribbon options **Home tab/Styles/Format as Table**
1. Select the cells that will become the Excel table, including one row of headings (optional).
2. Click the **Format as Table** button in the **Home** tab's Styles group to open the Table styles selector.
3. Click on one of the predefined table styles.

	A	B	C	D	E	F	G	H	I	J	K
1	Temperature Data										
2											
3					Temperatures (K)						
4	Sample #	Time (sec.)	T1	T2	T3	T4	T5	T avg		Check	
5	1	0	243.2	246.8	241.2	242.2	244.1			1	
6	2	1	243.3	246.9	242.0	242.6	244.5			2	
7	3	2	243.4	247.0	242.8	243.0	244.9			3	
8	4	3	243.5	247.2	243.6	243.4	245.3			4	
9	5	4	243.6	247.3	244.4	243.8	245.7			5	
10	6	5	243.7	247.4	245.2	244.2	246.1			6	
11	7	6	243.8	247.5	246.0	244.6	246.5			7	
12	8	7	243.9	247.6	246.9	245.0	246.9			8	
13	9	8	244.0	247.8	247.7	245.4	247.3			9	
14	10	9	244.1	247.9	248.5	245.8	247.7			10	
15	11	10	244.2	248.0	249.3	246.2	248.1			11	
16											

Figure 73
Temperature data with cells A4:H15 selected.

Figure 74
Format as Table dialog.

Method 2: Using Ribbon options **Insert tab/Table**
1. Select the cells that will become the Excel table, including one row of headings (optional).
2. Click the **Table** button in the **Insert** tab's Tables group.

The primary difference between the two methods is that Method 1 gives you a choice of table styles; Method 2 does not.

Once you have completed the steps for one of the methods, Excel will display the Format as Table dialog (Figure 74) to verify the cell range that will be defined as a table, and to ask if your table has a row of headings, such as row 4 in our temperature data.

Click **OK** to finish defining the table. The formatted table is shown in Figure 75. Notice that the formatting does not apply outside of the cell range used to define the table (A4:H15).

	A	B	C	D	E	F	G	H	I	J	K
1	Temperature Data										
2											
3						Temperatures (K)					
4	Sample	Time (sec.	T1	T2	T3	T4	T5	T avg		Check	
5	1	0	243.2	246.8	241.2	242.2	244.1			1	
6	2	1	243.3	246.9	242.0	242.6	244.5			2	
7	3	2	243.4	247.0	242.8	243.0	244.9			3	
8	4	3	243.5	247.2	243.6	243.4	245.3			4	
9	5	4	243.6	247.3	244.4	243.8	245.7			5	
10	6	5	243.7	247.4	245.2	244.2	246.1			6	
11	7	6	243.8	247.5	246.0	244.6	246.5			7	
12	8	7	243.9	247.6	246.9	245.0	246.9			8	
13	9	8	244.0	247.8	247.7	245.4	247.3			9	
14	10	9	244.1	247.9	248.5	245.8	247.7			10	
15	11	10	244.2	248.0	249.3	246.2	248.1			11	
16											

Figure 75
The defined table.

Sorting an Excel Table

Also notice that each of the headings now has a drop-down menu button (indicated for heading T5 in Figure 75) on the right side of the heading cell. Clicking any of these buttons opens a menu of filtering and sorting options. The menu for heading T5 is shown in Figure 76.

If we select **Sort Largest to Smallest** on the T5 menu, the values in the T5 column (worksheet column G) will be arranged in descending order—but the table rows are

	A	B	C	D	E	F	G	H	I	J	K
1	Temperature Data										
2											
3					Temperatures (K)						
4	Sample ▼	Time (sec. ▼	T1 ▼	T2 ▼	T3 ▼	T4 ▼	T5 ▼	T avg ▼		Check	
5	1	0	243							1	
6	2	1	243							2	
7	3	2	243							3	
8	4	3	243							4	
9	5	4	243							5	
10	6	5	243							6	
11	7	6	243							7	
12	8	7	243							8	
13	9	8	244							9	
14	10	9	244							10	
15	11	10	244							11	
16											
17											
18											
19											
20											
21											
22											
23											
24											

Menu overlay:
- ↑ Sort Smallest to Largest
- ↓ Sort Largest to Smallest (circled)
- Sort by Color ▸
- Clear Filter From 'T5'
- Filter by Color ▸
- Number Filters ▸
- Search 🔍
- ☑ (Select All)
- ☑ 244.1
- ☑ 244.5
- ☑ 244.9
- ☑ 245.3
- ☑ 245.7
- ☑ 246.1
- ☑ 246.5
- ☑ 246.9
- ☑ 247.3
- OK   Cancel

Figure 76
The filtering and sorting menu for heading T5.

kept together, so the rest of the table will be rearranged as well. The result of sorting on the T5 column is shown in Figure 77.

Notice:

1. The entire table has been rearranged, not just the T5 column. The rows in a table are kept together during a sort.
2. The button next to the T5 heading has changed; it now shows a small downward-pointing arrow as a reminder that the table has been sorted in descending order on the values in column T5.
3. The Check column (worksheet column J) has not been changed. The changes made to the table did not impact anything outside the table, and the Check column was outside of the cell range used to define the table (A4:H15).

Using the Total Row in an Excel Table

To insert a *total row* at the bottom of the Excel table, right-click anywhere on the table and select **Table/Totals Row** from the pop-up menu. An empty total row will be added to the table, as shown in Figure 78.

To use the total row, simply click in any cell in the total row, and a menu button will appear. Click the menu button and a list of options will be displayed, as shown in Figure 79.

In Figure 79, the total row for column T5 is being used to display the maximum value in that column (248.1 K).

The control next to the column heading changes to show how the table has been sorted.

	A	B	C	D	E	F	G	H	I	J
1	Temperature Data									
2										
3										
4	Sample	Time (sec.	T1	T2	T3	T4	T5	T avg		Check
5	11	10	244.2	248.0	249.3	246.2	248.1			1
6	10	9	244.1	247.9	248.5	245.8	247.7			2
7	9	8	244.0	247.8	247.7	245.4	247.3			3
8	8	7	243.9	247.6	246.9	245.0	246.9			4
9	7	6	243.8	247.5	246.0	244.6	246.5			5
10	6	5	243.7	247.4	245.2	244.2	246.1			6
11	5	4	243.6	247.3	244.4	243.8	245.7			7
12	4	3	243.5	247.2	243.6	243.4	245.3			8
13	3	2	243.4	247.0	242.8	243.0	244.9			9
14	2	1	243.3							10
15	1	0	243.2							11
16										

Values in cells outside of the defined table are not impacted when the table is resorted.

Figure 77
The result of filtering (descending order) on the T5 column.

	A	B	C	D	E	F	G	H	I	J
1	Temperature Data									
2										
3			Temperatures (K)							
4	Sample	Time (sec.	T1	T2	T3	T4	T5	T avg		Check
5	11	10	244.2	248.0	249.3	246.2	248.1			1
6	10	9	244.1	247.9	248.5	245.8	247.7			2
7	9	8	244.0	247.8	247.7	245.4	247.3			3
8	8	7	243.9	247.6	246.9	245.0	246.9			4
9	7	6	243.8	247.5	246.0	244.6	246.5			5
10	6	5	243.7	247.4	245.2	244.2	246.1			6
11	5	4	243.6	247.3	244.4	243.8	245.7			7
12	4	3	243.5	247.2	243.6	243.4	245.3			8
13	3	2	243.4	247.0	242.8	243.0	244.9			9
14	2	1	243.3	246.9	242.0	242.6	244.5			10
15	1	0	243.2	246.8	241.2	242.2	244.1			11
16	Total							0		
17										

Figure 78
The Excel table with added total row.

Deactivating a Defined Excel Table

If you are done working with the data in a table and want to turn the table back into a simple cell range, you can. Here's how:

1. Right-click anywhere on the table. A pop-up menu will appear.
2. Select **Table/Convert to Range** from the pop-up menu. Excel will display a prompt window to make sure you really want to eliminate the table (but leaving the data).
3. Say **Yes** to the prompt "Do you want to convert the table to a normal range?"

	A	B	C	D	E	F	G	H	I	J	K
1	Temperature Data										
2											
3						Temperatures (K)					
4	Sample	Time (sec.	T1	T2	T3	T4	T5	T avg		Check	
5	11	10	244.2	248.0	249.3	246.2	248.1			1	
6	10	9	244.1	247.9	248.5	245.8	247.7			2	
7	9	8	244.0	247.8	247.7	245.4	247.3			3	
8	8	7	243.9	247.6	246.9	245.0	246.9			4	
9	7	6	243.8	247.5	246.0	244.6	246.5			5	
10	6	5	243.7	247.4	245.2	244.2	246.1			6	
11	5	4	243.6	247.3	244.4	243.8	245.7			7	
12	4	3	243.5	247.2	243.6	243.4	245.3			8	
13	3	2	243.4	247.0	242.8	243.0	244.9			9	
14	2	1	243.3	246.9	242.0	242.6	244.5			10	
15	1	0	243.2	246.8	241.2	242.2	244.1			11	
16	Total							0			
17								None			
18								Average			
19								Count			
20								Count Numbers			
21								Max			
22								Min			
23								Sum			
								StdDev			
								Var			
								More Functions.			

Figure 79
The drop-down menu showing the options available for the total row.

When you eliminate the table definition, the formatting remains, and the cells contain the same values they held when the table was converted back to a range. That is, any sorting you did to the table remains. If the table was filtered, any data hidden by the filtering process is restored when the table definition is eliminated.

6.3 Using Conditional Formatting

With *conditional formatting*, particular format attributes are applied only if a certain condition is met. For example, you might want unsafe values to show up in bright red. Or, if you are the engineer in charge of quality control, you might want off-spec values to be highlighted so that they are easy to spot.

As an example of conditional formatting, consider again the temperature data from Section 4.4, shown again in Figure 80.

The temperature values have been selected. Next we will apply conditional formatting to make temperature values greater than 248 K stand out, since 248 K is considered the highest "safe" temperature for this freezer system. If the temperature gets too high, the contents of the freezer could go bad.

To apply conditional formatting:

1. Select the cells to which the conditional formatting should be applied (cells C5:G15, shown in Figure 80).
2. Use Ribbon options **Home/Styles/Conditional Formatting**, then menu options **Highlight Cell Rules/Greater Than...** to begin defining the condition when the

◢	A	B	C	D	E	F	G	H
1	Temperature Data							
2								
3			Temperatures (K)					
4	Sample #	Time (sec.)	T1	T2	T3	T4	T5	
5	1	0	243.2	246.8	241.2	242.2	244.1	
6	2	1	243.3	246.9	242.0	242.6	244.5	
7	3	2	243.4	247.0	242.8	243.0	244.9	
8	4	3	243.5	247.2	243.6	243.4	245.3	
9	5	4	243.6	247.3	244.4	243.8	245.7	
10	6	5	243.7	247.4	245.2	244.2	246.1	
11	7	6	243.8	247.5	246.0	244.6	246.5	
12	8	7	243.9	247.6	246.9	245.0	246.9	
13	9	8	244.0	247.8	247.7	245.4	247.3	
14	10	9	244.1	247.9	248.5	245.8	247.7	
15	11	10	244.2	248.0	249.3	246.2	248.1	
16								

Figure 80
Temperature data with temperature values (cells C5:G15) selected.

special format will be applied. These menu selections are shown in Figure 81. The Greater Than dialog will appear, as shown in Figure 82.

3. Excel tries to be helpful and fills in the fields in the Greater Than dialog. The value of 245.3 is the average of the selected temperature values. That's not the value we want. We want to know if there are any temperatures greater than 248 K, so we enter 248 in the Greater Than dialog, as shown in Figure 83.

4. A **Custom Format...** was specified (black fill with white text) so that it would show up well in this text. The resulting worksheet is shown in Figure 84.

The result indicates that there are four temperatures in the data set that are above the safety threshold. It's time to check the freezer.

Excel 2007 and 2010 come with a variety of predefined conditional formats to help show trends in data. Because of the Live Preview feature, the best way to learn about what the predefined conditional formats can do for you is to try them on some data.

Clearing Conditional Formatting

If you want to remove the conditional formatting, use one of the following Ribbon options:

• To remove conditional formatting from a selected range of cells:

  Home/Styles/Conditional Formatting/Clear Rules/Clear Rules from Selected Cells

• To remove conditional formatting from a current worksheet:

  Home/Styles/Conditional Formatting/Clear Rules/Clear Rules from Entire Sheet

Figure 81
Menu selections used to apply a "greater than" conditional formatting.

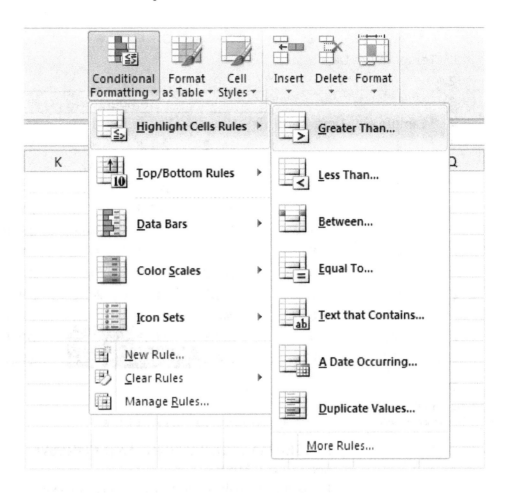

Figure 82
The Greater Than dialog with Excel's default values.

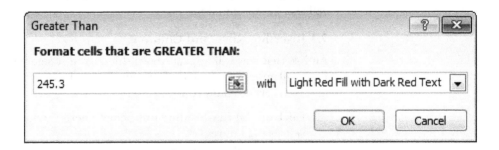

Figure 83
The completed Greater Than dialog.

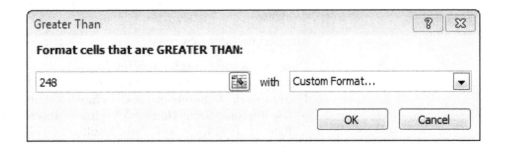

▲	A	B	C	D	E	F	G	H
1	Temperature Data							
2								
3			Temperatures (K)					
4	Sample #	Time (sec.)	T1	T2	T3	T4	T5	
5	1	0	243.2	246.8	241.2	242.2	244.1	
6	2	1	243.3	246.9	242.0	242.6	244.5	
7	3	2	243.4	247.0	242.8	243.0	244.9	
8	4	3	243.5	247.2	243.6	243.4	245.3	
9	5	4	243.6	247.3	244.4	243.8	245.7	
10	6	5	243.7	247.4	245.2	244.2	246.1	
11	7	6	243.8	247.5	246.0	244.6	246.5	
12	8	7	243.9	247.6	246.9	245.0	246.9	
13	9	8	244.0	247.8	247.7	245.4	247.3	
14	10	9	244.1	247.9	248.5	245.8	247.7	
15	11	10	244.2	248.0	249.3	246.2	248.1	
16								

Figure 84
The worksheet with conditional formatting to highlight temperatures above 248 K.

7 INSERTING, DELETING, AND FORMATTING ROWS AND COLUMNS

The *Cells group* on the Ribbon's Home tab provides access to buttons allowing you to insert, resize, and delete rows and columns. Many of these tasks have shortcuts that will also be presented here.

7.1 Inserting Rows and Columns

An inserted row will appear above the currently selected row, and an inserted column will appear to the left of the currently selected column.

To insert one new row:

1. Click on the row heading just below where the new row should be placed; this selects the entire row.
2. Use one of the following methods to insert a row:
   o Use Ribbon options **Home/Cells/Insert/Insert Sheet Rows**
   o Right-click on the selected row heading and choose **Insert** from the pop-up menu

To insert multiple new rows:

1. Drag the mouse across the row headings to select the number of rows to insert. The new rows will be inserted just above the selected rows.
2. Use one of the following methods to insert the new rows:
   o Use Ribbon options **Home/Cells/Insert/Insert Sheet Rows**
   o Right-click on the selected row heading and choose **Insert** from the pop-up menu

To insert one new column:

1. Click on the column heading just to the right of where the new column should be placed; this selects the entire column.
2. Use one of the following methods to insert a column:
   ○ Use Ribbon options **Home/Cells/Insert/Insert Sheet Columns**
   ○ Right-click on the selected column heading and choose **Insert** from the pop-up menu

To insert multiple new columns:

1. Drag the mouse across the column headings to select the number of columns to insert. The new columns will be inserted just to the left of the selected columns.
2. Use one of the following methods to insert the new columns:
   ○ Use Ribbon options **Home/Cells/Insert/Insert Sheet Columns**
   ○ Right-click on the selected row heading and choose **Insert** from the pop-up menu

7.2 Deleting Rows and Columns

To delete one or more rows from a worksheet:

1. Select the rows to be deleted by clicking (and dragging for multiple rows) on the row headings.
2. Use one of the following methods to delete the rows:
   ○ Use Ribbon options **Home/Cells/Delete/Delete Sheet Rows**
   ○ Right-click on a selected row heading and choose **Delete** from the pop-up menu

To delete one or more columns from a worksheet:

1. Select the columns to be deleted by clicking (and dragging for multiple columns) on the column headings.
2. Use one of the following methods to delete the columns:
   ○ Use Ribbon options **Home/Cells/Delete/Delete Sheet Columns**
   ○ Right-click on a selected column heading and choose **Delete** from the pop-up menu

7.3 Inserting a New Worksheet into the Current Workbook

You can use the following Ribbon options to insert a new worksheet into the current workbook:

Home/Cells/Insert/Insert Sheet

Alternatively, you can click the **Insert Worksheet** button on the worksheet tabs at the bottom of the Excel window (indicated in Figure 85).

7.4 Deleting the Currently Selected Worksheet

You can use the following Ribbon options to delete the current worksheet:

Home/Cells/Delete/Delete Sheet

Alternatively, you can right-click the worksheet's tab at the bottom of the Excel window and select **Delete** from the pop-up menu. This latter method can be used for any worksheet in the current workbook.

Figure 85
The **Insert Worksheet**
button.

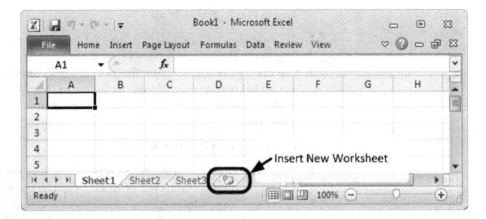

7.5 Adjusting Row Height and Column Width

Changing the displayed height of rows and width of columns is a common need and there are several ways to do each.

Changing row height with the mouse

The easiest way to adjust the height of a row is to grab the lower edge of the row heading and drag it to the size you want. When the mouse is positioned over the lower edge of the row heading, the mouse icon changes to a horizontal line with a vertical double-headed arrow through it, as shown in Figure 86. The row height is also displayed as the height is adjusted.

To change the height of several rows simultaneously:

1. Select the rows to be adjusted by dragging the mouse on the row headings.
2. Position the mouse over the lower edge of the bottom selected row (the icon will change as shown in Figure 86) and drag the edge to the desired height. The heights of all selected rows will be changed.

Changing row height with the Ribbon

To change the height of one or more rows using Ribbon options:

1. Select the rows to be adjusted.
2. Use Ribbon options **Home/Cells/Format/Row Height…**

Figure 86
The mouse icon while
adjusting row height.

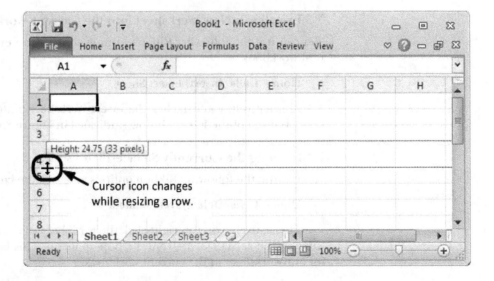

Figure 87
The Row Height dialog.

3. Enter the desired row height in the Row Height dialog, shown in Figure 87. A value of 15 is the default row height.

Changing column width with the mouse
To adjust the width of a column, grab the right edge of the column heading and drag it to the size you want. When the mouse is positioned over the right edge of the column heading, the mouse icon changes to a vertical line with a horizontal double-headed arrow through it, as shown in Figure 88. The column width is also displayed as the width is adjusted.

To change the width of several columns simultaneously:

1. Select the columns to be adjusted by dragging the mouse on the column headings.
2. Position the mouse over the right edge of the right-most selected row (the icon will change as shown in Figure 88) and drag the edge to the desired width. The widths of all selected columns will be changed.

Changing column width with the Ribbon
To change the height of one or more rows using Ribbon options:

1. Select the columns to be adjusted.
2. Use Ribbon options **Home/Cells/Format/Column Width...**
3. Enter the desired column width in the Column Width dialog, shown in Figure 89. A value of 8.43 is the default column width, but that can be changed with Ribbon options **Home/Cells/Format/Default Width...**

Figure 88
The mouse icon while adjusting column width.

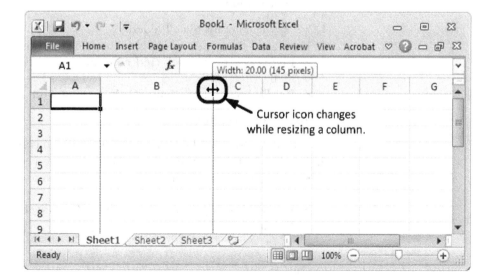

Figure 89
The Column Width dialog.

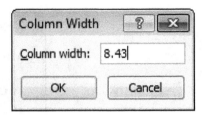

7.6 Hiding and Unhiding Rows and Columns

It is sometimes convenient to hide some of the rows and/or columns in a worksheet. This might be done when:

- The worksheet is very large and hiding unused rows or columns makes it easier to navigate to the areas that are being developed.
- You do not want parts of the worksheet to be seen by the end user. These might be company secrets, or just intermediate calculations that the end user is not interested in.

Hidden rows and *hidden columns* are still actively being kept up to date (recalculated) as the rest of the worksheet is created; they are simply not displayed. Hidden rows do not display when a worksheet is printed.

To hide rows:

1. Select the rows to be hidden.
2. Use one of these methods to hide the selected rows:
   - Right-click on the selected rows and choose **Hide** from the pop-up menu.
   - Use Ribbon options **Home/Cells/Format/Hide and Unhide/Hide Rows**

To unhide rows:

1. Select one row above and below the hidden rows.
2. Use one of these methods to unhide the selected rows:
   - Right-click on the selected rows and choose **Unhide** from the pop-up menu.
   - Use Ribbon options **Home/Cells/Format/Hide and Unhide/Unhide Rows**

To hide columns:

1. Select the columns to be hidden.
2. Use one of these methods to hide the selected columns:
   - Right-click on the selected columns and choose **Hide** from the pop-up menu.
   - Use Ribbon options **Home/Cells/Format/Hide and Unhide/Hide Columns**

To unhide columns:

1. Select one column above and below the hidden columns.
2. Use one of these methods to unhide the selected columns:
   - Right-click on the selected columns and choose **Unhide** from the pop-up menu.
   - Use Ribbon options **Home/Cells/Format/Hide and Unhide/Unhide Columns**

7.7 Renaming Worksheets

Many problems can be solved using a single worksheet, but when several worksheets are used it can be very helpful to give the worksheets meaningful names. To *rename* a worksheet, follow one of these methods:

Renaming a worksheet using the worksheet's tab

1. Double-click on a worksheet's tab. The name field on the tab will enter edit mode so that you can change the name.
2. Edit the name on the tab.
3. Click somewhere on the worksheet (away from the tab) to leave edit mode.

Renaming a worksheet using the Ribbon

1. Make sure the worksheet you wish to rename is the currently selected worksheet.
2. Use Ribbon options **Home/Cells/Format/Rename Sheet**. The name field on the worksheet's tab will enter edit mode.
3. Edit the name on the tab.
4. Click somewhere on the worksheet (away from the tab) to leave edit mode.

7.8 Protecting Worksheets

When a completed worksheet is made available to another person, it is often helpful to limit the other person's access to the calculations on the worksheet. This is done by *protecting* the worksheet.

As an example, consider the loan amortization table developed earlier (see Figure 90). Someone might want to use the table for their own car loan, and that would be OK, but we would want to protect the calculations in the table and only allow them to have access to the input values at the top of the worksheet.

In Figure 90, the input values that someone needs to enter are indicated. All of the other values in the table are calculated from those four numbers. We want to lock

Figure 90

The loan amortization table with unprotected cells indicated.

	A	B	C	D	E	F
1	Loan Amortization Table					
2						
3		Amount Borrowed:		$ 25,000.00		
4		APR:		6.0%		
5		Periodic Interest Rate:		0.5%		
6		Term:		5	years	
7		Payments/Year:		12		
8		Payments:		60		
9		Payment Amount:		$ 483.32		
10						
11	Payment	Principal Before Payment	Interest Payment	Paid on Principal	Principal After Payment	
12	1	$ 25,000.00	$ 125.00	$ 358.32	$ 24,641.68	
13	2	$ 24,641.68	$ 123.21	$ 360.11	$ 24,281.57	
14	3	$ 24,281.57	$ 121.41	$ 361.91	$ 23,919.66	
15	4	$ 23,919.66	$ 119.60	$ 363.72	$ 23,555.93	
16	5	$ 23,555.93	$ 117.78	$ 365.54	$ 23,190.39	

down the worksheet, except for those four cells. This keeps inexperienced Excel users from accidentally messing up the table by entering values on top of the formulas.

In Section 6, it was pointed out that cells formatted with the Normal style are, by default, locked. You can't tell they are locked until the worksheet is protected, but they are. Before we protect the worksheet we need to unlock the four cells that we want people to be able to use (cells C3:C4, C6:C7).

Unlocking Cells

The procedure for unlocking one or more cells is:

1. Select the cell(s) to be unlocked. In Figure 92, cells C3:C4, C6:C7 were selected.
2. Use Ribbon options **Home/Cells/Format/Lock Cell**. This toggles the Lock Cell button to unlock the cells. You can tell whether or not a cell is locked by looking at the icon in front of the **Lock Cell** button (shown in Figure 91). If

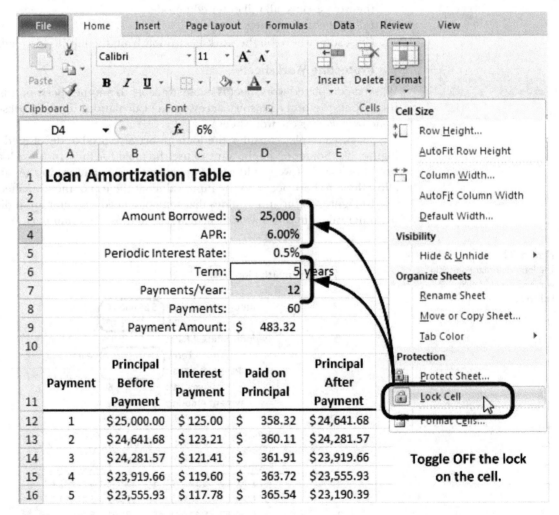

Figure 91
Unlocking cells.

110

the icon is selected (enclosed with a box), the cell is locked. The image shown in Figure 91 was taken just before the **Lock Cell** button was clicked to unlock cells C3:C4, C6:C7.

At this point, cells C3:C4, C6:C7 have been unlocked, but all cells are still accessible since the worksheet has not been protected.

Protecting the Worksheet

To protect the worksheet, use Ribbon options **Home/Cells/Format/Protect Sheet...** Excel 2003: Tools/Protection/Protect Sheet... The Protect Sheet dialog will appear, as shown in Figure 92.

Figure 92
The Protect Sheet dialog.

On this dialog you need to supply a password so that you can unprotect the sheet again, if needed. You should also review the items that users will be allowed to do in the worksheet. By default, users can select both locked and unlocked cells, and that's it. (They can also enter values into unlocked cells.)

When you enter a password and click **OK**, Excel will ask you to confirm the password by reentering the same password in the Confirm Password dialog, shown in Figure 93.

When you click **OK** on the Confirm Password dialog (and both passwords match), your worksheet has been protected, and only the four unlocked cells (C3:C4, C6:C7) can be edited.

As a service to people who will be using locked down worksheets, it helps if you provide some indication of which cells they are allowed to use. In Figure 94, the final loan amortization table is shown with borders around unlocked cells to help the user see that those are the cells they need to use.

Figure 93
The Confirm Password
dialog.

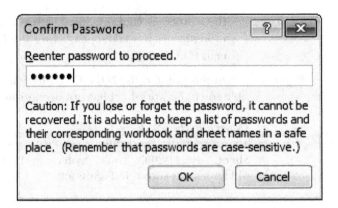

If a friend wants to see what the values look like for their loan, they just update the input values (and they can't accidentally break the formulas). For example, the loan amortization table for a $20,000 loan for 3 years at 7.25% is shown in Figure 95.

	A	B	C	D	E	F
1	**Loan Amortization Table**					
2						
3		Amount Borrowed:		$ 25,000.00		
4		APR:		6.0%		
5		Periodic Interest Rate:		0.5%		
6		Term:		5	years	
7		Payments/Year:		12		
8		Payments:		60		
9		Payment Amount:		$ 483.32		
10						
11	Payment	Principal Before Payment	Interest Payment	Paid on Principal	Principal After Payment	
12	1	$25,000.00	$ 125.00	$ 358.32	$24,641.68	
13	2	$24,641.68	$ 123.21	$ 360.11	$24,281.57	
14	3	$24,281.57	$ 121.41	$ 361.91	$23,919.66	
15	4	$23,919.66	$ 119.60	$ 363.72	$23,555.93	
16	5	$23,555.93	$ 117.78	$ 365.54	$23,190.39	

Figure 94
The locked loan amortization table (showing 5 of 60 payments).

◢	A	B	C	D	E	F
1	**Loan Amortization Table**					
2						
3		**Amount Borrowed:**		$ 20,000.00		
4		**APR:**		7.3%		
5		**Periodic Interest Rate:**		0.6%		
6		**Term:**		3	years	
7		**Payments/Year:**		12		
8		**Payments:**		36		
9		**Payment Amount:**		$ 619.83		
10						
11	Payment	Principal Before Payment	Interest Payment	Paid on Principal	Principal After Payment	
12	1	$20,000.00	$ 120.83	$ 499.00	$19,501.00	
13	2	$19,501.00	$ 117.82	$ 502.01	$18,998.99	
14	3	$18,998.99	$ 114.79	$ 505.05	$18,493.95	
15	4	$18,493.95	$ 111.73	$ 508.10	$17,985.85	
16	5	$17,985.85	$ 108.66	$ 511.17	$17,474.68	

Figure 95
The loan amortization table for a $20,000 loan for 3 years at 7.25% (showing 5 of 60 payments).

KEYWORDS

Accounting format
Cell fill
Clipboard Group
Clipboard pane
Conditional formatting
Copy
Currency
Cut
Decrease decimal
    (button)
Excel Options
Excel table
Fill Handle
Font Attributes (bold,
    italics, underline)
Font Group
Format Painter
Fraction format

General format
Groups
Hidden rows and
    columns
Horizontal alignment
Increase decimal
    (button)
Live Preview
Locked cells
Long Date
Merged cells
Named formats
Normal style
Number group
Paste
Paste Options menu
Paste Values
Paste/Transpose

Percentage format
Protected worksheet
Rename worksheet
Ribbon
Scientific format
Short Date format
Style
Styles group
Subscript
Superscript
Tabs
Text format
Text wrapping
Time format
Total row (Excel table)
Vertical alignment
Windows clipboard

SUMMARY

Cut, Copy, and Paste

- Cut

  Copies cell contents to the clipboard and (ultimately) removes them from the worksheet.

  Ribbon: **Home/Clipboard/Cut**

  Keyboard: [Ctrl-x]

- Copy

  Copies cell contents to the clipboard and leaves them from the worksheet.

  Ribbon: **Home/Clipboard/Copy**

  Keyboard: [Ctrl-c]

- Paste

  Copies cell contents from the clipboard to the currently selected worksheet location.

  Ribbon: **Home/Clipboard/Paste**

  Keyboard: [Ctrl-v]

- Paste Options Menu

  The Paste Options menu, located just below the Paste button, provides access to additional ways to paste information from the clipboard, such as:
  - **Paste Values**—pastes the result of formulas, not the formulas themselves.
  - **Transpose**—interchanges rows and columns during the paste.
  - **Paste Special...**—opens the Paste Special dialog to allow greater control during the paste operation.

Format Painter

Copies the formatting applied to a cell, not the cell contents.

  Ribbon: **Home/Clipboard/Format Painter**

- Click the **Format Painter** button once to copy formatting from one cell to another cell or cell range.
- Double-click the **Format Painter** button once to copy formatting from one cell to multiple cells or cell ranges. Then click the **Format Painter** button again to deactivate format painting.

Fill Handle

The Fill Handle is the small black square at the bottom-right corner of a selected cell or group of cells. It can be used to:

- Copy selected cells down or across a worksheet.
- Fill cells with a series of values.
  - For series values incremented by one, enter the first two values in adjacent cells, select both, and drag the Fill Handle to create the series.
  - For series values incremented by values other than one, enter the first two values in adjacent cells, select both, and drag the Fill Handle to create the series.
  - For nonlinear series, drag the Fill Handle with the right mouse button; a menu will open with fill options.

Font Group

Use the Font Group on the Ribbon's Home tab to set or modify:

- Font type
- Font size
- Font color
- Font attributes (bold, italics, underline)
- Cell border
- Fill color (cell background color)

> Ribbon: **Home/Font**

Excel Default Options

Use the Excel Options dialog to set Excel's default values, such as:

- Default font type and size
- Number of worksheets in a new workbook
- Enabling iterative calculations
- Setting workbook AutoRecovery options
- Changing the date system (1900 or 1904)
- Activate or deactivate Add-Ins

> Access the Excel Options dial as follows:

- Excel 2010: **File tab/Options**
- Excel 2007: **Office/Excel Options**
- Excel 2003: **File/Options**

Superscripts and Subscripts

Use the Format Cells dialog to include subscripts or superscripts in text in cells.

1. Select the cell containing the text to be modified.
2. Activate Edit mode by double-clicking the cell, or pressing [F2].
3. Select the character(s) to be sub- or superscripted.
4. Click the Font group **Expand** button to open the Format Cells dialog.
5. Check the **Subscript** or **Superscript** box.
6. Click **OK** to close the Format Cells dialog.
7. Click outside of the cell to leave Edit mode.

> Ribbon: **Home/Font/Expand**

Horizontal and Vertical Alignment

Use the Horizontal and Vertical Alignment buttons on the Alignment group of the Ribbon's **Home** tab to adjust how information is displayed in cells.

Horizontal Alignment

- left-justify (default for text)
- center-justify
- right-justify (default for values)

Vertical Alignment

- top-justify
- middle-justify
- bottom-justify (default)

> Ribbon: **Home/Alignment**

Wrapping Text in Cells

When labels are too long to fit in a cell, word wrapping can be used to show the labels on multiple lines.

Ribbon: **Home/Alignment/Wrap Text**

Merged Cells

Cells on a worksheet can be merged; the *merged cells* are treated as a single cell for calculations.

The **Merge & Center** button is located in the Alignment group on the Ribbon's Home tab.

There is also a Merge Options menu available that allows the following options:

• Merge & Center
• Merge Across
• Merge Cells
• Unmerge Cells

Ribbon: **Home/Alignment/Merge & Center**, or **Home/Alignment/Merge (menu)**

Formatting Numbers

The Number group on the Ribbon's Home tab provides numeric formats, including:

• General
• Number
• Currency (available as a button)
• Accounting
• Short Date
• Long Date
• Time
• Percentage (available as a button)
• Fraction
• Scientific

Ribbon: **Home/Number**, then use the named format drop-down list

Number of Displayed Decimal Places

The Number group on the Ribbon's Home tab provides buttons to increase or decrease the number of displayed decimal places.

Ribbon: **Home/Number/Increase Decimal**, or **Home/Number/Decrease Decimal**

Working with Monetary Units

Excel provides two named formats for monetary values: *Accounting format* and *Currency format*. The difference is in the way the currency symbols are displayed. Accounting format aligns all of the currency symbols in a column, currency format does not. There is a shortcut button in the Number group for the currency format.

Ribbon: **Home/Number**, then use the named format drop-down list

Working with Percentages

Excel provides the *Percentage format* for working with percentages. When the percentage format is applied, the displayed value is increased by a factor of 100, and the percentage symbol is displayed.

Ribbon: **Home/Number/Percent Style**

Date and Time Formats

If Excel recognizes a cell entry as a date or time, it automatically converts it to a date/time code and applies a date or time format to the cell, as appropriate.

If you change the contents of a cell from a date or time to a number or text, you may need to manually set the cell format back to General format.

Ribbon: **Home/Number**, then use the named format drop-down list

Styles

All cells are initially formatted using the Normal style.

Excel provides a lot of built-in styles that can be applied to change the appearance of cells. To apply a built-in style:

1. Select the cells to be formatted with the style.

2. Select the style from the Styles group on the Ribbon's Home tab.

By default, Excel uses Live Preview to allow you to see how the styles will look before they are applied. As you move the mouse over the style options, Live Preview will show what the style will look like in the selected cells.

Ribbon: **Home/Styles** then choose a style from the available selection.

Excel Tables

An Excel table is a set of rows and columns containing related information (a data set) that Excel treats as separate from the rest of the worksheet. Sorting and filtering is easy within tables.

Defining an Excel Table

1. Select the cells that will become the Excel table.

2. Click the **Format as Table** button in the Home tab's Styles group.

3. Click on one of the predefined table styles.

Sorting and Filtering: Use the drop-down menus available with each column heading to sort or filter based on the values in that column.

Inserting a Total Row in an Excel Table

1. Right-click anywhere on the table.

2. Select **Table/Totals Row** from the pop-up menu.

Using the Total Row in an Excel Table

1. Click in the Total Row below the desired column.

2. Select the desired quantity (average, sum, etc.) from the drop-down list.

Inserting a Row

1. Click on the row heading just below where the new row should be placed.

2. Use one of the following methods to insert a row:
   - Use Ribbon options **Home/Cells/Insert/Insert Sheet Rows**
   - Right-click on the selected row heading and choose **Insert** from the pop-up menu

Inserting a Column

1. Click on the column heading just to the right of where the new column should be placed.

2. Use one of the following methods to insert a column:

- Use Ribbon options **Home/Cells/Insert/Insert Sheet Columns**
- Right-click on the selected column heading and choose **Insert** from the pop-up menu

Deleting Rows or Columns

1. Select the rows or columns to be deleted.

2. Right-click on a selected row or column heading and choose **Delete** from the pop-up menu.

Inserting a New Worksheet

You can use Ribbon options **Home/Cells/Insert/Insert Sheet**

Alternatively, you can click the Insert Worksheet button just to the right of the worksheet tabs at the bottom of the Excel window.

Adjusting Row Height and Column Width

With the mouse, grab the lower edge of the row heading, or right edge of a column heading, and drag it to the size you want.

Alternatively you can use Ribbon options **Home/Cells/Format/Row Height...** or **Home/Cells/Format/Column Width...**

Hiding Rows and Columns

1. Select the rows or columns to be hidden.

2. Right-click on the selected rows or columns and choose **Hide** from the pop-up menu.

Unhiding Rows

1. Select one row above and below the hidden rows.

2. Use one of these methods to unhide the selected rows:

- Right-click on the selected rows and choose **Unhide** from the pop-up menu.
- Use Ribbon options **Home/Cells/Format/Hide and Unhide/Unhide Rows**

Unhiding Columns

1. Select one column above and below the hidden columns.

2. Use one of these methods to unhide the selected columns:

- Right-click on the selected columns and choose **Unhide** from the pop-up menu.
- Use Ribbon options **Home/Cells/Format/Hide and Unhide/Unhide Columns**

Renaming Worksheets

1. Double-click on a worksheet's tab. The name field on the tab will enter edit mode so that you can change the name.

2. Edit the name on the tab.

3. Click somewhere on the worksheet (away from the tab) to leave edit mode.

Protecting Worksheets

Cells are, by default, locked; but the locking is not activated until the worksheet is protected. Before you protect the worksheet, you should unlock any cells that you want to be accessible afterward.

To unlock specific cells:

1. Select the cell(s) to be unlocked.
2. Use Ribbon options **Home/Cells/Format/Lock Cell** to toggle the **Lock Cell** button for the selected cells.

To protect a worksheet:
Use Ribbon options **Home/Cells/Format/Protect Sheet...**

PROBLEMS

1 Paying Back Student Loans I

College students graduating from US universities often have accumulated $20,000 in loans. In recent years, the interest rate on those loans has been about 6% APR, and a common repayment plan is to pay the money back over 10 years. Such a loan would have a monthly payment of $222.04.

Create an amortization table similar to the one shown in Figure 96.
Be sure to include the following formatting features in your worksheet:

- Large, bold title
- Borders around the cells that require data entry (cells D3, D4, D6, and D7) in Figure 96

Figure 96
Student loan amortization table.

	A	B	C	D	E	F
1	**Loan Amortization Table**					
2						
3			Amount Borrowed:	$ 20,000.00		
4			APR:	6.0%		
5			Periodic Interest Rate:	0.5%		
6			Term:	10	years	
7			Payments/Year:	12		
8			Payments:	120		
9			Payment Amount:	$ 222.04		
10						
11	Payment	Principal Before Payment	Interest Payment	Paid on Principal	Principal After Payment	
12	1	$20,000.00	$ 100.00	$ 122.04	$19,877.96	
13	2	$19,877.96	$ 99.39	$ 122.65	$19,755.31	
14	3	$19,755.31	$ 98.78	$ 123.26	$19,632.04	
15	4	$19,632.04	$ 98.16	$ 123.88	$19,508.16	
16	5	$19,508.16	$ 97.54	$ 124.50	$19,383.66	

- Accounting format on all dollar amounts
- Use Percentage format on the APR and periodic interest rate
- For column headings
  - Text wrapping
  - Bold font
  - Centered headings
  - Heavy bottom border

Use your amortization table to determine:

a) Total amount paid on the loan.

b) Amount paid on interest.

2 Paying Back Student Loans II

The minimum monthly payment on the loan described in Problem 1 was $222.04, but there is (usually) no penalty for overpayment. Recalculate the loan amortization table assuming a monthly payment of $250.

a) How many months would it take to pay off the loan with the higher payment?

b) What is the total amount paid on the loan?

c) What percent of the total paid went toward interest?

3 Distances Between European Capitals

Perform an Internet search on "Travel Distances Between European Cities" and use the results to complete the grid shown in Figure 97.

Be sure to include the following formatting features in your worksheet:

- Large, bold title
- Border around the distance grid
- Center all headings and distance values
- Adjust column widths to fit all headings

4 Exponential Growth I

There is a legend that the inventor of chess asked for a small payment in return for the marvelous game he had developed: one grain of rice for the first square on the

	A	B	C	D	E	F	G	H	I	J
1	**Distances Between European Capitals (KM)**									
2										
3			Athens	Berlin	Bucharest	Copenhagen	London	Madrid	Rome	
4		Athens	0							
5		Berlin		0						
6		Bucharest			0				1140	
7		Copenhagen				0				
8		London					0			
9		Madrid						0		
10		Rome			1140				0	
11										

Figure 97
Distances between European capitals.

chess board, two for the second square, four for the third square, and so on. There are 64 squares on a chess board.

    a) How many grains of rice were placed on the 16th square?
    b) How many grains of rice were placed on the 64th square?
    c) How many grains of rice were placed on the chess board?

This problem is intended to give you some practice working with very large numbers in Excel. You may want to try using the scientific format. Creating a series of values from 1 to 64 for the "square number" column is a good place to use the Fill Handle.

5 Exponential Growth II

Bacteria grow by dividing, so one cell produces two, two cells produce four, and so on. This is another example of exponential growth. It is not uncommon for bacteria to double every hour; assuming, of course, that there is enough food about to sustain such growth. Use a worksheet something like the one shown in Figure 98 to find the answers to the following questions.

    a) How many hours does it take for one bacterium to turn into more than 10^{10} bacteria?

Figure 98
Calculating bacterial population.

⬗	A	B	C	D
1	**Bacterial Population**			
2				
3		**Hours**	**Population**	
4		0	1	
5		1	2	
6		2	4	
7		...	...	
8				

Graphing with Excel

From Chapter 3 of *Engineering with Excel*, Fourth Edition. Ronald W. Larsen. Copyright © 2013 by Pearson Education, Inc. Published by Pearson Prentice Hall. All rights reserved.

Graphing with Excel

Objectives

After reading this chapter, you will know

- How to organize data in a worksheet to make graphing easy
- How to create an XY scatter graph
- How to modify an existing graph
  - Adding additional data series to a graph

- Modifying plot formatting
- How to add trendlines to graphs
- How to add error bars to graphs
- Two ways to print a graph
- How to use Web data in an Excel graph
- How to import text files into Excel for graphing

1 INTRODUCTION

An Excel worksheet is a convenient place to generate graphs. The process is quick and easy, and Excel gives you a lot of control over the appearance of the graph. Once a graph is created, you can then begin analyzing your data by adding a trendline to a graphed data set with just a few mouse clicks. The majority of Excel's trendlines are regression lines, and the equation of the best-fit curve through your data set is immediately available. Excel graphs are great tools for visualizing and analyzing data.

1.1 Nomenclature

- The good folks at Microsoft use the term *chart* rather than *graph*. Graph is a more commonly used term in engineering and is used here. Chart and graph can be treated as synonymous in this text.
- The points displayed on a graph are called *markers*.

- Microsoft Excel uses the term *trendline* (one word), but Microsoft Word's spell-checker claims it should be *trend line* (two words). While common usage agrees with Microsoft Word, I have used Excel's "trendline" in this text for consistency with the menu options presented by the Excel program.

2 GETTING READY TO GRAPH

You must have some data in the worksheet before creating a graph, and those data can come from a variety of sources. Creating a graph from values that were calculated within the worksheet is probably the most common, but data can also be imported from data files, copied from other programs (such as getting data from the Internet by using a browser), or perhaps even read directly from an experiment that uses automated data acquisition. Once the data, from whatever source, are in your worksheet, there are some things you can do to make graphing quicker and easier. That is the subject of this section on getting ready to create a graph.

Excel attempts to analyze your data to automatically create a basic graph. You can assist the process by laying out your data in a standard form. A typical set of data for plotting might look something like Figure 1.

Excel is fairly flexible, but the typical data layout for an XY scatter graph, such as the temperature and time data in Figure 1, includes the following elements:

- The data to be plotted on the *x* axis (Time) are stored in a single column.
  - No blank rows exist between the first *x* value and the last *x* value, or between the column heading and the first *x* value.
- The data to be plotted on the *y* axis (Temperature) are stored in a single column to the right of the column of *x* values.
  - No blank rows exist between the first *y* value and the last *y* value.
  - The series name ("Temp. (°C)") may be included in the cell directly above the first *y* value. If the top cell in the *y* values column contains text rather than

Figure 1
A data set for graphing.

	A	B	C
1	**Temperature vs. Time Data**		
2			
3	Time (sec.)	Temp. (°C)	
4	0	54.23	
5	1	45.75	
6	2	28.41	
7	3	28.30	
8	4	26.45	
9	5	17.36	
10	6	17.64	
11	7	9.51	
12	8	5.76	
13	9	8.55	
14	10	6.58	
15	11	4.62	
16	12	2.73	
17	13	2.91	
18	14	0.32	
19	15	1.68	
20			

Wondering how the degree symbol got into cell B3?

- From the numeric keypad (not the numbers at the top of the keyboard), press [Alt-0176]; that is, hold down the [Alt] key while pressing 0176 on the numeric keypad, or
- Use Insert/Symbol, and select the degree symbol from the list of available symbols.

Figure 2
The temperature and time data in rows.

▲	A	B	C	D	E	F	G	H
1	**Temperature vs. Time Data**							
2								
3	Time (sec.)	0	1	2	3	4	5	6
4	Temp. (°C)	54.23	45.75	28.41	28.30	26.45	17.36	17.64
5								

a number, Excel will use that text as the name of the series and will include that name in the graph's legend and title (if these are displayed).

Keeping data in columns is the most common practice, but rows will also work. The temperature and time data set shown above would look like Figure 2, if it were stored in rows. (Only the first seven values of each row have been shown.)

By putting your data into a standard form, you make it possible for the logic programmed into Excel to recognize the structure in your data and assist in creating the graph; this makes creating graphs in Excel easier.

3 CREATING AN XY SCATTER GRAPH

The majority of graphs used by engineers are *XY scatter graphs*, so preparing this type of graph is covered here. Other types of graphs available in Excel are described in Section 6.

Once you have a block of data in the worksheet, it can be plotted by following these steps:

1. Select the Data Range (including the series names, if desired).
2. Use Ribbon options **Insert/Charts/Scatter** to select the graph type and create the graph.
   [In Excel 2003: Start the Chart Wizard and select the chart type.]

At this point, Excel 2010 will display a basic graph on the worksheet, but the graph is missing some key features, such as axis labels. Complete the graph by using formatting options on the Ribbon, with these steps:

3. Choose a Quick Layout (**Chart Tools/Design/Chart Layouts/Quick Layout**)
4. Edit the axis labels and graph title

Each of these steps will be explained in more detail in the following paragraphs.

Step 1. Select the data range. An XY scatter graph is made up of a set of data points that each has an *x* value and a *y* value, which determine the location of the point on the graph. To create an XY scatter plot in Excel, first select the two columns (or rows) of data to be graphed, as shown in Figure 3.

To select the data to be plotted, simply click on the cell containing the first *x* value and hold the left mouse button down as you move the mouse pointer to the cell containing the last *y* value. In the temperature vs. time data shown here, cells A3 through B19 have been selected for graphing.

Including the column headings (cells A3:B3) with the selected data (A3:B19) is optional, but Excel will use the heading in the graph's legend if included.

Step 2. Select the type of graph to be inserted on the worksheet. Use Ribbon options **Insert/Charts/Scatter** to open the Scatter drop-down graph type selector (shown in Figure 3 and Figure 4).

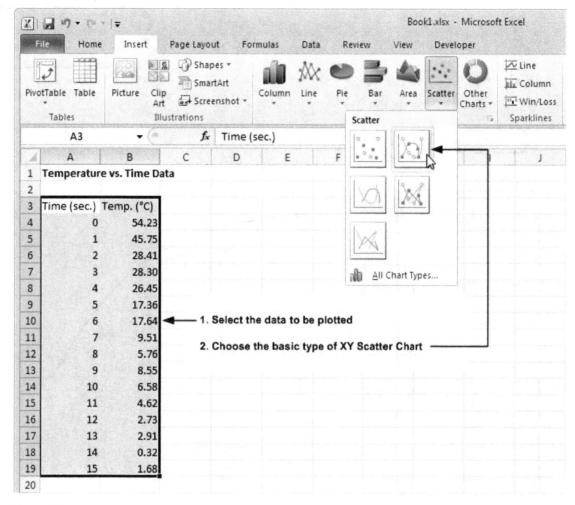

Figure 3
Select the data to be graphed, then choose the type of graph.

Excel provides five options for XY scatter graphs:

1. Markers (data points) only, no curves connecting the points in the *data series*.
2. Markers connected by *smoothed curves*. The curve will bend as needed to go through every data point.
3. No markers, just smoothed curves.
4. Markers connected by straight *line segments*.
5. No markers, just straight line segments.

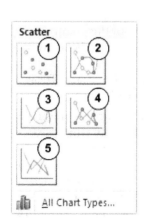

Figure 4
Scatter graph options.

When you choose one of the graph types (in Figure 3, markers connected with smoothed curves were selected), a basic graph of your selected data will be inserted on the worksheet, as shown in Figure 5.

Several important features have been indicated in Figure 5:

1. The basic graph (with markers connected with smoothed curves, as requested) has been inserted into the worksheet.
2. The data used to create the graph are indicated with colored borders. You can move these borders with the mouse to change the data range that appears on the graph.

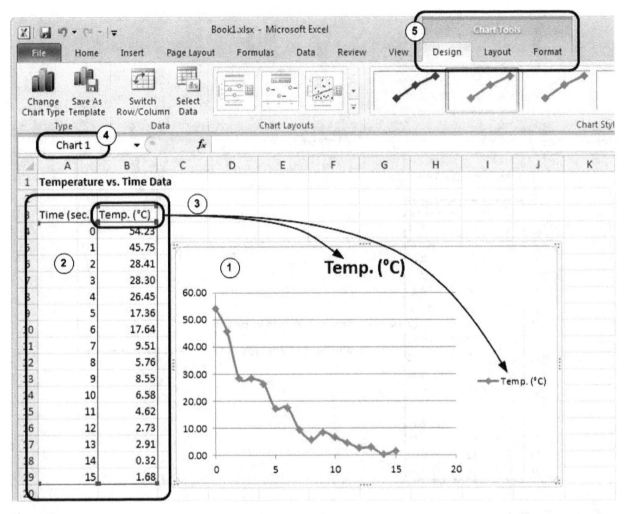

Figure 5
The basic graph inserted on the worksheet.

3. The column heading for the *y* values has been used as the *graph title* (above the graph) and appears on the *graph legend* (to the right of the graph).
4. The chart is an Excel *object* (this term is defined below) and has been given a name (Chart 1).
5. Three new tabs have appeared on the Ribbon. The **Chart Tools** tabs (**Design**, **Layout**, and **Format**) are used to modify the appearance of the graph.

An object, in a programming context, is an item that exists (has been created and stored in computer memory), has an identity (this graph is called "Chart 1"), and has properties that can be assigned values (e.g., diamond-shaped markers connected with smoothed curves, a location on the worksheet). The chart object has an associated data set (from cells A3:B19). Because the graph is a self-contained object, it can also be moved around, even between programs using copy and paste. We'll present moving graphs between programs (e.g., from Excel to Word) later in the chapter.

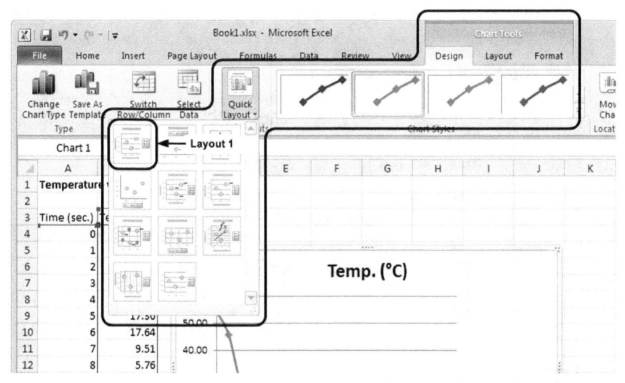

Figure 6
Select a graph layout.

Step 3. Choose a Quick Layout. The basic graph shown in Figure 5 is missing axis labels, but this is easy to fix using the Chart Tools on the Ribbon. Use Ribbon options **Chart Tools/Design tab/Chart Layouts group/Quick Layout** to open the Quick Layouts selector panel, shown in Figure 6.

The Quick Layout selector panel packs a lot of information into a tiny space. For now we will simply use Layout 1 (selected in Figure 6), but the features of the available layouts are summarized later in this chapter. Layout 1 is adequate for most engineering graphs, and features can be activated or deactivated at any time.

When Layout 1 is selected, Excel applies the additional features (axis titles) to the graph, as shown in Figure 7.

Excel has added axis titles with the text "Axis Title"; something a little more descriptive is needed. We need to edit the axis titles.

Step 4. Edit the axis titles and graph title. To edit the *axis titles*:

1. Make sure the graph is selected (a wide border is shown on a selected graph). Click on the graph to select it, if needed.
2. Click on the title to select it. A border around the title indicates that the title has been selected.
3. Select the text in the title (drag the mouse across it or triple-click on the text to select the entire text string).
4. Enter the desired text for the axis title.
5. Click outside the axis title, but inside the graph when you have finished editing the axis title.

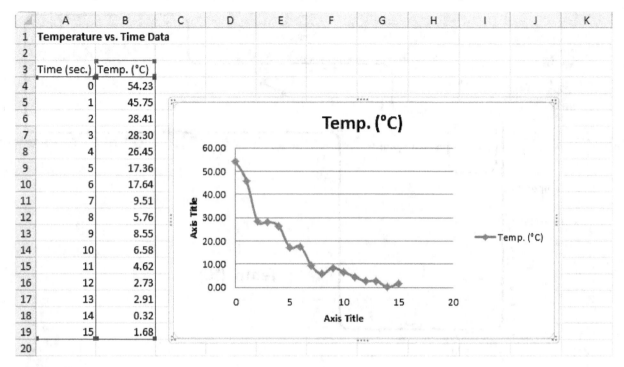

Figure 7
The XY scatter graph after Layout 1 has been applied.

The same process is used to edit the graph title. The result of editing the axis titles and graph title is shown in Figure 8.

The size and location of the graph are set using default values, but they can be changed with the mouse. A graph in edit mode is indicated by a thick border with groups of small dots (called *handles*) located around the border. Drag any of the handles to resize the graph and drag the borders between the handles to move the graph.

The colors used in the graph depend on the *theme* that has been applied to the workbook ("Office" theme by default). Themes are predefined collections of colors and font specifications. You can change the theme applied to your workbook using Ribbon options **Page Layout/ Themes (group)/Themes (button)** and then selecting a theme from the drop-down selector. Be aware that the theme impacts a lot more than just the selected graph; changing the theme will change the appearance (colors, font styles, font sizes) of everything in the workbook.

You can continue to edit the graph after it has been placed on the worksheet.

4 EDITING AN EXISTING GRAPH

Since Excel 2007, the Ribbon is the way to access and modify a graph's features. Whenever a graph has been selected, three **Chart Tools** tabs appear on the Ribbon. (If the graph is not selected, click anywhere on the graph to enter edit mode.) For now, each of the chart tabs will be presented briefly; then more information will be provided about how to use each tab in the next sections.

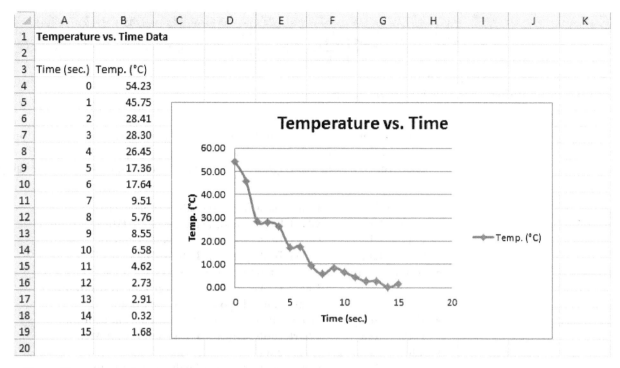

▲	A	B	C	D	E	F	G	H	I	J	K
1	Temperature vs. Time Data										
2											
3	Time (sec.)	Temp. (°C)									
4	0	54.23									
5	1	45.75									
6	2	28.41									
7	3	28.30									
8	4	26.45									
9	5	17.36									
10	6	17.64									
11	7	9.51									
12	8	5.76									
13	9	8.55									
14	10	6.58									
15	11	4.62									
16	12	2.73									
17	13	2.91									
18	14	0.32									
19	15	1.68									
20											

Figure 8
The XY scatter graph after updating the axis titles.

Chart Tools/Design Tab (Figure 9)—this tab is primarily used when creating the graph. See Section 4.2 for more information on using this tab.

- Modify the way Excel is plotting your data
  - Change rows/columns   **Chart Tools/Design/Data/[Switch Row/Column]**
  - Select graph data   **Chart Tools/Design/Data/Select Data**
- Set or change the basic appearance of the graph
  - Choose a basic layout   **Chart Tools/Design/Chart Layouts/Quick Layouts**
  - Choose a chart style   **Chart Tools/Design/Chart Styles**

Under the **Design** tab, the **Chart Layouts** group provides quick access to 11 basic chart layouts. The layout selector that is displayed using the **Quick Layout** button (Ribbon options **Chart Tools/Design/Chart Layouts/Quick Layout**). The 11 layouts are displayed graphically as small chart icons, as illustrated in Figure 10.

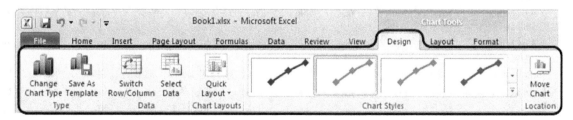

Figure 9
The **Chart Tools/Design** tab.

Figure 10
Available Quick Layouts for graphs (icons).

The icons are hard to read until you know the basic features of the various layouts. Table 1 lists the features of each layout.

Chart Tools/Layout Tab (Figure 11)—this tab is used to modify an existing graph.

- Add or modify labels
    - Chart Title   **Chart Tools/Layout/Labels/Chart Title**
    - Axis Titles   **Chart Tools/Layout/Labels/Axis Titles**
    - Legend   **Chart Tools/Layout/Labels/Legend**
    - Data Labels   **Chart Tools/Layout/Labels/Data Labels**
- Modify the appearance of axes and gridlines
    - Axes   **Chart Tools/Layout/Axes (group)/Axes (button)**
    - Gridlines   **Chart Tools/Layout/Axes/Gridlines**
- Modify the appearance of the plot area within the graph window
    - Plot Area   **Chart Tools/Layout Background/Plot Area**
- Add trendlines and error bars
    - Trendlines   **Chart Tools/Layout/Analysis/Trendline**
    - Error bars   **Chart Tools/Layout/Analysis/Error Bars**
         Chart Tools/Format Tab
- Add or modify the graph's border and/or background
    - Border/Background   **Chart Tools/Format/Shape Styles (selector)**

Table 1 Summary of Features of the Quick Layouts

Feature	Quick Layout										
	1	2	3	4	5	6	7	8	9	10	11
Graph Title	Top	Top	None	None	Top	Top	Top	Top	Top	None	None
X Axis Label	Yes	Yes	Yes	None	Yes	Yes	None	None	Yes	Yes	None
Y Axis Label	Yes	None	Yes	None	Yes	Yes	None	None	Yes	Yes	None
Legend	Right	Top	Right	Bottom	Right	Right	Right	Bottom	Right	Right	Right
X Axis Major Gridlines	No	No	Yes	No	No	No	Yes	No	No	Yes	No
X Axis Minor Gridlines	No	No	Yes	No	No	No	No	No	No	Yes	No
Y Axis Major Gridlines	Yes	No	Yes	No	Yes	Yes	Yes	Yes	Yes	Yes	Yes
Y Axis Minor Gridlines	No	No	Yes	No	No	No	No	No	Yes	Yes	No
Data Labels	None	All (x,y)	None	None	All (x,y)	All (x)	All (x,y)	None	None	None	None
Regression Line	No	No	Yes	No	No	No	No	No	Yes	No	No
Regression Equation	No	No	No	No	No	No	No	No	Yes	No	No
R^2 Value	No	No	No	No	No	No	No	No	Yes	No	No

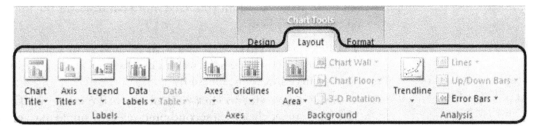

Figure 11
The **Chart Tools/Layout** tab (only a portion of this tab is shown here).

Note: If you are familiar with prior versions of Excel, you can still right-click on a feature and select "Format <feature>" from the pop-up menu or (in Excel 2010) double-click on the graph feature. This method opens the same dialog boxes that can be accessed from the Ribbon. But the Ribbon provides another quick way to access the dialogs:

- **Chart Tools/Layout/Current Selection/Format Selection**
- **Chart Tools/Format/Current Selection/Format Selection**

The **Current Selection** group is available from either the **Layout** tab or the **Format** tab (shown in Figure 12). If you click on the graph feature that you want to modify (or select the feature in the drop-down box in the **Current Selection** group) and then click the **Format Selection** button, the dialog box for that graph feature will open.

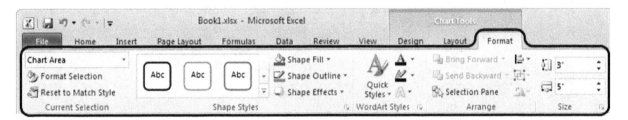

Figure 12
The **Chart Tools/Format** tab.

HINT

Once a Format dialog for a graph element is open, if you click on a different graph element Excel will automatically switch to the Format dialog for that graph element. For example, if you are changing the appearance of the x axis and want to also change the appearance of the y axis, don't close the Format x axis dialog. Instead, when you are done formatting the x axis, simply click on the y axis and Excel will display the Format y axis dialog.

4.1 Modifying the Appearance of the Plotted Curve

If you want to control the appearance of the plotted curve(s), Excel has been designed to have you choose a layout (**Chart Tools/Design/Chart Layouts/Quick Layouts**) and a style (**Chart Tools/Design/Chart Styles**) and that's it. Sometimes that's adequate; but often you need more control over the appearance of the plotted data. Here's how...

1. Click on the curve that you wish to modify to select it. (The one curve in Figure 13 has been selected.) The markers are highlighted to indicate that the curve has been selected.

    Note: Be careful to click only once on the curve; clicking once selects the entire curve, clicking a second time selects a single marker on the curve. (This allows you to change the appearance of a single marker if you wish to highlight one point on the curve.)

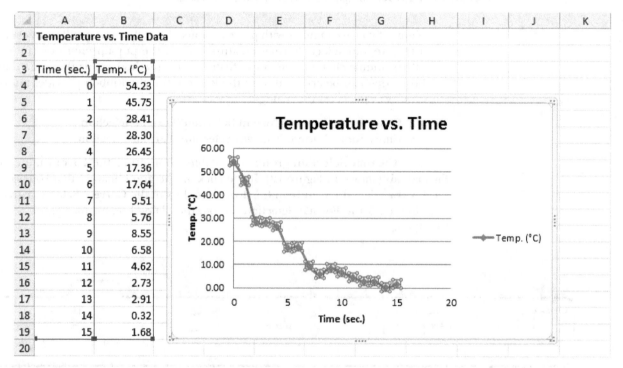

Figure 13
The graph with the plotted data curve selected.

2. Use one of the following (equivalent) Ribbon options:
    o **Chart Tools/Layout/Current Selection/Format Selection**
    o **Chart Tools/Format/Current Selection/Format Selection**
    Clicking the **Format Selection** button when the curve is selected will open the Format Data Series dialog shown in Figure 14.

    Note: In Excel 2010 (and Excel 2003, but not Excel 2007), you can simply double-click on the curve to open the Format Data Series dialog.

3. Choose the panel needed to make the desired change. The **Marker Options** panel is shown in Figure 14. This panel allows you to set the type and size of the marker—or choose **None** to deactivate markers altogether.

    The Format Data Series dialog panels listed below allow you to make the following common adjustments to the plotted data curves:
    o *Series Options:* Choose to plot the series on the primary (left) or secondary (right) *y* axis. This option is not available unless there are at least two curves on the graph.

Figure 14
The Format Data Series dialog, **Marker Options** panel.

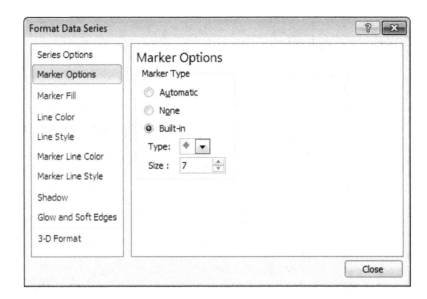

- ○ *Marker Options:* Set marker type and size.
- ○ *Marker Fill:* Allows you to create filled and unfilled markers (e.g., ◆, ◇).
- ○ *Line Color:* Set the line color and activate and deactivate the line between the markers.
- ○ *Line Style:* Set the line width, solid or dashed style, activate or deactivate smoothing of the connecting lines.
- ○ *Marker Line Color:* Set the color of the line used to draw the border of the marker. This is most useful for unfilled markers.
- ○ *Marker Line Style:* Set the width of the line used to draw the border of the marker.

4. Once you have made the desired changes, **Close** the Format Data Series dialog. In Figure 15, the Format Data Series dialog was used to create large, unfilled markers without connecting lines.

4.2 Adding a Second Curve to the Plot

If there is another column of data to plot on the same graph, such as the predicted temperature values shown in column C in Figure 15, the easiest way to add a second curve to the plot is to:

1. Click on the graph to select it. Be sure not to click on the plotted data points; you need the graph selected, not the original data series. When the graph is selected, the data used to create the graph are surrounded by colored borders, as shown in Figure 16.
2. Drag the corner (handle) of the box containing the y values over one column so that both columns of y values are included in the box. This is illustrated in Figure 17.

Expanding the border around the y values is all that is required to add a second curve to the graph, but there's one catch: This method works only when the two columns of y values share the same set of x values. If the two sets of y values correspond to different sets of x values, a different approach must be used.

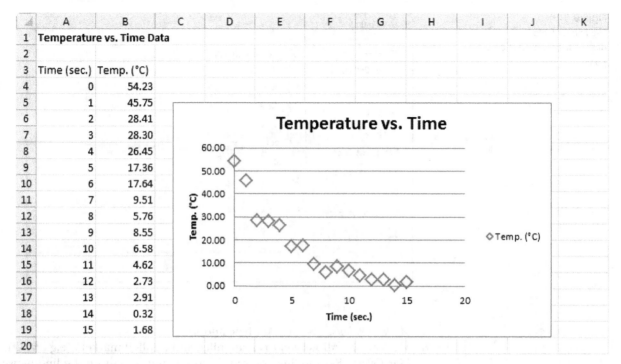

Figure 15
The modified graph.

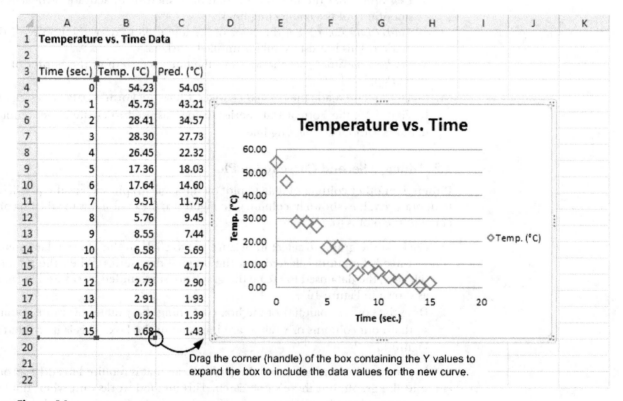

Drag the corner (handle) of the box containing the Y values to expand the box to include the data values for the new curve.

Figure 16
The selected graph, ready to add an additional curve.

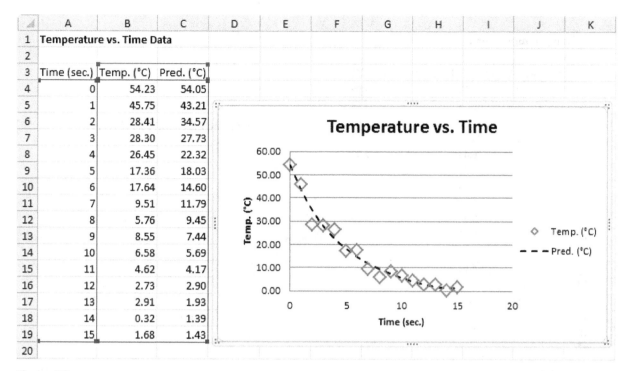

◢	A	B	C	D	E	F	G	H	I	J	K
1	Temperature vs. Time Data										
2											
3	Time (sec.)	Temp. (°C)	Pred. (°C)								
4	0	54.23	54.05								
5	1	45.75	43.21								
6	2	28.41	34.57								
7	3	28.30	27.73								
8	4	26.45	22.32								
9	5	17.36	18.03								
10	6	17.64	14.60								
11	7	9.51	11.79								
12	8	5.76	9.45								
13	9	8.55	7.44								
14	10	6.58	5.69								
15	11	4.62	4.17								
16	12	2.73	2.90								
17	13	2.91	1.93								
18	14	0.32	1.39								
19	15	1.68	1.43								
20											

Figure 17
The second data series has been added to the graph.

The dashed line used for the predicted temperature values in Figure 17 is not Excel's default for the second curve on a graph. The appearance of the second data series was modified using the Format Data Series dialog as described in the previous section.

Adding a Second Data Series with Different x Values

It is not uncommon to have two related data sets that do not share the same *x* values. This happens, for example, when you repeat an experiment but don't record the data values at exactly the same times in each experiment. Figure 18 shows two temperature vs. time data sets, but the columns of times are quite different.

The process of graphing the two sets of data begins as before: the first data series is graphed by itself (as shown in Figure 18). Then, to add the second data series:

1. Use Ribbon options **Chart Tools/Design/Data/Select Data**. This opens the Select Data Source dialog, as shown in Figure 19.
2. The "Temp. (°C)" shown just below the **Add** button in Figure 19 is the name of the data series that is already plotted. We need to add the new data series to the graph. To do so, click the **Add** button to open the Edit Series dialog, as shown in Figure 20.
3. The Edit Series dialog needs three pieces of information in order to create the new data series: the series name (used in the legend, optional), the cell range containing the *x* values, and the cell range containing the *y* values.

The small button at the right side of the Series name field (indicated in Figure 20) is supposed to look like an arrow pointing to a worksheet; clicking

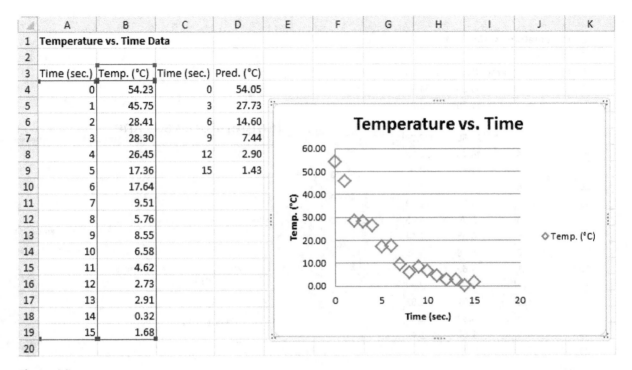

Figure 18
Two temperature and time data sets.

Figure 19
The Select Data Source dialog showing only one data series.

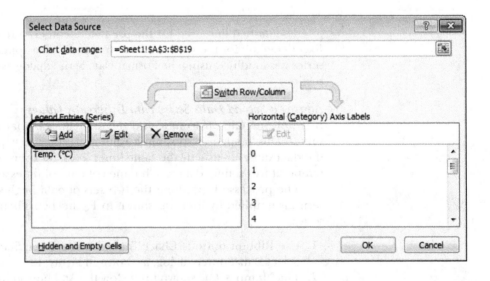

this button allows you to jump to the worksheet so that you can use the mouse to select the cell containing the new series name (cell D3, see Figure 18). When you do jump to the worksheet, yet another small Edit Series dialog opens, as shown in Figure 21.

Wherever you click on the worksheet, that cell address appears in the Edit Series dialog. In Figure 21, cell D3 was selected since that cell contains the name of the new data series.

Figure 20
The Edit Series dialog.

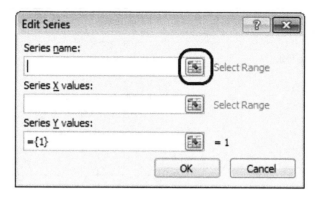

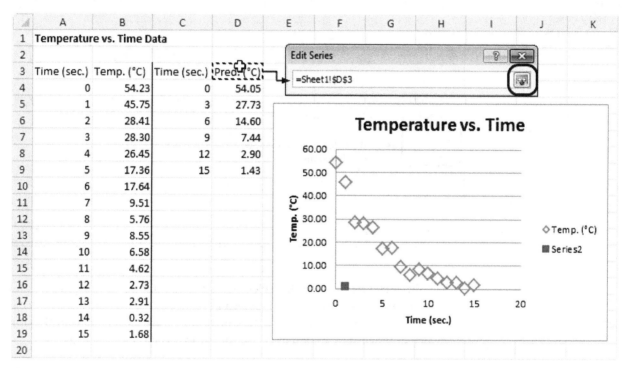

Figure 21
Pointing out the cell containing the new series name.

4. There is, again, a small button at the right side of the data entry field, indicated in Figure 21. This button will return back to the larger Edit Series dialog (shown in Figures 20 and 22). When you return to the larger Edit Series dialog, the information (cell address) gathered from the worksheet is automatically entered into the dialog.

5. The process of jumping to the worksheet is repeated two more times to point out (1) the cell range containing the new *x* values (cells C4:C9), and (2) the cell range containing the new *y* values (cells D4:D9). All of the necessary information has been collected in the Edit Series dialog shown in Figure 22.

6. Next, click **OK** to add the new data series to the Select Data Source dialog, as shown in Figure 23.

Figure 22

The Edit Series dialog (with information needed to create the new data series).

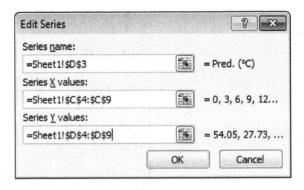

Figure 23

The Select Data Source dialog showing two data series.

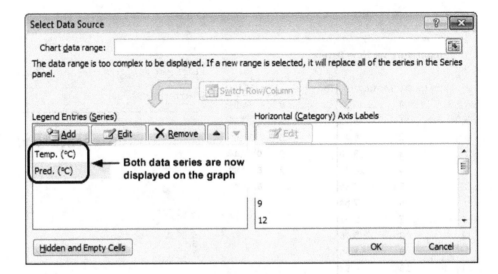

7. Finally, click **OK** to close the Select Data Source dialog and display the new curve on the graph. The result is shown in Figure 24. Again, the appearance of the new curve was modified using Ribbon options **Chart Tools/Layout/Current Selection/Format Selection** to access the Format Data Series dialog.

4.3 Changing the Appearance of the Plot using the Layout Tab

Once you have a graph with one or more curves (data series) displayed, you can use the **Layout** tab under **Chart Tools** to modify the appearance of the graph (Figure 25).

Changing Labels

The labels group (**Chart Tools/Layout/Labels**) is used primarily to activate or deactivate the various labels on a graph. If the labels are displayed, you do not need the Ribbon to edit the text displayed in the labels, simply:

1. Make sure the graph is selected.
2. Click on the label to select it.
3. Select the text in the label (drag the mouse across it or triple-click on the text to select the entire text string).
4. Enter the desired text for the label.
5. Click outside the label, but inside the graph when you have finished editing.

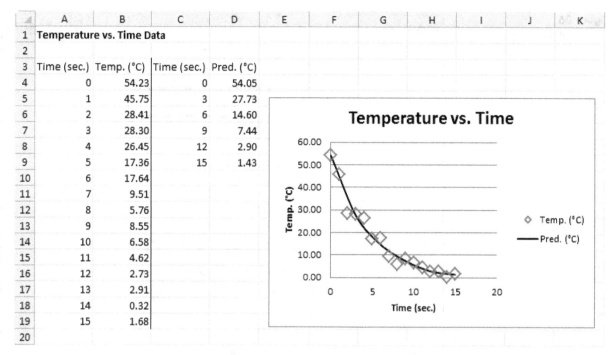

◢	A	B	C	D	E	F	G	H	I	J	K
1	Temperature vs. Time Data										
2											
3	Time (sec.)	Temp. (°C)	Time (sec.)	Pred. (°C)							
4	0	54.23	0	54.05							
5	1	45.75	3	27.73							
6	2	28.41	6	14.60							
7	3	28.30	9	7.44							
8	4	26.45	12	2.90							
9	5	17.36	15	1.43							
10	6	17.64									
11	7	9.51									
12	8	5.76									
13	9	8.55									
14	10	6.58									
15	11	4.62									
16	12	2.73									
17	13	2.91									
18	14	0.32									
19	15	1.68									
20											

Figure 24
The graph with two data series plotted.

Figure 25
The **Chart Tools/ Layout** tab.

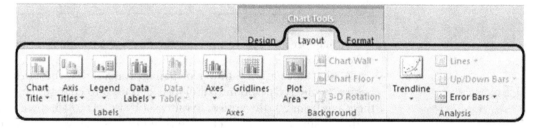

The exception to this is the legend. If the series names in the legend are coming from cells (such as cells B3 and D3 in Figure 24), then you cannot edit the legend directly. To change the legend, edit the cells that contain the series names and the legend will automatically be updated to reflect the changes.

Modify the Appearance of Axes and Gridlines

There are several ways to open the Format Axis dialog to make changes to the appearance of an axis or gridlines:

- Use Ribbon options **Chart Tools/Layout/Axes (group)/Axes (button)**, then select the desired axis to modify (primary or secondary, horizontal or vertical), then select **More Axis Options...**
- Click on the axis you want to modify to select it (click on the numbers, not the axis line), and then use Ribbon options **Chart Tools/Layout (or Format)/ Current Selection/Format Selection**.
- Right-click on the axis you want to modify (right-click on the numbers, not the axis line) and choose **Format Axis...** from the pop-up menu.
- In Excel 2010, double-click on the axis that you want to modify.

Figure 26
The Format Axis dialog.

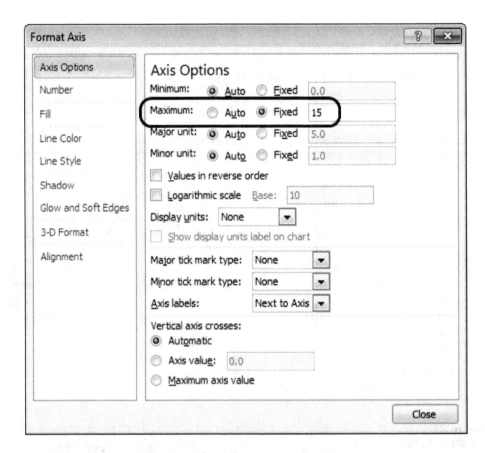

Whichever method you prefer, the Format Axis dialog shown in Figure 26 will open.

Again, there are a number of panels available on the Format Axis dialog. In Figure 26, the **Axis Options** panel has been used to change the **Maximum** value on the *x* axis from 20 (the autoscale value set by Excel) to 15, since 15 is the maximum *x* (time) value in the data sets. The result of this change is shown in Figure 27; the data fit the graph better with less wasted space.

To display vertical *gridlines*, use Ribbon options **Chart Tools/Layout/Axes/ Gridlines**, then choose **Primary Vertical Gridlines/Major Gridlines**. The graph with both horizontal and vertical gridlines is shown in Figure 28.

Figure 27
The result of rescaling the
x axis.

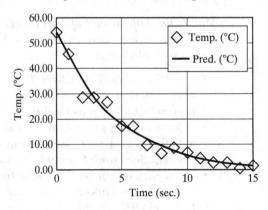

Figure 28

The graph after activating major vertical gridlines.

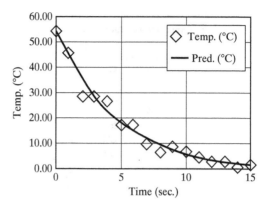

4.4 Adding a trendline to a graph

A *trendline* is a curve that goes through the data points (not through each point) to highlight the trend in the data. Most, but not all, of the trendlines available in Excel are best-fit regression lines. Specifically, Excel provides the following trendline options:

- Linear (straight line)
- Exponential
- Logarithmic
- Polynomial
- Power
- Moving Average (this is the only nonregression trendline)

Some options may not be available for some data sets if the math involved is not valid for all values in the set. For example, $\ln(0)$ is not defined, so logarithmic fits are not possible for data sets containing y values of zero. Excel will display an error message if the trendline cannot be calculated.

Because the trendlines (except for the moving average) are best-fit regression lines, the *equations of the trendlines* and the R^2 *values* (indicating the "goodness of the fit") are available and can be displayed on the graph.

The quickest way to add a trendline to a graph is to right-click on the data series that the trendline should be fit to, and then choose **Add Trendline** from the series' pop-up menu (illustrated in Figure 29). (To simplify the graph, the predicted temperature values have been eliminated in Figure 29.)

Ribbon options could also be used to add a trendline. Use **Chart Tools/Layout/ Analysis/Trendline**, then select More Trendline Options... If more than one curve has been plotted, you will be asked to select the data series to fit with a trendline.

Whether you right-click the data set, or use the Ribbon, the Format Trendline dialog will open, as shown in Figure 30.

On the Format Trendline dialog, we have requested an exponential fit to the temperature data and have asked that the equation of the trendline and the R^2 value be printed on the graph. The result is shown in Figure 31.

In Figure 31, the equation of the trendline and R^2 value were relocated and increased in size to improve readability. The exponential curve seems to go through the data values fairly well, but the R^2 value of 0.876 isn't that great. We can try a different type of trendline, say a polynomial, to see if we can get a better fit. The result of applying a fourth-order polynomial trendline is shown in Figure 32.

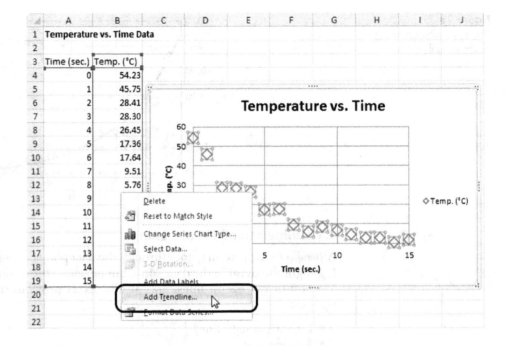

Figure 29
Adding a trendline
using the data series'
pop-up menu.

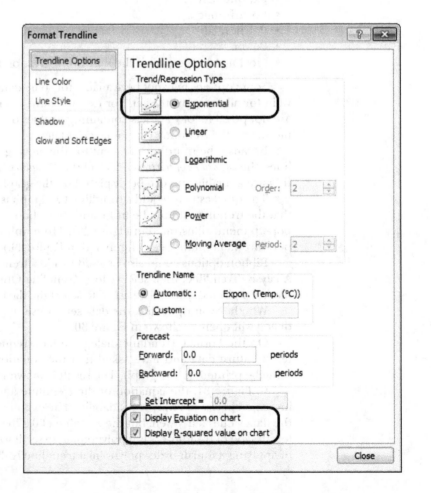

Figure 30
The Format Trendline
dialog.

Figure 31

The graph with the exponential trendline, trendline equation, and R^2 value.

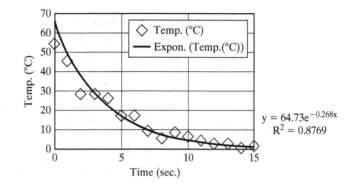

Figure 32

The graph with the fourth-order polynomial trendline, trendline equation, and R^2 value.

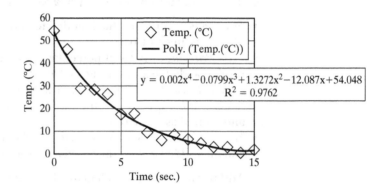

The R^2 value is closer to 1 (1 is a perfect fit), so the fourth-order polynomial trendline is doing a better job of fitting the data than the exponential trendline did. But be careful not to infer too much from the trendline because this data is imperfect. A very high-order polynomial could probably wiggle through every data point and give an R^2 value of 1, but that won't help us interpret the data. It is OK to use trendlines to show trends in the data, but don't forget to go back to the theory behind the experiment to seek a fitting equation that makes sense. Trendlines often get used because they are easy, but the trendlines available in Excel may not be appropriate for analyzing every data set.

4.5 Adding Error Bars

NOTE

With Excel 2007, a bug appeared in Excel's handling of error bars, and it is still present in Excel 2010. When you use the Ribbon to open the error bar dialog, only the vertical error bars are available for editing on the Format Error Bars dialog, and Excel automatically adds horizontal error bars whether you want them or not! Fortunately there is a workaround for this:

- If you want to edit vertical error bars, use the expected Ribbon commands (**Chart Tools/Layout/Analysis/Error Bars**, then choose **More Error Bars Options...**). The Format Error Bars dialog will work correctly to allow you to generate vertical error bars. However, Excel will add horizontal error bars whether you want them or not, and even if you want horizontal error bars, they may not be calculated correctly for your situation. But we can make this work:

o If you do not want horizontal error bars, click on any one of the horizontal error bars, then press the [Delete] key—problem solved.

o If you want horizontal error bars, right-click on any one of the horizontal error bars and select **Format Error Bars...** from the pop-up menu. The Format Error Bars dialog will open and allow you to calculate the horizontal error bars using any of the available methods.

o If you do not want vertical error bars, click on any one of the vertical error bars, then press the [Delete] key.

Excel can automatically add *x-* or *y-error bars*, calculated from the data in several ways:

- *Fixed Value:* A fixed value is added to and subtracted from each data value and plotted as an error bar.
- *Fixed Percentage:* A fixed percentage is multiplied by each data value, and the result is added to and subtracted from the data value and plotted as an error bar.
- *Standard Deviation:* The selected standard deviation of all of the values in the data set is computed and then added to and subtracted from each data value and plotted as an error bar.
- *Standard Error:* The standard error of all of the values in the data set is computed and then added to and subtracted from each data value and plotted as an error bar.

Additionally, you can calculate the values you want plotted as error bars by using the Custom error bar option.

To demonstrate how to add error bars to a graph, fixed-percentage (30%) error bars will be added to the temperature values (*y* values) shown in Figure 33.

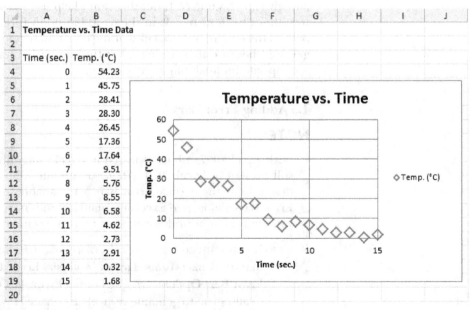

Figure 33
Temperature vs. time data.

Figure 34
The Format Error Bars
dialog.

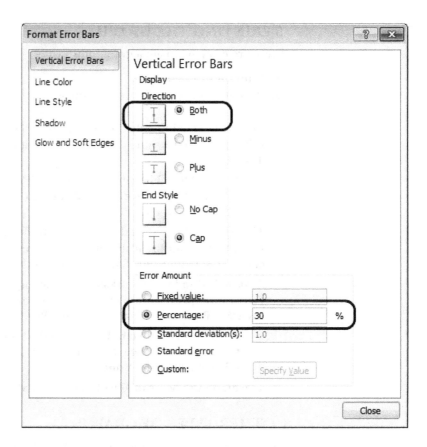

To bring up the Format Error Bars dialog, click on the graph to select it, then use Ribbon options **Chart Tools/Layout/Analysis/Error Bars**, then choose More Error Bar Options... from the menu. The Format Error Bars dialog will open as shown in Figure 34.

Select the **Both** option to display error bars both above and below the data marker and set the **Error Amount Percentage** to 30% as indicated in Figure 34. The graph with the vertical 30% error bars is shown in Figure 35.

Figure 35
The temperature vs. time
graph with 30% error bars.

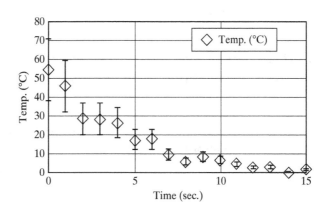

5 PRINTING THE GRAPH

There are two ways to get a graph onto paper:

1. Print the graph only.
2. Print the worksheet containing the graph.

Method 1. **Printing only the graph.** First, click the graph to select it. A border will be displayed around the edge of the graph to show that it has been selected. Then use:

- Excel 2010: **File tab/Print (panel)/Print (button)**
- Excel 2007: **Office/Print/Print (or Quick Print, or Print Preview)**
- Excel 2003: **File/Print**

The graph will, by default, be resized to fit the page. If you use Print Preview (Excel 2010 automatically includes a preview on the **Print** panel), you can change the margins to change the size of the printed graph.

Method 2. **Printing the worksheet containing the graph.** Include the graph when you set the print area with Ribbon options **Page Layout/Page Setup/Print Area/Set Print Area** [Excel 2003: File/Print Area/Set Print Area]. Then use:

- Excel 2010: **File tab/Print (panel)/Print (button)**
- Excel 2007: **Office/Print/Print (or Quick Print, or Print Preview)**
- Excel 2003: **File/Print**

The graph will be printed with the specified worksheet print area.

6 OTHER TYPES OF GRAPHS

Most of this chapter has focused on XY scatter graphs, the most common type of graph for engineering work; however, engineers use other types of graphs too. Other standard types include the following:

- Line graphs
- Column and bar graphs
- Pie charts
- Surface plots

CAUTION: A common error is to use a line graph when an XY scatter graph is needed. You will get away using a line graph if the x values in your data set are uniformly spaced. But if the x values are not uniformly spaced, your curve will appear distorted on the line graph. The following example is intended to illustrate how a line graph will misrepresent your data if your x values are not uniformly spaced.

EXAMPLE 2

The x values in the worksheet shown in Figure 33 are calculated as

$$x_{i+1} = 1.2 \cdot x_i \tag{1}$$

This creates nonuniformly spaced x values. The y values are calculated from the x values as

$$y_i = 3 \cdot x_i \tag{2}$$

so that the relationship between x and y is linear. On the XY scatter graph shown in Figure 36, the linear relationship is evident in the straight-line relationship between x and y.

However, when the same data are plotted on a line graph (shown in Figure 37), the relationship between x and y appears to be nonlinear.

The apparent nonlinear relationship between x and y in the line graph is an artifact of the line graph, because the actual x values were not used to plot the points on the graph. Excel's line graph simply causes the y values to be distributed evenly across the chart (effectively assuming uniform x spacing), and the x values (if included when the graph is created) are simply used as labels on the x axis. This can be misleading on a line graph, because the x values are displayed on the x axis, but they were not used to position the data points.

Figure 36
The data plotted on and XY scatter graph.

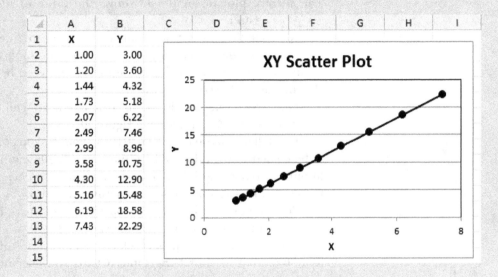

Figure 37
The same data plotted as a line graph.

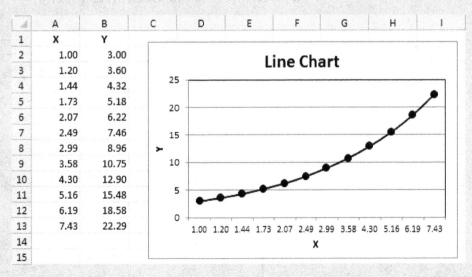

(*continued*)

Excel's line, column, bar, and pie charts all require only y values to create the graph. If you provide two columns (or rows) of data, the left column (or top row) will be used as labels for the graph. If you need to plot x and y values on a graph, you must use an XY scatter plot.

Surface Plots

A surface plot takes the values in a two-dimensional range of cells and displays the values graphically.

EXAMPLE 3

The surface plot in Figure 38 shows the value of $F(x,y) = \sin(x)\cos(y)$ for $-1 \leq x \leq 2$ and $-1 \leq y \leq 2$.

To create the plot, x values ranging from -1 to 2 were entered in column A, and y values ranging from -1 to 2 were entered in row 2, as shown in Figure 39. To create these series, the first two values were entered by hand, and then the Fill Handle was used to complete the rest of each series.

The first value for $F(x,y)$ is calculated in cell B3 using the formula =SIN($A3)*COS(B$2), as shown in Figure 40.

The dollar signs on the A in SIN($A3) and the 2 in COS(B$2) allow the formula to be copied to the other cells in the range (both x and y directions). When the formula is copied, the **SIN** functions will always reference x values in column A, and **COS** functions will always reference y values in row 3.

Next, the formula in cell B3 is copied to all of the cells in the range B3:Q18, to fill the two-dimensional array (Figure 41).

Then the array of values is selected before inserting a surface graph using Ribbon options **Insert/Charts/Other Charts** and selecting the **Wire-frame** icon in the **Surface** category (illustrated in Figure 42).

Figure 38
Surface plot of $F(x,y) = \sin(x)\cos(y)$.

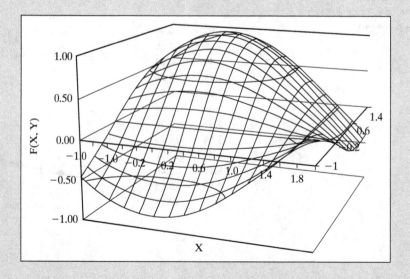

	A	B	C	D	E	F	G	H	I	J	K	L	M	N	O	P	Q	R
1		Y >>>																
2	X	-1.0	-0.8	-0.6	-0.4	-0.2	0.0	0.2	0.4	0.6	0.8	1.0	1.2	1.4	1.6	1.8	2.0	
3	-1.0																	
4	-0.8																	
5	-0.6																	
6	-0.4																	
7	-0.2																	
8	0.0																	
9	0.2																	
10	0.4																	
11	0.6																	
12	0.8																	
13	1.0																	
14	1.2																	
15	1.4																	
16	1.6																	
17	1.8																	
18	2.0																	
19																		

Figure 39
x and y values.

B3 f_x =SIN($A3)*COS(B$2)

	A	B	C	D	E	F	G	H	I	J	K	L	M	N	O	P	Q	R
1		Y >>>																
2	X	-1.0	-0.8	-0.6	-0.4	-0.2	0.0	0.2	0.4	0.6	0.8	1.0	1.2	1.4	1.6	1.8	2.0	
3	-1.0	-0.45																
4	-0.8																	
5	-0.6																	
6	-0.4																	
7	-0.2																	
8	0.0																	
9	0.2																	
10	0.4																	
11	0.6																	
12	0.8																	
13	1.0																	
14	1.2																	
15	1.4																	
16	1.6																	
17	1.8																	
18	2.0																	
19																		

Figure 40
The first calculated cell, cell B3.

(*continued*)

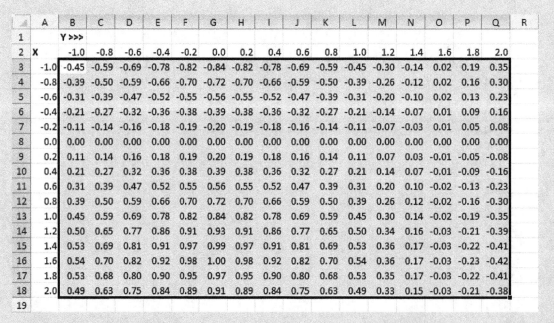

Figure 41
Cell B3 has been copied to cells B3:Q18.

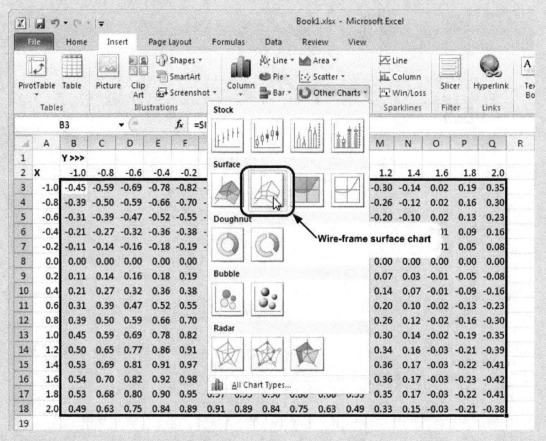

Figure 42
Inserting a surface graph into the worksheet.

The surface graph is inserted into a window on top of the data (see Figure 43), but it can be moved.

The basic graph has been inserted, but some better labels will help people understand what they are seeing. First, we add three axis labels and a title, as shown in Figure 44. This was accomplished from the Ribbon using **Chart Tools/Layout/Labels/Chart Title** and **Chart Tools/Layout/Labels/Axis Titles**.

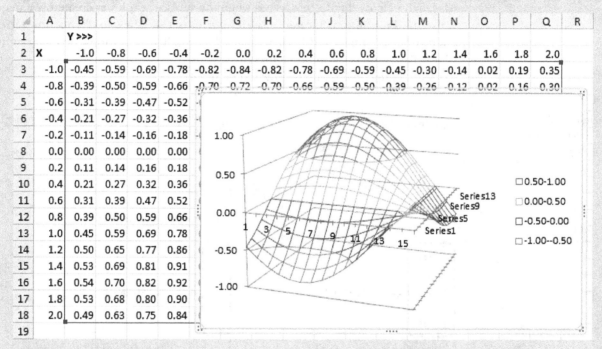

Figure 43
The surface graph inserted into the worksheet.

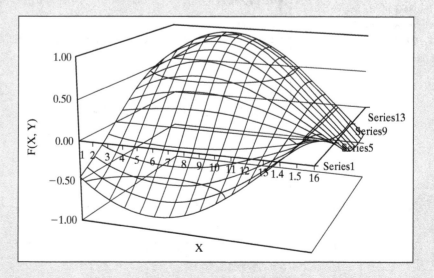

Figure 44
The surface graph with axis labels and title.

Next, we want to replace the labels on the x axis (1 ... 16) and the y axis (Series1 ... Series13) with something more meaningful. The x and y values both range from –1 to 2, so we want to get these values into the labels on the x and y axes.

Opening the Select Data Source dialog (**Chart Tools/Design/Data/Select Data**), we can quickly see where the labels on the x and y axes are coming from (Figure 45).

The x and y axis labels are coming from the series names (y axis) and horizontal axis labels (x axis) that Excel created when the surface graph was created. We need to use the **Edit** buttons located just above each set of labels to change the series names (one at a time) and horizontal axis labels (all at once) to more meaningful values. The result is shown in Figure 46.

And the updated graph is shown in Figure 47.

Figure 45
The Select Data Source dialog.

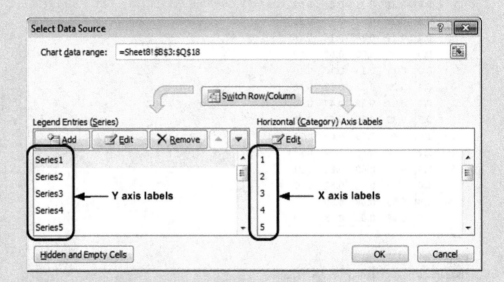

Figure 46
The Select Data Source dialog with updated x and y axis labels.

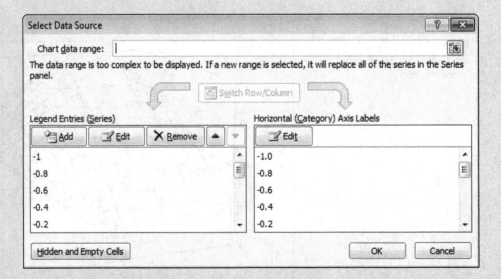

Figure 47
The surface plot with updated *x* and *y* axis labels.

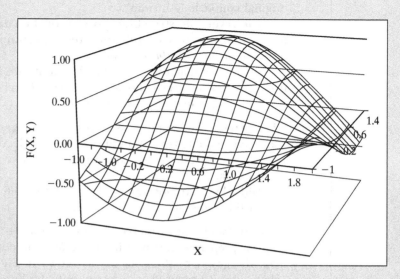

Note that the *x* and *y* values on the worksheet (column A and row 2) were never used to plot the points on the surface plot. The F(*x,y*) values in cells B3 through Q18 were plotted with uniform spacing in the *x* and *y* directions. This is a significant limitation of surface plotting in Excel.

MATERIALS TESTING

Stress–Strain Curve I

Strength testing of materials often involves a *tensile test* in which a sample of the material is held between two mandrels while increasing force—actually, *stress* (i.e., force per unit area)—is applied. A stress vs. strain curve for a typical ductile material is shown in Figure 48.

During the test, the sample first stretches reversibly (A to B). Then irreversible stretching occurs (B to D). Finally, the sample breaks (point D).

Point C is called the material's *ultimate stress*, or *tensile strength*, and represents the greatest stress that the material can endure (with deformation) before coming

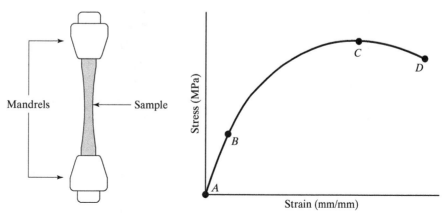

Figure 48
Tensile test.

apart. The *strain* is the amount of elongation of the sample (mm) divided by the original sample length (mm).

The reversible stretching portion of the curve (A to B) is linear, and the proportionality constant relating stress and strain in this region is called *Young's modulus*, or the *modulus of elasticity.*

Tensile test data on a soft, ductile sample are listed in Table 2 (available electronically at http://www.chbe.montana.edu/Excel).

To analyze the data we will want to:

1. Plot the tensile test data as a stress vs. strain graph.
2. Evaluate the tensile strength from the graph (or the data set).
3. Create a second graph containing only the elastic-stretch (linear) portion of the data.
4. Add a linear trendline to the new plot to determine the modulus of elasticity for this material.

First, the data are entered into the worksheet (Figure 49). Then, an XY scatter graph is prepared, as shown in Figure 50. The ultimate tensile stress can be read from the graph or the data set, as shown in Figure 50. Finally, another graph (Figure 51) is prepared, containing only the linear portion of the data (the first eight data points).

A linear trendline with the intercept forced through the origin has been added to the graph in Figure 48. We will use the slope from the equation for the trendline to compute the modulus of elasticity; the R^2 value, 1, provides reassurance that we have indeed plotted the linear portion of the test data.

From slope of the regression line, we see that the modulus of elasticity for this material is 1793 MPa, or 1.79 GPa.

Table 2 Tensile test data

Strain (mm/mm)	Stress (MPa)
0.000	0.00
0.003	5.38
0.006	10.76
0.009	16.14
0.012	21.52
0.014	25.11
0.017	30.49
0.020	33.34
0.035	44.79
0.052	53.29
0.079	57.08
0.124	59.79
0.167	60.10
0.212	59.58
0.264	57.50
0.300	55.42

◢	A	B	C	D
1	**Stress-Strain Curve I**			
2				
3		**Strain (mm/mm)**	**Stress (MPa)**	
4		0.000	0.00	
5		0.003	5.38	
6		0.006	10.76	
7		0.009	16.14	
8		0.012	21.52	
9		0.014	25.11	
10		0.017	30.49	
11		0.020	33.34	
12		0.035	44.79	
13		0.052	53.29	
14		0.079	57.08	
15		0.124	59.79	
16		0.167	60.10	
17		0.212	59.58	
18		0.264	57.50	
19		0.300	55.42	
20				

Figure 49
Strain and stress data.

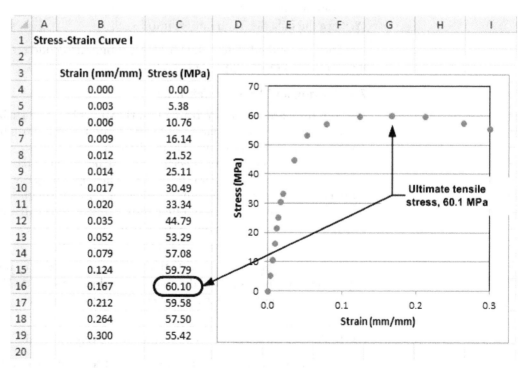

Figure 50
Stress–strain curve.

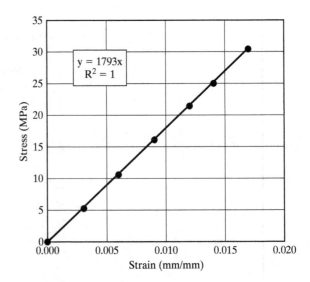

Figure 51
The linear portion of the stress–strain curve, with trendline.

7 GRAPHING WEB DATA

The Internet's World Wide Web is becoming an increasingly common place to locate data, but those data may be in many different forms. Web pages may provide links to data files or embed the data as HTML tables. There is no single way to move Web data into Excel for graphing, but the following two methods frequently work:

1. Copy and paste; or
2. Save the data file, then import into Excel.

The first method is described in this section; the second method is introduced, then described more fully in Section 9.

7.1 Copying and Pasting Web Data

Data sets presented on the Web are often HTML tables. It is usually possible to copy the information from such tables and paste it into Excel, but you have to copy entire rows; you can't select portions. Then, when you want to paste the data into Excel, you might need to use Paste Special ... to instruct Excel to paste the values as text and ignore the HTML format information. The copy and paste process will be presented using the same temperature vs. time data used throughout this chapter. This data is available on the text's website in two forms: as an HTML table and as text file Ex_Data.prn. The text's website is located at

http://www.chbe.montana.edu/Excel

To copy the data from the HTML table, simply select all of the rows (and headings, if desired) and copy the data to the Windows clipboard. This is illustrated in Figure 52. Options for copying the selected data to the Windows clipboard include:

- Press [Ctrl-c]
- Right-click on the selected data and choose **Copy** from the pop-up menu

Then, you can paste the data into Excel. Frequently, you will find it necessary to use Ribbon options **Home/Clipboard/Paste/Paste Special...** to paste the data into the worksheet as **Text**. Pasting as **Text** tells Excel to ignore HTML formatting information and paste just the data into the cells. This approach was used to paste the data into the worksheet shown in Figure 53.

[Excel 2003: Edit/Paste Special..., then paste as "Text"]

Figure 52
Copying Web data.

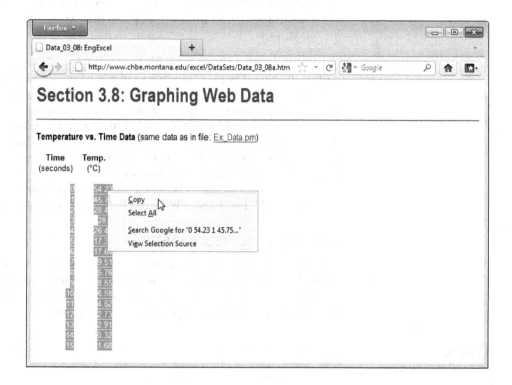

Figure 53
The Web data pasted into an Excel worksheet.

	A	B	C
1	0	54.23	
2	1	45.75	
3	2	28.41	
4	3	28.3	
5	4	26.45	
6	5	17.36	
7	6	17.64	
8	7	9.51	
9	8	5.76	
10	9	8.55	
11	10	6.58	
12	11	4.62	
13	12	2.73	
14	13	2.91	
15	14	0.32	
16	15	1.68	
17			

7.2 Importing Data Files from the Web

A Web page could provide a link to a data file, such as the link to file Ex_Data.prn from the text's website. What happens when you click on a link to a .prn file depends on how your browser is configured:

1. The browser might display the contents of the file on the screen.
2. The browser might present an option box asking whether you want to open the file or save it.

If your browser displays the file contents on the screen, you can try copying and pasting the data. The process is exactly like that used in the previous section. If copying and pasting the data fails (or if your browser will not display the data-file contents), then you might need to save the file to your computer and import the file into Excel.

If you right-click on the data-file link, a pop-up menu will offer a **Save Target As...** option (Microsoft Internet Explorer) or **Save Link As...** option (Mozilla Firefox), as shown in Figure 54. These options allow you to save a copy of the link's target (the data file) to your own computer.

Once the data file has been saved on your own computer, it can be imported into Excel by Excel's Text Import Wizard. That process is described in the next section.

8 IMPORTING TEXT FILES

Text files are a common way to move data from one program to another, and Excel is good at creating graphs that use data from other programs. Importing a text file is one way to get the data to be plotted into Excel. Excel provides a Text Import Wizard to make it easy to import data from text files.

Figure 54
Saving a linked file from the Web.

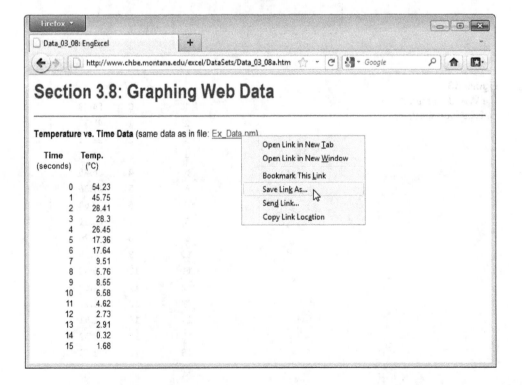

Two types of text files are used to store data:

- *delimited*
- *fixed width*

Delimited data has a special character, called a *delimiter*, between data values. Commas, spaces, and tabs are the most common delimiters, but any non-numeric character can be used. Quotes are frequently used as text-string delimiters.

The following is an example of comma-delimited data:

```
0, 54.23
1, 45.75
2, 28.41
```

Fixed-width files align the data values in columns and use character position to distinguish individual data values. The comma-delimited data shown previously would look quite different in a fixed-width data file. In the following example, the data have been written to the file with eight-character fields, using four decimal places (a couple of header lines have been included to show the layout of the data fields):

```
Field 1 Field 2
1234567812345678
0.0000 54.2300
1.0000 45.7500
3.0000 28.4100
```

Excel can read the data from either type of file, but Excel must know the format used in the data file before the data can be imported. The Text Import Wizard allows you to select the appropriate format as part of the import process. Fixed-width files were once very common, but delimited data seem to be more common at this time. Both types of data files are used regularly, and Excel's Text Import Wizard can handle either type of file.

8.1 Using the Text Import Wizard

The temperature–time data set used throughout this chapter consists of 16 temperature values measured at one-second intervals from 0 to 15 seconds. The values are available as a space-delimited text file called Ex_Data.prn. The file is available at the text's website, http://www.chbe.montana.edu/Excel. The following example assumes that the data file is available on a drive labeled M: in a folder called "Excel Data."

You begin importing a text file into Excel by attempting to open the file.

1. To open the Open dialog, use:
   - Excel 2010: **File tab/Open**
   - Excel 2007: **Office/Open**
   - Excel 2003: **File/Open**
2. Enter the name of the data file in the **File name** field, or, to select the data file from the files on the drive, change the displayed file type (near the bottom of the Open dialog) to **Text Files (*.prn; *.txt; *.csv)** and browse for the file. This is illustrated in Figure 55.

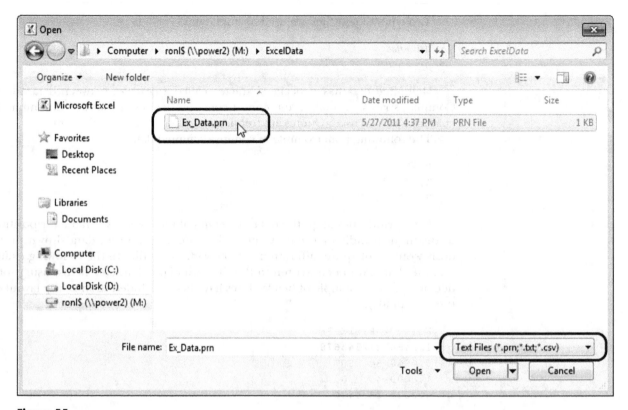

Figure 55
Change the file type to **Text Files (*.prn; *.txt; *.csv)** to display text data files.

3. Click the **Open** button to open the file.

When Excel attempts to open the file and finds that it is not saved as an Excel workbook, it starts the Text Import Wizard to guide you through the import process. The steps in the process are as follows:

Step 1. **Select the type of text file.** Excel will analyze the file contents and make a recommendation on the best way to import the data, but you should verify the data format. You can see how the data will import in the preview, as shown in Figure 56.

Excel determined that the data in Ex_Data.prn are delimited, which it is.

Notice that the Text Import Wizard allows you to begin importing data at any row by changing the value in the Start import at row: field. This is very useful if your data file contains heading or title information that you do not want to import into the worksheet.

Click **Next >** to move to Step 2 of the import process.

Step 2. **Select the type of delimiter(s).** If you selected **Delimited** data in the previous step, then you can choose the type(s) of delimiters. In file Ex_Data. prn, the values have leading spaces at the left of each line and spaces between two columns of values. When **Space** delimiter is checked (see Figure 57), Excel treats the spaces in the files as delimiters and adds lines in the **Data preview** panel to show how the values will be separated into columns.

Click **Next >** to go to the next step in the process.

Figure 56
The Text Import Wizard.

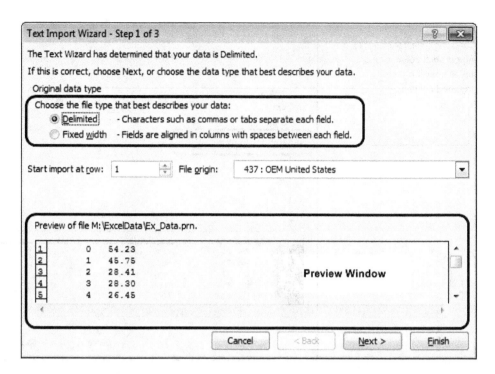

Figure 57
Choosing the delimiter(s).

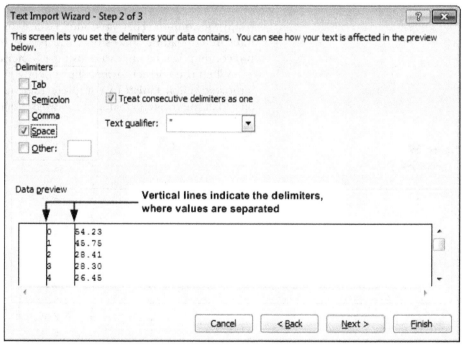

Step 3. Select the data to be imported and the data formats to be used. The third step allows you to tell Excel the number format you want to be used for each imported column, or you can choose not to import one or more columns. To select a column, click on the column heading. In Figure 58, the first column heading was selected, and then we chose **Do not import column**

Figure 58

Choosing whether or not to import each column, and the number format for imported columns.

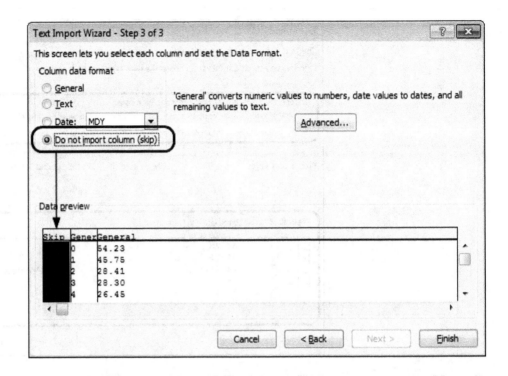

(**skip**) the column. This was done because the first column is empty. (Excel interpreted leading spaces on each line as an empty column.) The other two columns will be imported, using a **General** number format.

When the correct formats have been specified for each column to be imported, click **Finish** to complete the import process. The values are placed at the top-left corner of the worksheet, as shown in Figure 59.

Figure 59

The imported data.

	A	B	C
1	0	54.23	
2	1	45.75	
3	2	28.41	
4	3	28.3	
5	4	26.45	
6	5	17.36	
7	6	17.64	
8	7	9.51	
9	8	5.76	
10	9	8.55	
11	10	6.58	
12	11	4.62	
13	12	2.73	
14	13	2.91	
15	14	0.32	
16	15	1.68	
17			

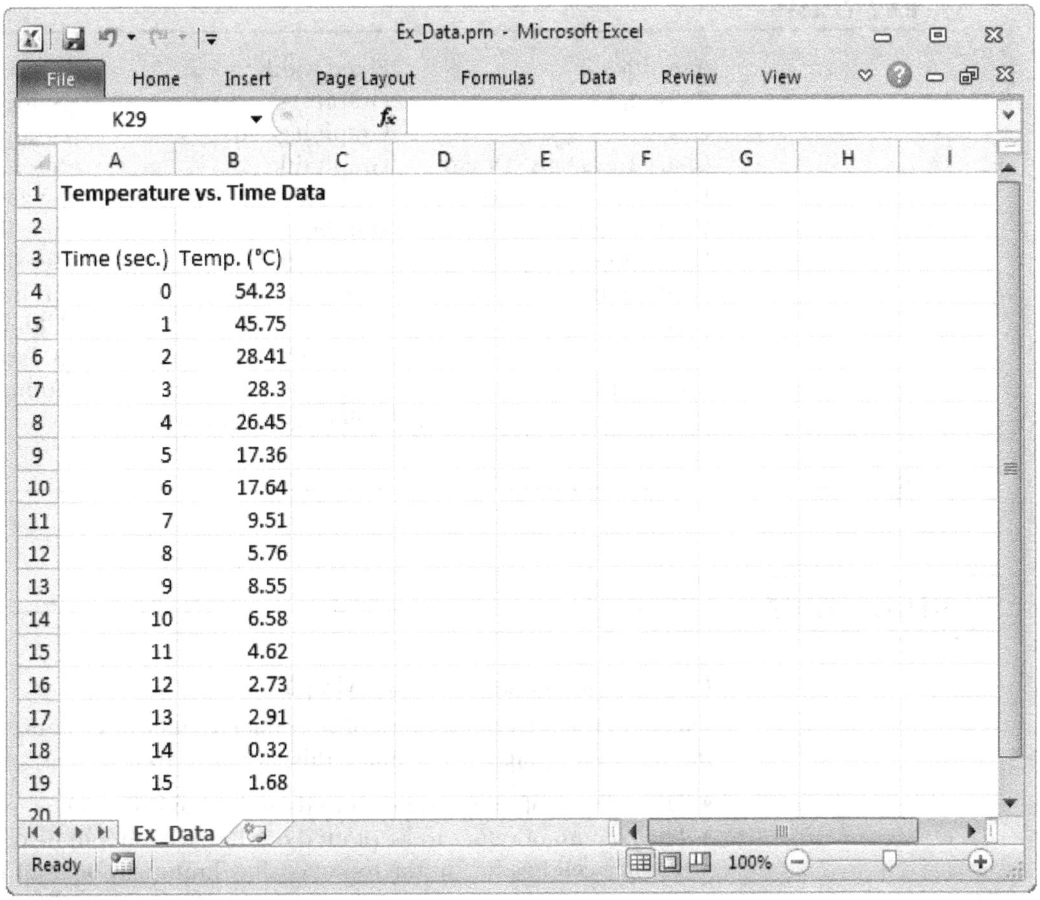

Figure 60
The imported data, moved down to allow a title and column headings to be inserted.

You can move the cells to a different location within the same worksheet or copy and paste them to another worksheet. In Figure 60, the values were moved down to make room for a title and column headings.

Note: Since file Ex_Data.prn was opened, Excel named the workbook shown in Figure 60 Ex_Data.prn. Excel will allow you to use the workbook just as you would a standard workbook (.xlsx) file, but any nonalphanumeric content (e.g., graphs) will be lost if the file is saved as a .prn file. Excel will show a warning if you attempt to save the file with a .prn extension. It is a good idea to immediately save the file with an Excel workbook file extension, .xlsx. To do this, use:

- Excel 2010: **File tab/Save As…**
- Excel 2007: **Office/Save As…**
- Excel 2003: **File/Save As…**

Then, select **Excel Workbook** as the file type.

KEY TERMS

Axis titles
Bar graphs
Chart
Chart Tools tabs (Design,
Layout, and Format)
Column graphs
Data series
Delimited
Delimiter
Equation of the
trendline
Error bars

Fixed width
Graph
Graph legend
Graph title
Gridlines
Handles
Line graphs
Line segments
Markers
Modulus of elasticity
Pie charts
Quick (Graph) Layout

R^2 value
Smoothed curves
Strain
Stress
Surface plots
Tensile strength
Tensile test
Trendline
Ultimate stress
XY scatter graphs
Young's modulus

SUMMARY

Preparing to Plot an XY Scatter Graph

Excel will use the organization of your data to infer information necessary to create the XY scatter graph. To facilitate this, organize your data as follows:

- The column of values to be plotted on the x axis should be on the left.
- The column of values to be plotted on the y axis should be on the right.
- A single-cell heading at the top of each column may be used (optional).

The cell heading on the y values (if used) will be used as the graph title and in the graph legend.

Creating an XY Scatter Plot from Existing Data

1. Select the data range (including the series names, if desired).
2. Use Ribbon options **Insert/Charts/Scatter** to select the graph type and create the graph.
3. Choose a Quick Layout (**Chart Tools/Design/Chart Layouts/Quick Layout**).
4. Edit the axis labels and graph title.

Editing an Existing Graph

Select the item you wish to modify, then use Ribbon options **Chart Tools/Layout/Format Selection** to open a dialog to edit the selected chart element. (With Excel 2010 you can also double-click a chart element to directly open the Format dialog for that element.) Items that can be modified include:

- Axes
- Gridlines
- Legend

- Markers and lines
- Plot area
- Titles

Add Another Curve or Modify Existing Data Series

Use Ribbon options **Chart Tools/Design/Data/Select Data**. This opens the Select Data Source dialog which is used to add a new data series or edit the existing data series.

Adding a Trendline to a Graph

Right-click on the data series that the trendline should be fit to and then choose **Add Trendline** from the series' pop-up menu. The following trendlines are available:

- Linear (straight line)
- Exponential
- Logarithmic
- Polynomial
- Power
- Moving average (nonregression)

Printing a Graph

There are two ways to print a graph:

1. Print the graph only—select the graph, then choose one of the printing options listed below.
2. Print the worksheet containing the graph—set the print area to include the graph, then use one of the printing options listed below.

Printing Options

- Excel 2010: **File tab/Print (panel)/Print (button)**—opens the Print dialog (including a preview panel) to allow you to set printer options before printing.
- Excel 2007:
  - **Office/Print/Print**—opens the Print dialog to allow you to set printer options before printing.
  - **Office/Print/Quick Print**—prints directly to the default printer using default printer settings.
  - **Office/Print/Print Preview**—shows what the printout will look like on the screen to allow you to change margins, scale to fit a page, etc., before printing.
- Excel 2003: **File/Print**—opens the Print dialog to allow you to set printer options before printing.

Available Graph Types

- XY scatter plots
- Line graphs
- Column and bar graphs
- Pie charts
- Surface plots

PROBLEMS

1 Stress–Strain Curve II

The following tabulated data represent stress–strain data from an experiment on an unknown sample of a white metal (modulus of elasticity values for various white metals are also listed):

a. Graph the stress–strain data. If the data include values outside the elastic-stretch region, discard those values.
b. Use a linear trendline to compute the modulus of elasticity for the sample.
c. What type of metal was tested?

Stress	Strain	Material	Modulus of Elasticity
(mm/mm)	(MPa)		(GPa)
0.0000	0	Mg Alloy	45
0.0015	168	Al Alloy	70
0.0030	336	Ag	71
0.0045	504	Ti Alloy	110
0.0060	672	Pt	170
		SS	200

Note: The modulus of elasticity depends on the type of alloy or purity of a non-alloyed material. The values listed here are typical.

2 Tank Temperature During a Wash-Out

One evening, a few friends come over for a soak, and you discover that the water in the hot tub (Figure 61) is at 115°F (46°C)—too hot to use. As your friends turn on the cold water to cool down the tub, the engineer in you wants to know how long this is going to take, so you write an energy balance on a well-mixed tank (ignoring heat losses to the air). You end up with the following differential equation relating

Figure 61
Hot tub.

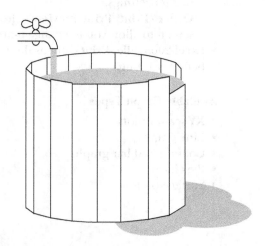

the temperature in the tank, T, to the temperature of the cold water flowing into the tank, T_{in}, the volume of the tank, $\dot{V}$, and the volumetric flow rate of the cold water, $\dot{V}$:

$$\frac{dT}{dt} = \frac{\dot{V}}{V}(T_{in} - T).$$ (3)

Integrating, you get an equation for the temperature in the tank as a function of time:

$$T = T_{in} - (T_{in} - T_{init.})e^{\frac{-\dot{V}}{V}t}.$$ (4)

If the initial temperature $T_{init.}$ is 115°F, the cold water temperature is 35°F (1.7°C), and the volume and volumetric flow rate are 3000 liters and 30 liters per minute, respectively,

    a. Calculate the expected water temperature at 5-minute intervals for the first 60 minutes after the flow of cold water is established.

    b. Plot the water temperature in the hot tub as a function of time.

    c. Calculate how long it should take for the water in the tub to cool to 100°F (37.8°C).

    d. Explain whether a hot tub is really a well-mixed tank. If it is not, will your equation predict a time that is too short or too long? Explain your reasoning.

3 Fluid Statics: Manometer

Manometers used to be common pressure-measurement devices, but, outside of laboratories, electronic pressure transducers are now more common. Manometers are sometimes still used to calibrate the pressure transducers.

In the calibration system shown in Figure 62, the mercury manometer on the right and the pressure transducer on the left are both connected to a piston-driven pressure source filled with hydraulic oil ($\rho = 880\,\text{kg/m}^3$). The bulbs connected to the transducer and the right side of the manometer are both evacuated ($\rho = 0$).

During the calibration, the piston is moved to generate a pressure on both the manometer and the transducer. The manometer reading R is recorded, along with the output of the pressure transducer A (assuming a 4- to 20-mA output current from the transducer).

Figure 62
Calibrating pressure transducers.

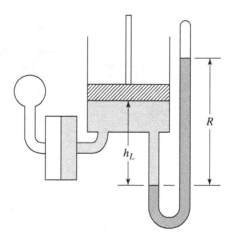

Consider the following calibration data:

a. Calculate pressures from the manometer readings.
b. Create a calibration table and graph showing the transducer output (mA) as a function of measured pressure.

		Calibration Data	
Piston Setting	hL (mm Oil)	Manometer Reading (mm Hg)	Transducer Output (mA)
1	300	0	4.0
2	450	150	5.6
3	600	300	7.2
4	750	450	8.8
5	900	600	10.4
6	1050	750	13.0
7	1200	900	13.6
8	1350	1050	15.2
9	1500	1200	16.8
10	1650	1350	18.4
11	1800	1500	20.0

4 Thermocouple Calibration Curve

A type J (iron/constantan) thermocouple was calibrated by using the system illustrated in Figure 63. The thermocouple and a thermometer were dipped into a beaker of water on a hot plate. The power level was set at a preset level (known only as 1, 2, 3, ... on the dial) and the thermocouple readings were monitored on a computer screen. When steady state had been reached, the thermometer was read, and 10 thermocouple readings were recorded. Then the power level was increased and the process repeated.

The accumulated calibration data (steady-state data only) are as follows (available electronically at http://www.coe.montana.edu/che/Excel):

Power Setting	Thermometer (°C)	Thermocouple Average (mV)	Thermocouple Standard Deviation (mV)
0	24.6	1.264	0.100
1	38.2	1.841	0.138
2	50.1	3.618	0.240
3	60.2	3.900	0.164
4	69.7	3.407	0.260
5	79.1	4.334	0.225
6	86.3	4.506	0.212
7	96.3	5.332	0.216
8	99.8	5.084	0.168

Figure 63
Calibrating thermocouples.

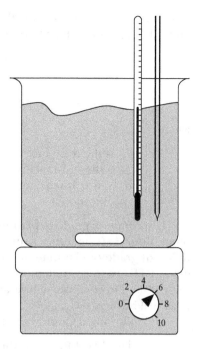

a. Plot the thermocouple calibration curve with temperature on the x axis and average thermocouple reading on the y axis.

b. Add a linear trendline to the graph and have Excel display the equation for the trendline and the value.

c. Use the standard deviation values to add error bars (± 1 standard deviation) to the graph.

d. The millivolt output of an iron/constantan thermocouple can be related to temperature by the correlation equation[1]

$$T = aV^b, \tag{5}$$

where

T is temperature in °C,
V is the thermocouple output in millivolts,
a is 19.741 for iron/constantan, and
b is 0.9742 for iron/constantan.

Use this equation to calculate predicted thermocouple outputs at each temperature and add these to the graph as a second data series. Do the predicted values appear to agree with the average experimental values?

5 Resistance Temperature Detector

The linear temperature coefficient α of a resistance temperature detector (RTD) is a physical property of the metal used to make the RTD that indicates how the

[1]Thermocouple correlation equation from *Transport Phenomena Data Companion*, L.P.B.M. Janssen and M.M.C.G. Warmoeskerken, Arnold DUM, London, 1987, p. 20.

electrical resistance of the metal changes as the temperature increases. The equation relating temperature to resistance[1] is

$$R_T = R_0[1 + \alpha\, T],\qquad(6)$$

or

$$R_T = R_0 + (R_0\alpha)^T \quad \text{(in linear regression form)},\qquad(7)$$

where

> R_T is the resistance at the unknown temperature, T,
> R_0 is the resistance at $0°C$ (known, one of the RTD specifications), and
> α is the linear temperature coefficient (known, one of the RTD specifications).

The common grade of platinum used for RTDs has an α value equal to 0.00385 ohm/ohm/°C (sometimes written simply as $0.00385°C^{-1}$), but older RTDs used a different grade of platinum and operated with $\alpha = 0.003902°C^{-1}$, and laboratory grade RTDs use very high-purity platinum with $\alpha = 0.003923°C^{-1}$. If the wrong α value is used to compute temperatures from RTD readings, the computed temperatures will be incorrect.

The following data show the temperature vs. resistance for an RTD:

    a. Use Excel to graph the data and add a trendline to evaluate the linear temperature coefficient.

    b. Is the RTD of laboratory grade?

Temperature	Resistance
°C	Ohms
0	100.0
10	103.9
20	107.8
30	111.7
40	115.6
50	119.5
60	123.4
70	127.3
80	131.2
90	135.1
100	139.0

6 Experimentally Determining a Value for π

The circumference and diameter of a circle are related by the equation

$$C = \pi D \qquad(8)$$

A graph of diameter (x axis) and circumference (y axis) for a number of circles of various sizes should produce a plot with a slope of π.

- Find at least six circular objects of various sizes.
- Measure the diameter and circumference of each circle.

- Create an XY scatter plot with diameter on the x axis and circumference on the y axis.
- Add a linear trendline through your data.
  - Force the intercept through the origin.
  - Display the equation and R^2 value on the graph.
  a. What is the experimentally determined value of π?
  b. What is the percent error in your experimental result compared with the accepted value of 3.141593?

$$\% \text{ error} = \frac{\text{measured value} - \text{true value}}{\text{true value}} \times 100$$

7 Predicting Wind Speed

As part of an experiment looking into how energy losses depend on wind speed, some data were collected on air velocity at three distances from a portable fan. The data are shown in Table 3.

The data were collected with a tape measure and a hand-held anemometer, and there are mixed unit systems in the data in Table 3.

Create an Excel worksheet containing:

a. The original data (from Table 3).
b. The distance data converted inches to meters [2.54 cm/inch].
c. A plot of the distance (x axis) and air velocity (y axis) values.
d. An exponential trendline through the data, with the trendline equation and R^2 value shown on the graph.

Use the trendline equation to predict air velocity values at 0.3 m and 0.6 m.

Table 3 Air velocity at three distances from a portable fan

Distance (in.)	Air Velocity (m/s)
8	2.0
8	1.9
8	2.0
8	2.2
8	2.1
16	1.3
16	1.2
16	1.1
16	1.2
16	1.2
32	0.5
32	0.4
32	0.5
32	0.5
32	0.5

8 Using a Pie Chart

A pie chart is used to show how a complete entity is divided into parts. The data in Table 4 show how the total cost of bringing a new product to market can be attributed to various aspects of the development process.

Table 4 Costs associate with new product development

Category	As Budgeted	Actual
Research	$1,200,000	$1,050,000
Patenting	$87,000	$89,000
Development	$1,600,000	$2,400,000
Legal	$32,000	$104,000
Marketing	$134,000	$85,000
Packaging	$48,000	$36,000
TOTAL:	$3,101,000	$3,764,000

The budgeted and actual costs associated with bringing a new product to market are listed in the worksheet shown in Figure 64. The "As Budgeted" *pie chart* is shown and was created by:

1. Selecting cells B4:C9.
2. Using Ribbon Options **Insert/Charts/Pie** and choosing the first pie chart option.

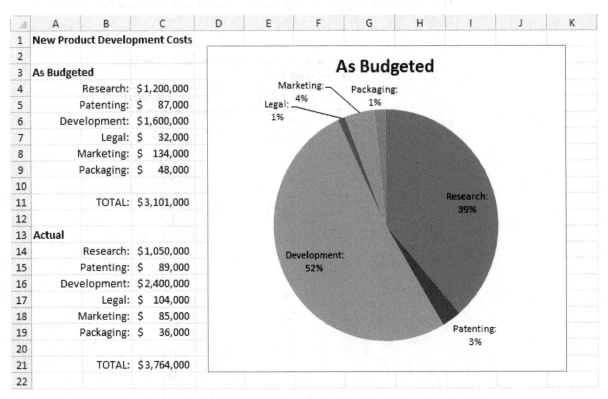

Figure 64
Budgeted and actual product development costs.

3. Using Ribbon Options **Chart Tools/Design/Chart Layouts** and selecting the first chart layout.
4. Editing the chart title.

Create an Excel worksheet similar to Figure 64 that shows the As Budgeted and Actual data values, and two pie charts, one for the "as budgeted" values (as shown) and another for the "actual" values.

9 Using a Column Chart

The data shown in Figure 64 can also be plotted with a *column chart* (commonly called a *bar chart*, but a bar chart is different in Excel), as shown in Figure 65. A pie chart is used to show how costs are distributed, whereas a column chart focuses attention on the differences between "as budgeted" and "actual" costs for each category. The column chart was created by:

1. Selecting cells B3:D9.
2. Using Ribbon Options **Insert/Charts/Column** and choosing the first column chart option.
3. Moving the legend to allow the plot area to be larger.

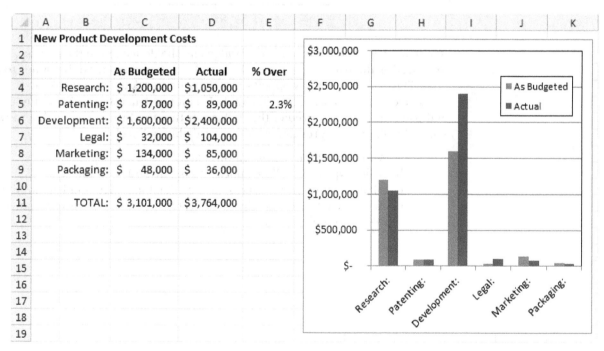

Figure 65
Budgeted and actual product development costs as column chart.

Recreate the worksheet shown in Figure 65 and complete the "% over" column to show much each category was over budget (or under budget, if the percentage is negative).

10 Safety of an Old Bridge

An old bridge over a river was constructed with steel beams and wood planking. The owner tried to test the safety of the bridge by measuring deflections in the main span under various loadings. Specifically, a truck with a 1000-gallon water tank

Table 5 Span deflections

Load (lbs)	Deflection (mm)
5400	3.2
5400	3.2
5400	3.1
7400	4.8
7400	4.9
7400	4.8
9400	7.6
9400	7.5
9400	7.7
11,400	10.8
11,400	10.9
11,400	11.1
13,400	Broke

was driven back and forth across the bridge and the deflection in the main span was measured as the truck went across. The load was increased by adding water to the tank. The experiment was stopped when the water truck fell into the river.

The collected data are listed in Table 5. Plot the data using an XY scatter graph and use a trendline to predict the deflection that the bridge was unable to withstand. Try all of the regression trendlines available in Excel.

a. Which trendlines do not fit this data?
b. Which type of trendline appears to be the best fit to this data?
c. What is your estimate of the deflection that the bridge could not withstand?
d. How much does the predicted deflection value change as you change the type of trendline used?

Excel Functions

Objectives

After reading this chapter, you will

- Know how to use Excel's built-in functions
- Know the common functions for
  - Basic math operations
  - Computing sums
  - Trigonometric calculations
  - Advanced math operations

- Be aware of Excel's specialized functions that may be useful in some engineering disciplines
- Be familiar with the quick reference to the Excel functions included in the summary at the end of this chapter

1 INTRODUCTION TO EXCEL FUNCTIONS

In a programming language, the term *function* is used to mean a piece of the program dedicated to a particular calculation. A function accepts input from a list of *arguments* or *parameters*, performs calculations using the values passed in as arguments, and then returns a value or a set of values. Excel's functions work the same way and serve the same purposes. They receive input from an argument list, perform a calculation, and return a value or a set of values.

Excel provides a wide variety of functions that are predefined and immediately available. This chapter presents the functions most commonly used by engineers.

Functions are used whenever you want to:

- Perform the same calculations multiple times, using different input values.
- Reuse the calculation in another program without retyping it.
- Make a complex program easier to comprehend by assigning a section a particular task.

2 EXCEL'S BUILT-IN FUNCTIONS

Excel provides a wide assortment of built-in functions. Several commonly used classes of functions are as follows:

- Elementary math functions
- Trigonometric functions
- Advanced math functions
- Matrix math functions (not described in this chapter)
- Functions for financial calculations (not described in this chapter)
- Functions for statistical calculations (not described in this chapter)
- Date and time functions
- String functions
- Lookup and reference functions
- File-handling functions
- Functions for working with databases (not described in this chapter)

If Excel does not provide a necessary built-in function, you can always write your own functions, directly from Excel, by using Visual Basic for Applications (VBA).

2.1 Function Syntax

Built-in functions are identified by a *name* and usually require an *argument list.* They use the information supplied in the argument list to compute and return a value or set of values. One of the simplest functions in Excel, but still a very useful one, is **PI**(). When this function is called (without any arguments inside the parentheses), it returns the value of π.

In the Figure 1, cell B2 is assigned the value π by the formula =PI().

Figure 1
Using the **PI** function.

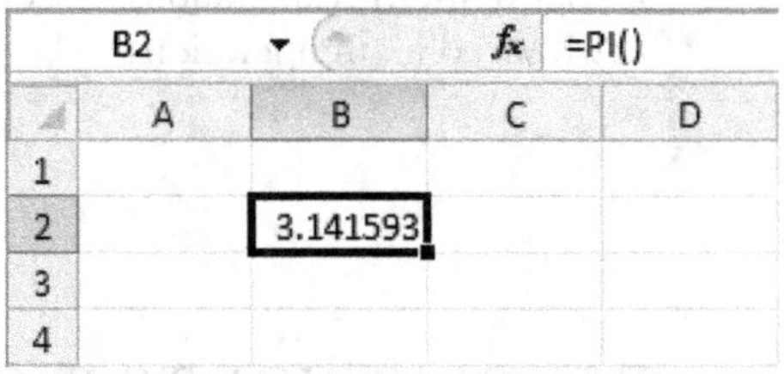

Functions can also be built into formulas. In Figure 2, the function **PI** is used in a formula to calculate the area of a circle.

Figure 2
Using a function within a formula.

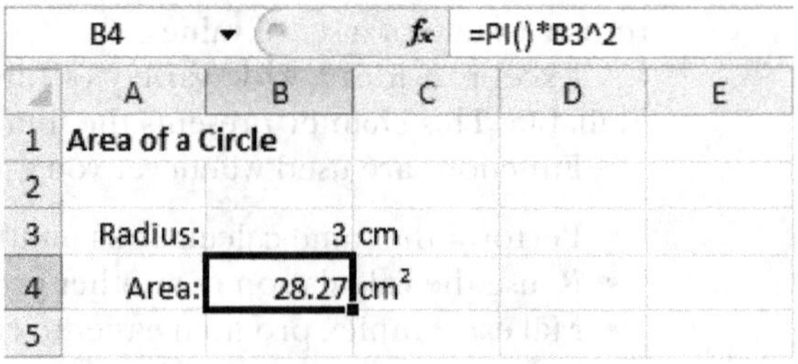

Most functions take one or more values as arguments. An example of a function that takes a single value as its argument is the factorial function, **FACT(x)**. The factorial of 4 is 24 (4 $\times$ 3 $\times$ 2 $\times$ 1 = 24). This can be computed by using the **FACT** function, as seen in Figure 3.

Figure 3
Using the **FACT** function.

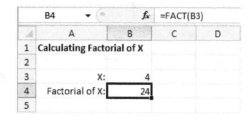

Some functions take a range of values as arguments, such as the **SUM(range)** function which calculates the sum of all of the values in the cell range specified as the function's argument. In Figure 4, the **SUM** function is used to compute the sum of three values.

Figure 4
Using the **SUM** function to compute the sum of the values in a range of cells.

An easy way to enter a function that takes a range of cells as an argument is to type in the function name and the opening parenthesis and then use the mouse to highlight the range of cells to be used as an argument. For the preceding example, this would be done as:

1. Type =sum(in cell B6.
2. Then use the mouse to select cells B3:B5.

The worksheet will look like Figure 5.

In Figure 5, the dashed line around cells B3:B5 indicates a range of cells currently selected, and the selected range is automatically included in the formula in cell B7. When you type the opening parenthesis and then move the mouse, Excel jumps into Point mode and expects you to use the mouse to point out the cells that will be used as arguments in the function.

The *ScreenTip* below the formula lets you know what arguments the function requires. Once the complete range has been selected, type the closing parenthesis and press [Enter], or simply press [Enter], and Excel will automatically add the final parenthesis.

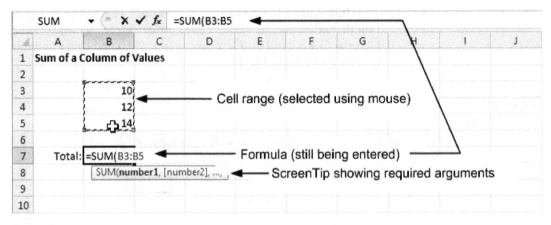

Figure 5
Entering the **SUM** function.

The cells to be included in the summation do not have to be next to each other on the worksheet; in Figure 6 two cell ranges appear in the **SUM** function.

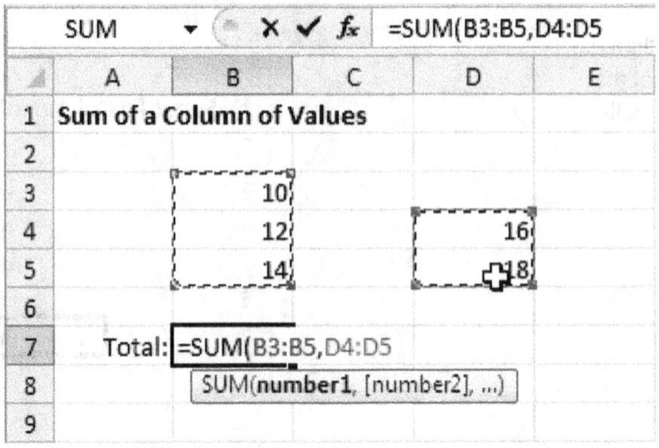

Figure 6
Using noncontiguous cell ranges as arguments in a function.

To select noncontiguous cells, you first select the first portion of the cell range (B3:B5) with the mouse. Then, either type a comma or hold down the control key while you select the second range (D4:D5) with the mouse. This completed formula is shown in Figure 7.

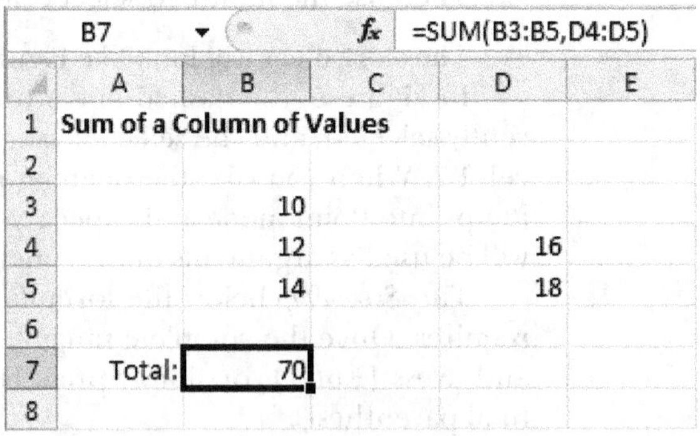

Figure 7
The completed summation of noncontiguous cells.

PROFESSIONAL SUCCESS

When do you use a calculator to solve a problem, and when should you use a computer? The following three questions will help you make this decision:

1. Is the calculation long and involved?
2. Will you need to perform the same calculation numerous times?
3. Do you need to document the results for the future, either to give them to someone else or for your own reference?

A "yes" answer to any of these questions suggests that you consider using a computer. Moreover, a "yes" to the second question suggests that you might want to write a reusable function to solve the problem.

3 USING THE CONVERT FUNCTION TO CONVERT UNITS

Excel provides an interesting function called **CONVERT** to convert units. The **CONVERT** function receives (as an argument) a value in certain units and then calculates and returns an equivalent value in different units. The **CONVERT** function has the syntax

CONVERT(value, from_units, to_units)

For example, =CONVERT(1, "in", "cm") returns 2.54; this is illustrated in Figure 8.

Figure 8
Converting inches to centimeters.

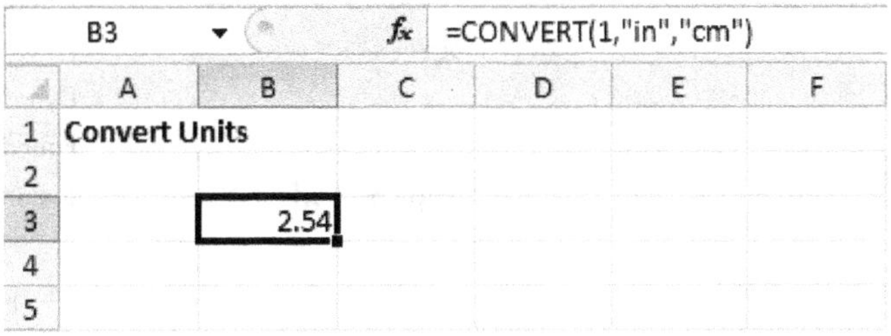

The **CONVERT** function can be useful for converting a table from one set of units to another. As an example, the fractional part sizes (in inches) are converted to centimeters in Figure 9.

Figure 9
Converting units on a table of part sizes.

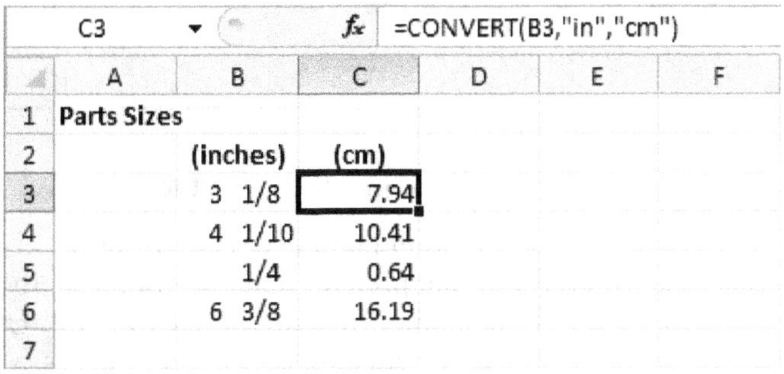

Note: Cells B3:B6 in Figure 9 are formatted using Fraction format, one of the less commonly used numeric formats.

Excel looks up the unit abbreviations in a list, so you can only use the abbreviations in Excel's list. These are available in Excel's help system (press [F1] and search on **CONVERT**). A list of commonly used units is provided in Table 1.

Table 1 Common unit abbreviations for the CONVERT function

Unit Type	Unit	Abbreviation
Mass	Gram	g
	Pound	lbm
Length	Meter	m
	Mile	mi
	Inch	in
	Foot	ft
	Yard	yd
Time	Year	yr
	Day	day
	Hour	hr
	Minute	mn
	Second	sec
Pressure	Pascal	Pa
	Atmosphere	atm
	mm of Mercury	mmHg
Force	Newton	N
	Dyne	dyn
	Pound force	lbf
Energy or Work	Joule	J
	Erg	e
	Foot-pound	flb
	BTU	BTU
Power	Horsepower	HP
	Watt	W
Temperature	Degree Celsius	C
	Degree Fahrenheit	F
	Degree Kelvin	K
Volume	Quart	qt
	Gallon	gal
	Liter	l

When using the **CONVERT** function, it is important to remember the following:

- The unit names are case sensitive.
- SI unit prefixes (e.g., "k" for kilo) are available for metric units. In the following example, the "m" prefix for milli can be used with the meter name "m" to report the part sizes in millimeters, as shown in Figure 10.

Figure 10
Reporting part sizes
in millimeters.

	C3	▼		fx	=CONVERT(B3,"in","mm")

	A	B	C	D	E	F
1	Parts Sizes					
2		(inches)	(mm)			
3		3 1/8	79.38			
4		4 1/10	104.14			
5		1/4	6.35			
6		6 3/8	161.93			
7						

- A list of prefix names is included in Excel's help system for the **CONVERT** function.
- Combined units such as gal/mn (gallons per minute) are not supported.

4 SIMPLE MATH FUNCTIONS

Most common math operations beyond multiplication and division are implemented as functions in Excel. For example, to take the square root of four, you would use =SQRT(4). SQRT() is Excel's square root function.

4.1 Common Math Functions

Table 2 presents some common mathematical functions in Excel.

Table 2 Excel's common mathematical functions

Operation	Function Name
Square Root	**SQRT(x)**
Absolute Value	**ABS(x)**
Factorial	**FACT(x)**
Summation	**SUM(range)**
Greatest Common Divisor	**GCD(x1, x2, …)**
Least Common Multiple	**LCM(x1, x2, …)**

Many additional mathematical operations are available as built-in functions. To see a list of the functions built into Excel, first click on an empty cell and then click on the **Insert Function** button on the Formula bar. This is illustrated in Figures 11 and 12.

Figure 11
Use the **Insert Function** button to obtain a list of available functions.

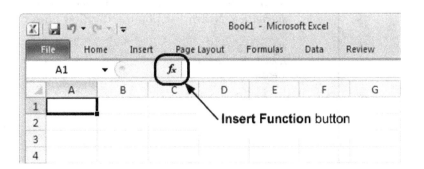

Insert Function button

Figure 12
The Insert Function dialog.

Clicking the **Insert Function** button opens the Insert function dialog, shown in Figure 12. The Insert Function dialog provides access to all of Excel's built-in functions.

Note: Excel's help files include descriptions of every built-in function, including information about the required and optional arguments.

FLUID MECHANICS

Fluid Velocity from Pitot Tube Data

A *pitot tube* is a device that allows engineers to obtain a *local velocity* (velocity value in the immediate vicinity of the pitot tube). A pitot tube measures a pressure drop, but that pressure drop can be related to local velocity with a little math. The theory behind the operation of the pitot tube comes from Bernoulli's equation (without the usual potential energy terms) and relates the change in kinetic energy to the change in fluid pressure.

$$\frac{P_a}{\rho} + \frac{u_a^2}{2} = \frac{P_b}{\rho} + \frac{u_b^2}{2}. \tag{1}$$

In Figure 13, part of the flow hits point *a*, which is a dead end tube; there is nowhere for the flow hitting point *a* to go, so it has to come to a stop; this is called *stagnation.* Nearby, at point *b*, the flow goes right past the point *b* and does not

Figure 13
A pitot tube in a flow stream.

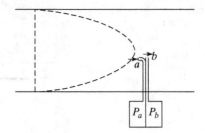

slow down at all; it is flowing at the *local free stream velocity.* The pressure measured at point *b* is called the *free stream pressure.* At point *a,* when the flowing fluid came to a stop, the kinetic energy in the fluid had to turn into something else because the total energy carried by the fluid has to be conserved. The kinetic energy of the moving fluid at point *a* is transformed to pressure energy as the velocity goes to zero. (You've felt this if you have ever stood in a river and felt the water pushing at you.) The pitot tube measures a higher pressure at point *a* than it does at point *b,* and the pressure difference can be used to determine the local free stream velocity at point *b.*

When the velocity at point *a* has been set to zero, and Bernoulli's equation is rearranged to solve for the local velocity at point *b,* we get

$$u_b = \sqrt{\frac{2}{\rho}(p_a - p_b)}. \tag{2}$$

If we used a pitot tube with a real flowing fluid with a specific gravity 0.81, and the pressure transducer indicated the pressure difference $p_a - p_b = 0.25$ atm, what was the local velocity at point *b*? A worksheet designed to solve this problem is shown in Figure 14. The formulas used in column C in the following have been displayed in column F.

The fluid is moving past the pitot tube at 7.9 m/s.

Figure 14
Solving for local velocity at *b*.

C8 | *fx* =SQRT((2/C6)*C4)

	A	B	C	D	E	F	G
1	**Pitot Tube**						
2						**Formulas in Column C**	
3		Pressure Difference:	0.25	atm			
4		Pressure Difference SI:	25331	Pa		=CONVERT(C3,"atm","Pa")	
5		Specific Gravity:	0.81				
6		Density:	810	kg/m³		=C5*1000	
7							
8		Velocity at b:	7.91	m/s		=SQRT((2/C6)*C4)	
9							

PRACTICE!

If the velocity at point *b* is doubled, what pressure difference would be measured across the pitot tube? [Answer: 1 atm]

5 COMPUTING SUMS

Calculating the sum of a row or column of values is a common worksheet operation. Excel provides the **SUM** function for this purpose, but also tries to simplify the process even further by putting the [AutoSum] button on the Ribbon's Home tab. Both approaches to calculating sums will be presented.

5.1 The SUM Function

The **SUM(range)** function receives a range of cell values as its argument, computes the sum of all of the numbers in the range, and returns the sum. The use of the **SUM** function is illustrated for several situations in Figures 15 through 18.

Figure 15
Basic use of the **SUM** function.

	B7	▾	f_x	=SUM(B3:B5)		
	A	B	C	D	E	F	G
1	Using the SUM Function - Case 1					
2						
3		10				
4		12				
5		14				
6						
7	Total:	36				
8						

If the 12 becomes "twelve," that is, if one of the cells being summed contains text rather than a numeric value, the non-numeric value is ignored. This is illustrated in Figure 16.

Figure 16
The **SUM** function ignores empty cells and cells containing text.

	B7	▾	f_x	=SUM(B3:B5)		
	A	B	C	D	E	F	G
1	Using the SUM Function - Case 2					
2						
3		10				
4	twelve					
5		14				
6						
7	Total:	24				
8						

The values to be summed don't have to be in a column, they can be in a row, a rectangular cell range, or a set of noncontiguous cells. These situations are illustrated in Figure 17.

5.2 The AutoSum Button

The **AutoSum** button on the Ribbon's Home tab is designed to seek out and find a column or row of values to sum. If you select the cell at the bottom of a column of numbers or to the right of a row of numbers and then press the **AutoSum** button, Excel will automatically include the entire column or row in the **SUM** function.

Note: There is a keyboard shortcut for the **AutoSum** button: [Alt =]; hold the [Alt] key down and press the [=] key.

For example, to sum the values in an expense report, first enter the expenses and select the cell immediately below the list of values. Then click the **AutoSum** button. This is illustrated in Figure 18.

Figure 17
The **SUM** function can handle any arrangement of cells.

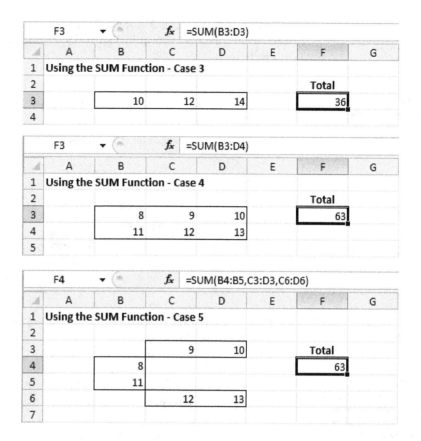

Note: The **AutoSum** button is on the far right side of the Ribbon's Home tab, so a section of the worksheet has been omitted from Figure 18 to show both the values to be added and the **AutoSum** button in the same figure.

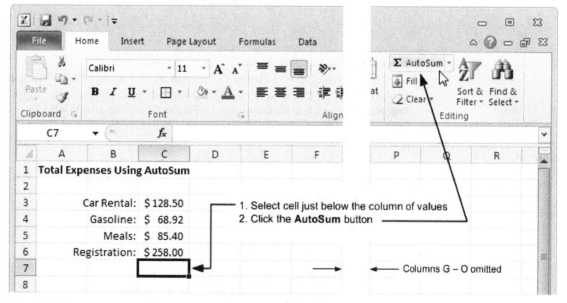

Figure 18
Using the **AutoSum** button.

When you click the **AutoSum** button, Excel shows you the nearly completed summation formula (shown in Figure 19) so that you can be sure that the correct cells were included.

Figure 19
Excel shows the nearly completed summation formula when the **AutoSum** button is pressed.

	A	B	C	D	E	F
1	Total Expenses Using AutoSum					
2						
3		Car Rental:	$ 128.50			
4		Gasoline:	$ 68.92			
5		Meals:	$ 85.40			
6		Registration:	$ 258.00			
7			=SUM(C3:C6)			
8			SUM(**number1**, [number2], ...)			
9						

Formula bar: SUM — X ✓ *fx* =SUM(C3:C6)

If the summation is correct, press [Enter] to complete the calculation. The result is shown in Figure 20.

Figure 20
The completed summation, with an added label in cell B7 and formatting (bottom border) on cell C6 to improve clarity.

	A	B	C	D	E	F
1	Total Expenses Using AutoSum					
2						
3		Car Rental:	$ 128.50			
4		Gasoline:	$ 68.92			
5		Meals:	$ 85.40			
6		Registration:	$ 258.00			
7		TOTAL:	$ 540.82			
8						

More than just summations ...

Like many of the Ribbon's features, the **AutoSum** button acts like both a button and a drop-down menu. If you click the small down arrow at the right side of the **AutoSum** button, the menu shown in Figure 21 will be displayed.

Figure 21
The **AutoSum** button's drop-down menu.

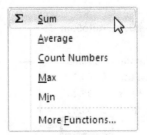

This menu provides quick access to some useful functions that work with cell ranges.

5.3 Logarithm and Exponentiation Functions

Excel's *logarithm* and *exponentiation functions* are listed in Table 3.

Excel also provides functions for working with logarithms and exponentiation of *complex numbers* (Table 4).

Table 3 Logarithm and exponentiation functions

Function Name	Operation
EXP(x)	Returns e raised to the power x
LN(x)	Returns the natural log of x
LOG10(x)	Returns the base-10 log of x
LOG(x, base)	Returns the logarithm of x to the specified base

Table 4 Functions for working with complex numbers

Function Name	Operation
IMEXP(x)	Returns the exponential of complex number x
IMLN(x)	Returns the natural log of complex number x
IMLOG10(x)	Returns the base-10 log of complex number x
IMLOG2(x)	Returns the base-2 logarithm of complex number x

PRACTICE!

Try out Excel's functions. First try these easy examples:

  a. =SQRT(4)
  b. =ABS(-7)
  c. =FACT(3)
  d. =LOG 10(100)

Then try these more difficult examples and check the results with a calculator:

  a. =FACT(20)
  b. =LN(2)
  c. =EXP(-0.4)

6 TRIGONOMETRIC FUNCTIONS

Excel provides all of the common *trigonometric functions,* such as **SIN(x), COS(x),** and **SINH(x).** The x in these functions is an angle, measured in radians. If your angles are in degrees, you don't have to convert them to radians by hand; Excel provides a **RADIANS** function to convert angles in degrees to radians. This is illustrated in Figure 22.

Similarly, the **DEGREES** function takes an angle in radians and returns the same angle in degrees. Also, the **PI** function is available whenever π is required in a calculation. Both of these functions have been used in the example in Figure 23.

Figure 22
Using the **RADIANS**
function.

	B11	▼		f_x	=RADIANS(A11)	
	A	B	C	D	E	F
1	Converting Degrees to Radians					
2						
3		Angle				
4	Degrees	Radians				
5	0	0.0000				
6	30	0.5236				
7	60	1.0472				
8	90	1.5708				
9	120	2.0944				
10	150	2.6180				
11	180	3.1416				
12						

Figure 23
Using the **DEGREES**
function.

	B7	▼		f_x	=DEGREES(A7)	
	A	B	C	D	E	F
1	Converting Radians to Degrees					
2						
3		Angle			Formulas Used	
4	Radians	Degrees		Col A	Col B	
5	0.0000	0		=0*PI()	=DEGREES(A5)	
6	0.7854	45		=PI()/4	=DEGREES(A6)	
7	1.5708	90		=PI()/2	=DEGREES(A7)	
8	3.1416	180		=PI()	=DEGREES(A8)	
9	6.2832	360		=2*PI()	=DEGREES(A9)	
10						

6.1 Standard Trigonometric Functions

Excel's trigonometric functions are listed in Table 5.

Table 5 Trigonometric functions

Function Name	Operation
SIN(x)	Returns the sine of x
COS(x)	Returns the cosine of x
TAN(x)	Returns the tangent of x

To test these functions, try $\sin(30°)$, which should equal 0.5. The 30° may be converted to radians as a preliminary step, as illustrated in Figure 24.

But the conversion to radians and the calculation of the sine can be combined in a single formula, as shown in Figure 25.

190

Figure 24
Testing Excel's **SIN** function.

C5				f_x	=SIN(B5)	
	A	B	C	D	E	F
1	Testing the Sine Function, SIN( ) - Case 1					
2						
3		X	SIN(X)			
4	Degrees:	30				
5	Radians:	0.5236	0.5			
6						

Figure 25
Combining the **SIN** and **RADIANS** functions in a formula.

C4				f_x	=SIN(RADIANS(B4))	
	A	B	C	D	E	F
1	Testing the Sine Function, SIN( ) - Case 2					
2						
3		X	SIN(X)			
4	Degrees:	30	0.5			
5						

APPLICATIONS

KINEMATICS

Projectile Motion I

A projectile is launched at an angle of 35° from the horizontal with velocity equal to 30 m/s. Neglecting air resistance and assuming a horizontal surface, determine how far away from the launch site the projectile will land.

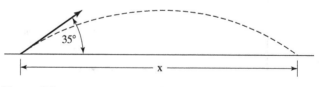

Figure 26
Projectile motion.

To answer this problem, we will need:

1. Excel's trigonometry functions to handle the 35° angle
2. Equations relating distance to velocity and acceleration

When the velocity is constant, as in the horizontal motion of our particle (since we're neglecting air resistance), the distance traveled is simply the initial horizontal velocity times the time of flight.

$$x(t) = v_{ox} t \tag{3}$$

What keeps the projectile from flying forever is gravity. Since the gravitational acceleration is constant, the vertical distance traveled becomes

$$y(t) = v_{oy} t + \frac{1}{2}g t^2 \tag{4}$$

Because the projectile ends up back on the ground, the final value of y is zero (a horizontal surface was specified), so equation (4) can be used to determine the time of flight, t.

The initial velocity is stated (30 m/s at the angle 35° from the horizontal). We can compute the initial velocity components in the horizontal and vertical directions with Excel's trigonometry functions as shown in Figure 27.

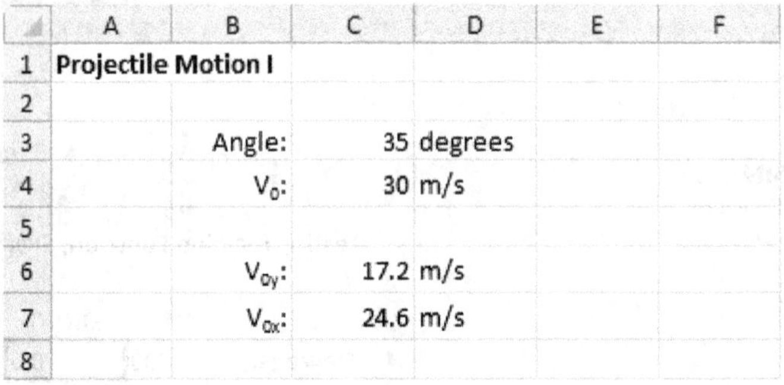

Figure 27
Determining the initial horizontal and vertical velocity components.

In Figure 27, cells C6 and C7 contain the following formulas:

```
C6: =C4*SIN(RADIANS(C3))
C7: =C4*COS(RADIANS(C3))
```

The **RADIANS** function has been used to convert 35° to radians for compatibility with Excel's trigonometric functions.

We now use equation (4) to solve for the time of flight in Figure 28.

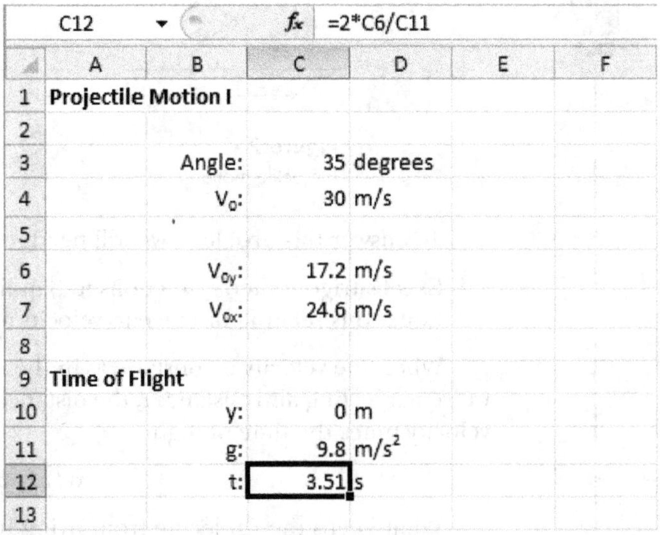

Figure 28
Solving for time of flight.

The time of flight can then be used in equation (3) to find the horizontal distance traveled. This is illustrated in Figure 29.

	C16		f_x	=C7*C12		
	A	B	C	D	E	F
7		V$_{ox}$:	24.6 m/s			
8						
9	**Time of Flight**					
10		y:	0 m			
11		g:	9.8 m/s^2			
12		t:	3.51 s			
13						
14	**Horizontal Travel Distance**					
15						
16		x:	86.3 m			
17						

Figure 29
Determine the horizontal distance travelled.

PRACTICE!

If the launch angle is changed to 55°:

1. What is the time of flight?
2. How far away will the projectile land?
3. What is the maximum height the projectile will reach? (Without air resistance, the maximum height is attained at half the time of flight.)

[Answers: 5 seconds, 86 m, 61 m]

6.3 Inverse Trigonometric Functions

Excel's *inverse trigonometric functions* are listed in Table 6. These functions return an angle in radians (the **DEGREES** function is available if you would rather see the result in degrees).

Table 6 Inverse trigonometric functions

Function Name	Operation
ASIN(x)	Returns the angle (between $-\pi/2$ and $\pi/2$) that has a sine value equal to x
ACOS(x)	Returns the angle (between 0 and π) that has a cosine value equal to x
ATAN(x)	Returns the angle (between $-\pi/2$ and $\pi/2$) that has a tangent value equal to x

STATICS

Resolving Forces

If one person pulls to the right on a rope connected to a hook imbedded in a floor, using the force 400 N at 20° from the horizontal, while another person pulls to the left on the same hook, but using the force 200 N at 45° from the horizontal, what is the net force on the hook? The situation is illustrated in Figure 30.

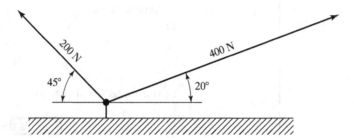

Figure 30
Forces on a fixed point.

Because both people are pulling up, their vertical contributions combine; but one is pulling left and the other right, so they are (in part) counteracting each other's efforts. To quantify this distribution of forces, we can calculate the horizontal and vertical components of the force being applied by each person. These components are illustrated in Figure 31. Excel's trigonometric functions are useful for calculating components of forces.

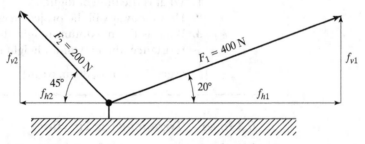

Figure 31
Horizontal and vertical components of the applied forces.

The 400-N force from person 1 resolves into a *vertical component*, f_{v1}, and a *horizontal component*, f_{h1}. The magnitudes of these force components can be calculated as follows:

$$f_{v1} = 400 \sin(20°) = 136.8 \text{ N},$$
$$f_{h1} = 400 \cos(20°) = 375.9 \text{ N}. \tag{5}$$

Figure 32 illustrates how these component forces are calculated using Excel.

Similarly, the 200-N force from the person on the left can be resolved into component forces as

$$f_{v2} = 200 \sin(45°) = 141.4 \text{ N},$$
$$f_{h2} = 200 \cos(45°) = 141.4 \text{ N}. \tag{6}$$

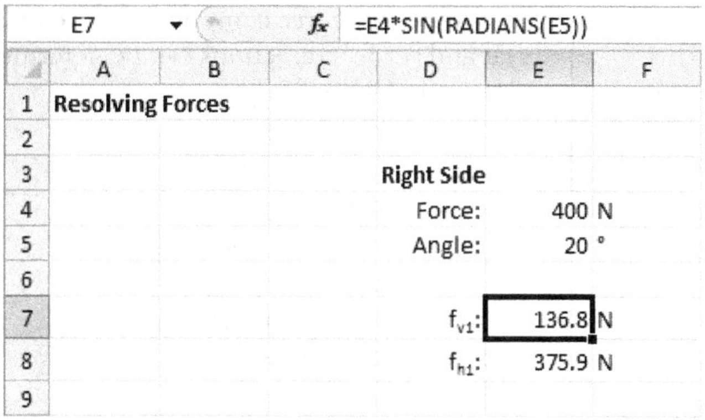

Figure 32
Calculating force components (right side) in Excel.

These calculations have been added to the worksheet in Figure 33.

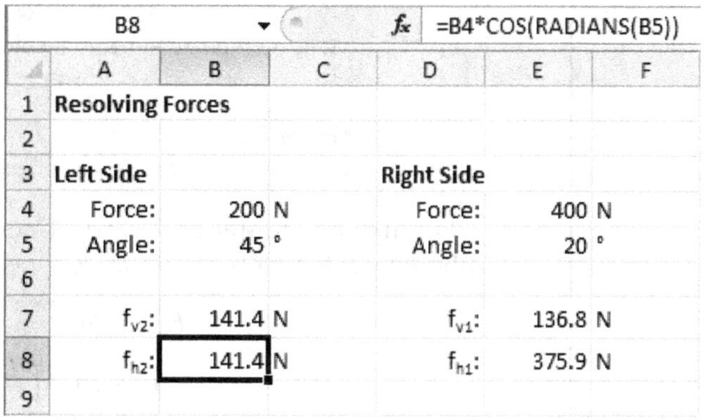

Figure 33
Calculating force components (left side) in Excel.

Actually, force component f_{h2} would usually be written as $f_{h2} = -141.421$ N, since it is pointed in the negative x direction. If all angles had been measured from the same position (typically counterclockwise from horizontal), the angle on the 200-N force would have been 135°, and the signs would have taken care of themselves, as shown in the updated worksheet in Figure 34.

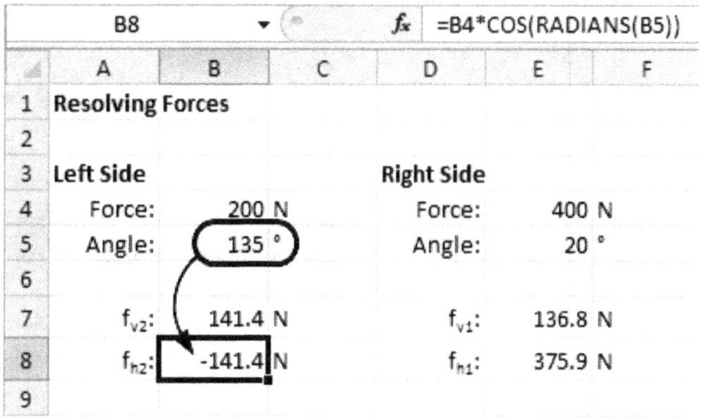

Figure 34
Calculating force components using angles measured from the same position.

Once the force components have been computed, the net force in the horizontal and vertical directions can be determined. This has been done in the worksheet shown in Figure 35.

	D10		▾	f_x	=B7+E7	
▦	A	B	C	D	E	F
1	**Resolving Forces**					
2						
3	**Left Side**			**Right Side**		
4	Force:	200	N	Force:	400	N
5	Angle:	135	°	Angle:	20	°
6						
7	f_{v2}:	141.4	N	f_{v1}:	136.8	N
8	f_{h2}:	-141.4	N	f_{h1}:	375.9	N
9						
10	Combined Vertical Force:			278.2	N	
11	Combined Horizontal Force:			234.5	N	
12						

Figure 35
Calculating net forces in the horizontal and vertical directions.

The net horizontal and vertical components can be recombined to find a combined net force on the hook, F_{net}, at angle θ:

$$F_{net} = \sqrt{f_h^2 + f_v^2} = 363.84 \text{ N},$$

$$\theta = a\tan\left(\frac{f_v}{f_h}\right) = 49.88°. \tag{7}$$

These calculations are shown in Figure 36.

	D13		▾	f_x	=SQRT(D11^2+D10^2)	
▦	A	B	C	D	E	F
1	**Resolving Forces**					
2						
3	**Left Side**			**Right Side**		
4	Force:	200	N	Force:	400	N
5	Angle:	135	°	Angle:	20	°
6						
7	f_{v2}:	141.4	N	f_{v1}:	136.8	N
8	f_{h2}:	-141.4	N	f_{h1}:	375.9	N
9						
10	Combined Vertical Force:			278.2	N	
11	Combined Horizontal Force:			234.5	N	
12						
13	Net Force:			363.8	N	
14	Angle from Horizontal, θ:			49.9	°	
15						

Figure 36
Calculating the net force and resultant angle.

The formulas in cells D13 and D14 are:

```
D13: =SQRT(D10^2+D11^2)
D14: =DEGREES(ATAN(D11/D10))
```

At the beginning of this application example the question was asked: What is the net force on the hook? The answer is 363.8 N at an angle of 49.9° from horizontal.

6.4 Hyperbolic Trigonometric Functions

Excel provides the common *hyperbolic trigonometric* and *inverse hyperbolic trigonometric functions*; they are listed in Table 7.

Table 7 Hyperbolic trigonometric functions

Function Name	Operation
SINH (x)	Returns the hyperbolic sine of x
COSH (x)	Returns the hyperbolic cosine of x
TANH (x)	Returns the hyperbolic tangent of x
ASINH (x)	Returns the inverse hyperbolic sine of x
ACOSH (x)	Returns the inverse hyperbolic cosine of x
ATANH (x)	Returns the inverse hyperbolic tangent of x

PRACTICE!

Use Excel's trigonometric functions to evaluate each of the following:

a. $\sin(\pi/4)$
b. $\sin(90°)$ (Don't forget to convert to radians.)
c. $\cos(180°)$
d. $\mathrm{asin}(0)$
e. $\mathrm{acos}(0)$

7 ADVANCED MATH FUNCTIONS

Some of the built-in functions in Excel are pretty specialized. The advanced math functions described here will be very useful to engineers in certain disciplines and of little use to many others.

7.1 Logical Functions

Excel provides the *logical functions* listed in Table 8.

A simple test of these functions is shown in Figure 37, where two unequal values are tested with an **IF** function to see if x_1 is less than x_2.

In this example, Excel tests to see whether 3 is less than 4. Because the test is true, the value **TRUE** is returned.

The following example (Figure 38) shows how a worksheet might be used to monitor the status of a tank being filled.

Table 8 Logical functions

Function Name	Operation
IF(*test, Tvalue, Fvalue*)	Performs the operation specified by the test argument and then returns *Tvalue* if the test is true, *Fvalue* if the test is false
TRUE()	Returns the logical value TRUE
FALSE()	Returns the logical value FALSE
NOT(*test*)	Reverses the logic returned by the test operation. If test returns TRUE, then NOT (*test*) returns FALSE
AND(*x1, x2, ...*)	Returns TRUE if all arguments are true, FALSE if any argument is false
OR(*x1, x2, ...*)	Returns TRUE if any argument is true, FALSE if all arguments are false

Figure 37
Comparing two values with
an **IF** function.

	A	B	C	D	E	F
1						
2		x_1:	3			
3		x_2:	4			
4						
5		test:	TRUE			
6						

C5 — f_x =IF(C2<C3,TRUE(),FALSE())

B9 — f_x =IF(B5>B4,TRUE(),FALSE())

	A	B	C	D	E	F
1	**Tank Monitor**					
2						
3	Tank Operating Capacity:	1200	liters			
4	Tank Maximum Capacity:	1350	liters			
5	Actual Volume in Tank:	800	liters			
6	Is the tank filling?	TRUE				
7					**Formulas Used**	
8	Is the tank full to operating capacity?	FALSE			=IF(B5>=B3,TRUE(),FALSE())	
9	Is the tank overflowing?	FALSE			=IF(B5>B4,TRUE(),FALSE())	
10						
11	Operator Action:	No action required			=IF(B9,"SHUT THE VALVE!","No action required")	
12						

Figure 38
A worksheet to monitor a tank-filling operation.

In this example,

- The **IF** function in cell B8 checks to see whether the volume in the tank (B5) has reached or exceeded the operating volume (B3).
- The **IF** function in cell B9 checks to see whether the volume in the tank (B5) has reached or exceeded the tank capacity (B4).

If the volume has exceeded the tank capacity (i.e., if the tank is overflowing), the **IF** function in cell B11 tells the operator to shut the valve. To test this, let's make the actual volume in the tank equal to the tank capacity (1350 liters). The result is shown in Figure 39.

	A	B	C	D	E	F
1	**Tank Monitor**					
2						
3	Tank Operating Capacity:	1200	liters			
4	Tank Maximum Capacity:	1350	liters			
5	Actual Volume in Tank:	1350	liters			
6	Is the tank filling?	TRUE				
7					**Formulas Used**	
8	Is the tank full to operating capacity?	TRUE			=IF(B5>=B3,TRUE(),FALSE())	
9	Is the tank overflowing?	TRUE			=IF(B5>=B4,TRUE(),FALSE())	
10						
11	Operator Action:	SHUT THE VALVE!			=IF(B9,"SHUT THE VALVE!","No action required")	
12						

Figure 39
What happens when the tank starts overflowing . . .

PRACTICE!

How would you modify the preceding worksheet to give the operators instructions in the following situations?

1. If the volume in the tank reaches or exceeds the operating volume, tell the operators to shut the valve. [ANSWER: =IF(B8, "Shut the valve.", "none required")]
2. If the volume in the tank is less than 200 liters and the tank is not filling, tell the operators to open the valve. [ANSWER: =IF(AND(B5<200,NOT(B6)),"Open the valve", "none required")]

8 ERROR FUNCTION

Excel provides two functions for working with *error functions*: **ERF** and **ERFC** (**Table 9**). **ERF**(x) returns the error function integrated between 0 and x, defined as

$$\text{ERF}(x) = \frac{2}{\sqrt{\pi}} \int_0^x e^{-t^2} dt. \tag{8}$$

Or you can specify two integration limits, as ERF($x1$, $x2$):

$$\text{ERF}(x_1, x_2) = \frac{2}{\sqrt{\pi}} \int_{x_1}^{x_2} e^{-t^2} dt. \tag{9}$$

The complementary error function, **ERFC**(x), is also available:

$$\text{ERFC}(x) = 1 - \text{ERF}(x) \tag{10}$$

Table 9 Error function functions

Function Name	Operation
ERF(*x*)	Returns the error function integrated between 0 and *x*
ERF(*x1,x2*)	Returns the error function integrated between x_1 and x_2.
ERFC(*x*)	Returns the complementary error function integrated between *x* and ∞

9 BESSEL FUNCTIONS

Bessel functions are commonly needed when integrating differential equations in cylindrical coordinates. These functions are complex and commonly available in tabular form. Excel's functions for using Bessel and modified Bessel functions are listed in Table 10.

Table 10 Bessel functions

Function Name	Operation
BESSELJ(*x,n*)	Returns the Bessel function, J_n, of *x* (*N* is the order of the Bessel function)
BESSELY(*x,n*)	Returns the Bessel function, Y_n, of *x*
BESSELI(*x,n*)	Returns the modified Bessel function, I_n, of *x*
BESSELK(*x,n*)	Returns the modified Bessel function, K_n, of *x*

The worksheet shown in Figure 40 uses the **BESSELJ**(*x,n*) function to create graphs of the $J_0(x)$ and $J_1(x)$ Bessel functions.

In Figure 40, the **BESSELJ** function has been used as follows:

Cell B4: =BESSELJ(A4,0)
Cell C4: =BESSELJ(A4,1)

10 WORKING WITH COMPLEX NUMBERS

Excel does provide functions for handling *complex numbers,* although working with complex numbers by using built-in functions is cumbersome at best. Still, if you occasionally need to handle complex numbers, the functions listed in Table 11 are available.

11 WORKING WITH BINARY, OCTAL, AND HEXADECIMAL VALUES

Excel provides the functions listed in Table 12 for converting *binary, octal, decimal,* and *hexadecimal* values.

In the next example (Figure 41), the decimal value 43 has been converted to binary, octal, and hexadecimal. In each case, eight digits were requested, and Excel added leading zeros to the result. The formulas used in column C are listed in column E.

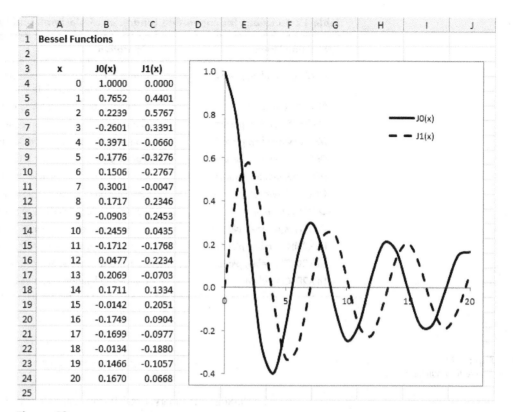

	A	B	C
1	**Bessel Functions**		
2			
3	x	J0(x)	J1(x)
4	0	1.0000	0.0000
5	1	0.7652	0.4401
6	2	0.2239	0.5767
7	3	-0.2601	0.3391
8	4	-0.3971	-0.0660
9	5	-0.1776	-0.3276
10	6	0.1506	-0.2767
11	7	0.3001	-0.0047
12	8	0.1717	0.2346
13	9	-0.0903	0.2453
14	10	-0.2459	0.0435
15	11	-0.1712	-0.1768
16	12	0.0477	-0.2234
17	13	0.2069	-0.0703
18	14	0.1711	0.1334
19	15	-0.0142	0.2051
20	16	-0.1749	0.0904
21	17	-0.1699	-0.0977
22	18	-0.0134	-0.1880
23	19	0.1466	-0.1057
24	20	0.1670	0.0668
25			

Figure 40
$J_0(x)$ and $J_1(x)$ Bessel functions.

Table 11 Functions for complex numbers

Function Name	Operation
COMPLEX(*real, img, suffix*)	Combines real and imaginary coefficients into a complex number. The suffix is an optional text argument allowing you to use a "j" to indicate the imaginary portion ("i" is used by default)
IMAGINARY(*x*)	Returns the imaginary coefficient of complex number x
IMREAL(*x*)	Returns the real coefficient of complex number x
IMABS(*x*)	Returns the absolute value (modulus) of complex number x
IMCOS(*x*)	Returns the cosine of complex number x
IMSIN(*x*)	Returns the sine of complex number x
IMLN(*x*)	Returns the natural logarithm of complex number x
IMLOG10(*x*)	Returns the base-10 logarithm of complex number x
IMLOG2(*x*)	Returns the base-2 logarithm of complex number x
IMEXP(*x*)	Returns the exponential of complex number x
IMPOWER(*x,n*)	Returns the value of complex number x raised to the integer power n
IMSQRT(*x*)	Returns the square root of complex number x
IMSUM(*x1, x2, …*)	Adds complex numbers
IMSUB(*x1, x2*)	Subtracts two complex numbers
IMPROD(*x1, x2, …*)	Determines the product of up to 29 complex numbers
IMDIV(*x1, x2*)	Divides two complex numbers

Table 12 Functions for converting binary, octal, decimal, and hexadecimal values

Function Name	Operation
BIN2OCT(*number, places*)	Converts a binary number to octal. Places can be used to pad leading digits with zeros
BIN2DEC(*number*)	Converts a binary number to decimal
BIN2HEX(*number, places*)	Converts a binary number to hexadecimal
DEC2BIN(*number, places*)	Converts a decimal number to binary
DEC2OCT(*number, places*)	Converts a decimal number to octal
DEC2HEX(*number, places*)	Converts a decimal number to hexadecimal
OCT2BIN(*number, places*)	Converts an octal number to binary
OCT2DEC(*number*)	Converts an octal number to decimal
OCT2HEX(*number, places*)	Converts an octal number to hexadecimal
HEX2BIN(*number, places*)	Converts a hexadecimal number to binary
HEX2OCT(*number, places*)	Converts a hexadecimal number to octal
HEX2DEC(*number*)	Converts a hexadecimal number to decimal

Figure 41
Converting numbers.

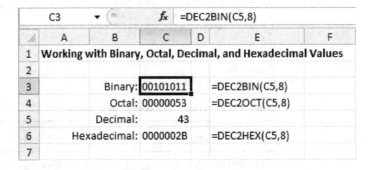

12 MISCELLANEOUS FUNCTIONS

Here are a few built-in functions that, although less commonly used, can be very handy on occasion.

12.1 Working with Random Numbers

The **RAND** and **RANDBETWEEN** functions generate *random numbers*. The **RAND** function returns a value greater than or equal to zero and less than 1. The **RANDBETWEEN**(*low, high*) function returns a value between the *low* and *high* values you specify.

Excel also provides a *random number tool* that will create columns of random numbers with unique properties, such as a column of normally distributed random numbers with a specific mean and standard deviation. This random number tool is part of Excel's Analysis ToolPak Add-In which is installed, but not activated when Excel is installed. You activate Add-Ins from the Excel Options dialog, as

- Excel 2010: **File tab/Options**
- Excel 2007: **Office/Excel Options**

Once the Excel Options dialog is open (illustrated in Figure 42), use the **Add-Ins** panel. The available Excel Add-Ins will vary greatly from one computer to the next, so your screen may look quite different.

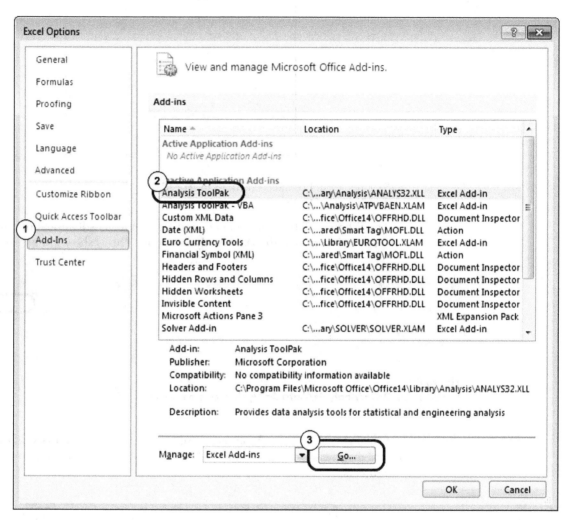

Figure 42
Activating the Analysis ToolPak Add-In.

The Add-Ins panel lists Active Application Add-Ins and Inactive Application Add-Ins.

- If the Analysis ToolPak is in the active list, you're good to go.
- If the Analysis ToolPak is not on any list, it wasn't installed; you will have to get out the CD's to install the Analysis ToolPak.
- If it is in the inactive list, you need to activate it. To activate the Analysis ToolPak:
  1. Click on the **Analysis ToolPak** list item (the name in the list).
  2. Click the **Go ...** button.
     These steps will cause the Add-Ins dialog to open, as shown in Figure 43.

Figure 43
The Add-Ins dialog.

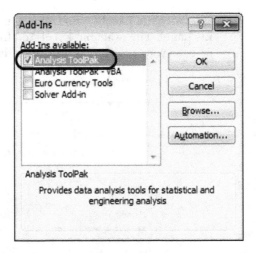

3. Check the box labeled **Analysis ToolPak.**
4. Click the **OK** button.

The Ribbon will then be updated, and a new button will appear on the **Data** tab in the Analysis group as the **Data Analysis** button. This is shown in Figure 44.

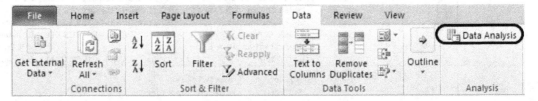

Figure 44
Ribbon options **Data/Analysis/Data Analysis** access the Analysis ToolPak.

Clicking on the **Data Analysis** button opens the Data Analysis dialog (Figure 45) and displays a list of available analysis tools. Many of these tools are very useful to engineers.

Figure 45
The Analysis Tools available through the Data Analysis dialog.

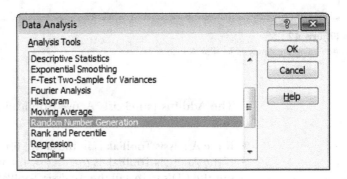

If you select **Random Number Generation** (as in Figure 45) and click the **OK** button, the Random Number Generation dialog will open (Figure 46). This dialog provides a quick way to create sets of random numbers with various distributions.

Figure 46
The Random Number
Generation dialog.

Random Number Generation

Number of Variables:	1	OK
Number of Random Numbers:	50	Cancel
Distribution:	Normal ▾	Help

Parameters

Mean = 0

Standard deviation = 1

Random Seed:

Output options

○ Output Range:

◉ New Worksheet Ply:

○ New Workbook

Example: Normally Distributed Random Values

If you want to test some of Excel's statistical functions, you might want to create a set of values that are normally distributed (the "bell curve") with a specific mean and standard deviation.

To generate a set of 15 random numbers, normally distributed with a mean of 5 and a standard deviation of 1, the Random Number Generation dialog should be filled out as shown in Figure 47.

Figure 47
Using the Random Number
Generation dialog.

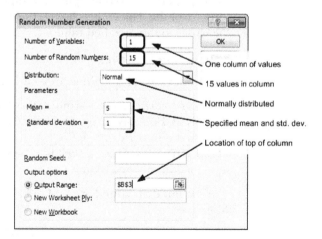

The result (after clicking **OK**) is a set of 15 values placed in the requested position on the worksheet. In Figure 48, the mean and standard deviation have been computed to verify that the random number generator did generate values with the requested characteristics.

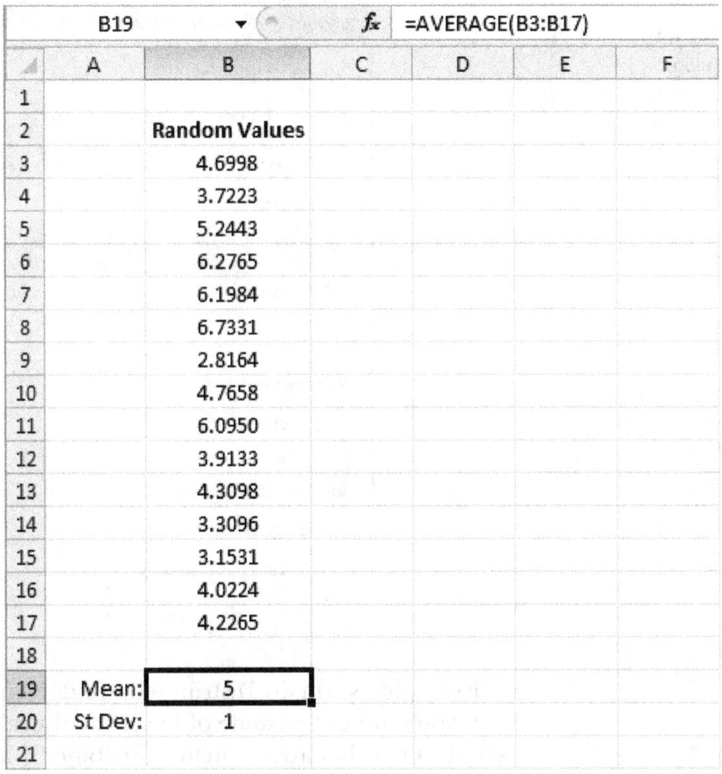

Figure 48
The calculated random numbers.

	A	B	C	D	E	F
				B19	▼	*fx* =AVERAGE(B3:B17)

	A	B	C	D	E	F
1						
2		**Random Values**				
3		4.6998				
4		3.7223				
5		5.2443				
6		6.2765				
7		6.1984				
8		6.7331				
9		2.8164				
10		4.7658				
11		6.0950				
12		3.9133				
13		4.3098				
14		3.3096				
15		3.1531				
16		4.0224				
17		4.2265				
18						
19	Mean:	5				
20	St Dev:	1				
21						

Note: The actual mean and standard deviation of the 15 values shown here are 4.6 and 1.2, respectively. Using a small data set, like the 15 values created in this example, you will not get precisely the requested mean and standard deviation (except perhaps, to one significant digit) because these are random values. As the size of the data set gets larger, the data set mean and standard deviation will be closer to the specified values.

12.2 Rounding Functions

Excel provides several functions for rounding numbers.

- **ROUND**(*Number, Digits*)—rounds the *Number* to the specified number of Digits.
- **ROUNDUP**(*Number, Digits*)—rounds the *Number* up (away from zero) to the specified number of Digits.
- **ROUNDDOWN**(*Number, Digits*)—rounds the *Number* down (toward zero) to the specified number of Digits.

For example, to round π (3.14159 ...) to three digits, the following formula could be used:

```
=ROUND(PI(),3)
```

The result would be 3.142.

Excel also provides functions that round away from zero to the next *odd* or *even* value.

- **ODD**(*Number*)—rounds the *Number* up (away from zero) to the next odd integer value.

- **EVEN**(*Number*)—rounds the *Number* up (away from zero) to the next even integer value.

If we round π to the next even value using the **EVEN** function, we should get 4. This is illustrated in Figure 49.

Note: The **ODD** function rounds zero to 1; **EVEN**(*0*) returns a zero.

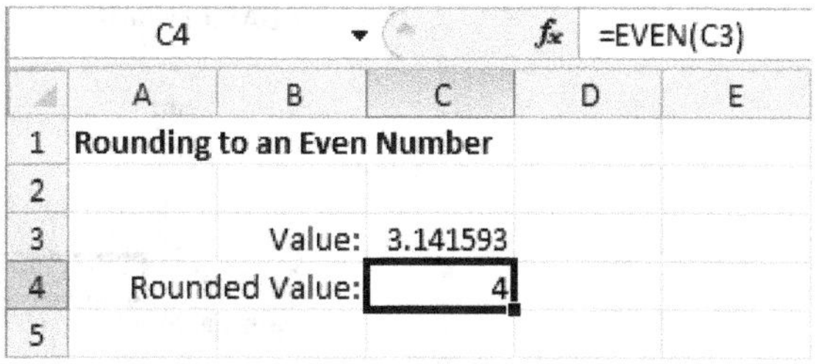

Figure 49
Rounding to an even
integer using the **EVEN**
function.

	C4			f_x	=EVEN(C3)
	A	B	C	D	E
1	Rounding to an Even Number				
2					
3		Value:	3.141593		
4		Rounded Value:	4		
5					

12.3 Date and Time Functions

Excel provides a number of *date* and *time functions* that read the calendar and clock on your computer to make date and time information available to your worksheets. The date and time is stored as a *date–time code*, such as 6890.45834. The number to the left of the decimal point represents the number of days after the defined start date. By default, the start date is January 1, 1900, for PCs, and January 1, 1904, for Macintosh computers. You can tell Excel to use a non-default date system by modifying the Excel options. For example, to use Macintosh-style date–time codes on a PC, first open the Excel Options dialog, as:

- Excel 2010: **File tab/Options**
- Excel 2007: **Office/Excel Options**

Then select the **Advanced** panel. Find the **When Calculating this Workbook** section and check **Use 1904 Date System**.

The date–time code 6890.45833 represents a unique moment in history; the eleventh hour (11/24 = 0.45833) of the eleventh day, of the eleventh month of 1918: the time of the signing of the armistice that ended World War I. November 11, 1918 is 6890 days after the PC start date of 1/1/1900.

You can find the date code for any date after 1900 (or 1904 if the 1904 date system is in use) by using the **DATE**(*year, month, day*) function. Using the **DATE** function with Armistice Day returns the date value, 6890, as shown in Figure 50.

Excel tries to make date codes more readable to the user by formatting cells containing date codes with a *Date format*. The worksheet in the preceding example actually displayed 11/11/18 in cell B8 until the formatting for that cell was changed from date format to Number format.

If you enter a date or time into a cell, Excel converts the value to a date–time code, but formats the cell to display the date or the time. Some examples are shown in Figure 51.

Date–time codes (also called *serial date values*) are used to allow Excel to perform calculations with dates and times. For example, Excel can calculate the number of days that were left until Christmas on August 12, 1916, by using the **DATE** function (the result is 135 days):

```
=DATE(1916,12,25)-DATE(1916,8,12)
```

Figure 50
Using the **DATE** function to return a date value from a date.

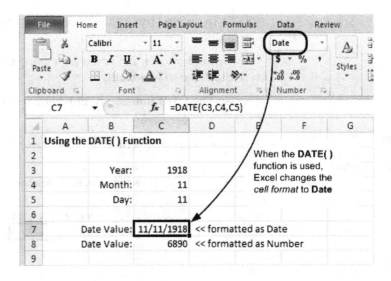

Figure 51
Examples of how Excel converts and displays dates and times.

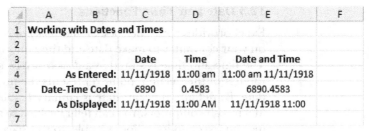

Excel provides a number of functions for working with dates and times. Some of these functions are listed in Table 13.

Table 13 Functions for working with dates and times

Function Name	Operation
TODAY()	Returns today's date code. Excel displays the date with a date format
DATE(*year, month, day*)	Returns the date code for the specified *year*, *month*, and *day*. Excel displays the date code with a date format (shows the date, not the date code). Change the cell format to number or general to see the date code
DATEVALUE(*date*)	Returns the date code for the *date*, which is entered as text such as "12/25/1916" or "December 25, 1916." The quotes are required. Excel displays the date code with a general format (i.e., shows the date code, not the date)
NOW()	Returns the current time code. Excel displays the time with a time format
TIME(*hour, minute, second*)	Returns the time code for the specified *hour*, *minute*, and *second*. Excel displays the time code with a time format (shows the time, not the time code). Change the cell format to number or general to see the time code
TIMEVALUE(*time*)	Returns the date code for the *time*, which is entered as text such as "11:00 am." The quotes are required. Excel displays the time code with a general format (i.e., shows the time code, not the time)

Table 14 Functions for extracting portions of date–time codes

Function Name	Operation
YEAR (*date code*)	Returns the year referred to by the date represented by the *date code*. For example, =YEAR(6890) returns 1918
MONTH (*date code*)	Returns the month referred to by the date represented by the *date code*. For example, =MONTH(6890) returns 11
DAY (*date code*)	Returns the day referred to by the date represented by the *date code*. For example, =DAY(6890) returns 11
HOUR (*time code*)	Returns the hour referred to by the time represented by the *time code* or date–time code. For example, =HOUR(6890.45833) returns 11. So does =HOUR(0.45833)
MINUTE (*time code*)	Returns the minute referred to by the time represented by the *time code* or date–time code
SECOND (*time code*)	Returns the second referred to by the time represented by the *time code* or date–time code

Excel also provides a series of functions for pulling particular portions from a date–time code (Table 14).

When using Excel's date–time codes, remember the following:

- Date–time codes work only for dates on or after the starting date (1/1/1900 or 1/1/1904).
- Using four-digit years avoids ambiguity. By default, 00 through 29 is interpreted to mean 2000 through 2029, while 30 through 99 is interpreted to mean 1930 through 1999.
- Excel tries to be helpful when working with date–time codes. You can enter a date as text when the function requires a date–time code, and Excel will convert the date to a date–time code before sending it to the function. This is illustrated in Figure 52.

Figure 52

Sending dates into functions that use date–time codes.

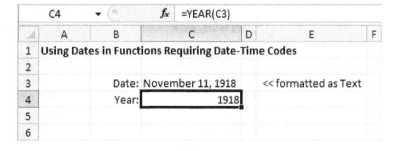

Note: Cell C3 in Figure 52 was formatted as Text before entering the date to keep Excel from immediately recognizing and converting the date.

- Whenever Excel interprets an entry in a cell as a date, it changes the format to Date format and changes the cell contents to a date code. This can be frustrating if the cell contents happen to look like a date, but are not intended to be interpreted as such. For example, if several part sizes are indicated in inches as 1/8, 1/10, and 1/16, they would appear in a worksheet as shown in Figure 53.

Figure 53
How Excel can incorrectly interpret values as dates.

Excel interpreted the 1/8 typed into cell B4 as a date (January 8th of the current year), converted the entry to a date code, and changed the cell formatting to display the date. Because Excel has changed the cell contents to a date code, simply fixing the cell format will not give you the fraction back. You need to tell Excel that it should interpret the entry as a fraction by setting the format for cells B4:B6 to Fraction before entering the values in the cell.

12.4 Text-Handling Functions

Excel's standard *text-manipulation functions* are listed in Table 15.

12.5 Lookup and Reference Functions

Because of the tabular nature of an Excel worksheet, lists of numbers are common and Excel provides ways to look up values in tables. Excel's *lookup functions* are summarized in Table 16.

Table 15 Text-handling functions

Function Name	Operation
CHAR (*number*)	Returns the character specified by the code *number*
CONCATENATE (*text1, text2*)	Joins several text items into one text item
	(The & operator can also be used for concatenation)
EXACT (*text1, text2*)	Checks to see if two text values are identical. Returns **TRUE** if the text strings are identical, otherwise **FALSE** (case sensitive)
FIND (*text_to_find, text_to_search, start_pos*)	Finds one text value within another (case sensitive)
LEFT (*text, n*)	Returns the leftmost *n* characters from a text value
LEN (*text*)	Returns the number of characters in text string, *text*
LOWER (*text*)	Converts *text* to lowercase
MID (*text, start_pos, n*)	Returns *n* characters from a text string starting at *start_pos*
REPLACE (*old_text, start_pos, n, new_text*)	Replaces *n* characters of *old_text* with *new_text* starting at *start_pos*
RIGHT (*text, n*)	Returns the rightmost *n* characters from a text value
SEARCH (*text_to_find, text_to_search, start_pos*)	Finds one text value within another (not case sensitive)
TRIM (*text*)	Removes spaces from *text*
UPPER (*text*)	Converts *text* to uppercase

Table 16 Lookup and reference functions

Function Name	Operation
VLOOKUP	Vertical lookup
(*value, table, N, matchType*)	Looks up a value in the left column of a *table*, jumps to column *N* of the table (the matched column is column 1), and returns the value in that location
	If *matchType* is set to **TRUE,** the lookup will fail unless the match is exact. If *matchType* is omitted or set to **FALSE,** Excel will use the next highest value as the match
HLOOKUP	Horizontal Lookup
(*value, table, N, matchType*)	Looks up a value in the top row of a *table*, jumps down to row *N* of the same table (same column), and returns the value in that location

The worksheet example in Figure 54 uses the **VLOOKUP** function to determine letter grades for students from a grade table.

Figure 54
Looking up grades.

	A	B	C	D	E	F	G	H
		D6			▼	*fx*	=VLOOKUP(C6,$F$3:$G$15,2)	
1	Class Grades							
2							Grade Table	
3		Student	Score	Grade		0	F	
4		John A.	85	B		59.9	D-	
5		Jane B.	93	A		62.9	D	
6		Jim G.	78	C+		66.9	D+	
7		Pris L.	82	B-		69.9	C-	
8						72.9	C	
9						76.9	C+	
10						79.9	B-	
11						82.9	B	
12						86.9	B+	
13						89.9	A-	
14						92.9	A	
15						96.9	A+	
16								

KEY TERMS

Argument list
Arguments
AutoSum button
Bessel functions
Binary
Complex numbers
Date format
Date functions

Date–time code
Decimal
Error functions
Even
Exponentiation
  functions
Function
Function name

Hexadecimal
Horizontal component
Hyperbolic trigonometric
  functions
Inverse hyperbolic
  trigonometric functions
Inverse trigonometric
  functions

SUMMARY

A *function* is a reusable equation that accepts arguments, uses the argument values in a calculation, and returns the result(s). In this section, the commonly used built-in functions in Excel are collected and displayed in tabular format. Also, descriptions of some other functions (matrix math functions, statistical functions, time-value-of-money functions) are included in the section in an attempt to provide a single source for descriptions of those commonly used functions.

Common math functions

SQRT (*x*)	Square root
ABS (*x*)	Absolute value
FACT (*x*)	Factorial
SUM (*range*)	Summation
GCD (*x1, x2, ...*)	Greatest common divisor
LCM (*x1, x2, ...*)	Least common multiple

Log and Exponentiation	Operation
EXP (*x*)	Returns e raised to the power *x*
LN (*x*)	Returns the natural log of *x*
LOG10 (*x*)	Returns the base-10 log of *x*
LOG (*x, base*)	Returns the logarithm of *x* to the specified base

Trigonometry Functions	Operation
SIN (*x*)	Returns the sine of *x*
COS (*x*)	Returns the cosine of *x*
TAN (*x*)	Returns the tangent of *x*
RADIANS (*x*)	Converts *x* from degrees to radians
DEGREES (*x*)	Converts *x* from radians to degrees

Inverse Trignometric Functions	Operation
ASIN (x)	Returns the angle (between $-\pi/2$ and $\pi/2$) that has a sine value equal to x
ACOS (x)	Returns the angle (between 0 and π) that has a cosine value equal to x
ATAN (x)	Returns the angle (between $-\pi/2$ and $\pi/2$) that has a tangent value equal to x

Hyperbolic Trignometric Functions	Operation
SINH (x)	Returns the hyperbolic sine of x
COSH (x)	Returns the hyperbolic cosine of x
TANH (x)	Returns the hyperbolic tangent of x
ASINH (x)	Returns the inverse hyperbolic sine of x
ACOSH (x)	Returns the inverse hyperbolic cosine of x
ATANH (x)	Returns the inverse hyperbolic tangent of x

Logical Functions	Operation
IF(*test, Tvalue, Fvalue*)	Performs the operation specified by the test argument and then returns *Tvalue* if the *test* is true, or *Fvalue* if the *test* is false
TRUE ()	Returns the logical value TRUE
FALSE ()	Returns the logical value FALSE
NOT (*test*)	Reverses the logic returned by the test operation. If *test* returns TRUE, then NOT (*test*) returns FALSE
AND $(x1, x2, \ldots)$	Returns TRUE if all arguments are true or FALSE if any argument is false
OR $(x1, x2, \ldots)$	Returns TRUE if any argument is true or FALSE if all arguments are false

Error Functions	Operation
ERF (x)	Returns the error function integrated between 0 and x
ERF $(x1, x2)$	Returns the error function integrated between x_1 and x_2.
ERFC (x)	Returns the complementary error function integrated between x and ∞.

Bessel Functions	Operation
BESSELJ (x, n)	Returns the Bessel function, J_n, of x (n is the order of the Bessel function)
BESSELY (x, n)	Returns the Bessel function, Y_n, of x
BESSELI (x, n)	Returns the modified Bessel function, I_n, of x
BESSELK (x, n)	Returns the modified Bessel function, K_n, of x

Complex Number Functions	Operation
COMPLEX(*real, img, suffix*)	Combines real and imaginary coefficients into a complex number. The *suffix* is an optional text argument in case you wish to use a "j" to indicate the imaginary portion ("i" is used by default)
IMAGINARY (*x*)	Returns the imaginary coefficient of complex number *x*
IMREAL (*x*)	Returns the real coefficient of complex number *x*
IMABS (*x*)	Returns the absolute value (modulus) of complex number *x*
IMCOS (*x*)	Returns the cosine of complex number *x*
IMSIN (*x*)	Returns the sine of complex number *x*
IMLN (*x*)	Returns the natural logarithm of complex number *x*
IMLOG10 (*x*)	Returns the base-10 logarithm of complex number *x*
IMLOG2 (*x*)	Returns the base-2 logarithm of complex number *x*
IMEXP (*x*)	Returns the exponential of complex number *x*
IMPOWER (*x, n*)	Returns the value of complex number *x* raised to the integer power *n*
IMSQRT (*x*)	Returns the square root of complex number *x*
IMSUM (*x1, x2, ...*)	Adds complex numbers
IMSUB (*x1, x2*)	Subtracts two complex numbers
IMPROD (*x1, x2, ...*)	Computes the product of up to 29 complex numbers
IMDIV (*x1, x2*)	Divides two complex numbers

Conversion Functions	Operation
BIN2OCT(*number, places*)	Converts a binary *number* to octal. *Places* can be used to pad leading digits with zeros
BIN2DEC (*number*)	Converts a binary *number* to decimal
BIN2HEX (*number, places*)	Converts a binary *number* to hexadecimal
DEC2BIN (*number, places*)	Converts a decimal *number* to binary
DEC2OCT (*number, places*)	Converts a decimal *number* to octal
DEC2HEX (*number, places*)	Converts a decimal *number* to hexadecimal
OCT2BIN (*number, places*)	Converts an octal *number* to binary
OCT2DEC (*number*)	Converts an octal *number* to decimal
OCT2HEX (*number, places*)	Converts an octal *number* to hexadecimal
HEX2BIN (*number, places*)	Converts a hexadecimal *number* to binary
HEX2OCT (*number, places*)	Converts a hexadecimal *number* to octal
HEX2DEC (*number*)	Converts a hexadecimal *number* to decimal

Date and Time Functions	Operation
TODAY()	Returns today's date code. Excel displays the date with a date format
DATE(*year, month, day*)	Returns the date code for the specified *year, month*, and *day*. Excel displays the date code with a date format (i.e., shows the date, not the date code). Change the cell format to number or general to see the date code

DATEVALUE (*date*)	Returns the date code for the *date*, which is entered as text such as "12/25/1916" or "December 25, 1916." The quotes are required. Excel displays the date code with a general format (i.e., shows the date code, not the date)
NOW ()	Returns the current time code. Excel displays the time with a time format
TIME(*hour, minute, second*)	Returns the time code for the specified *hour, minute,* and *second.* Excel displays the time code with a time format (i.e., shows the time, not the time code). Change the cell format to number or general to see the time code
TIMEVALUE (*time*)	Returns the date code for the *time,* which is entered as text such as "11:00 am." The quotes are required. Excel displays the time code with a general format (i.e., shows the time code, not the time)
YEAR (*date code*)	Returns the year referred to by the date represented by the *date code.* Example: =YEAR(6890) returns 1918
MONTH (*date code*)	Returns the month referred to by the date represented by the *date code.* Example: =MONTH(6890) returns 11
DAY (*date code*)	Returns the day referred to by the date represented by the *date code.* Example: =DAY(6890) returns 11
HOUR (*time code*)	Returns the hour referred to by the time represented by the *time code* or date–time code. Example: =HOUR (6890.45833) returns 11. So does =HOUR(0.45833)
MINUTE (*time code*)	Returns the minute referred to by the time represented by the *time code* or date–time code
SECOND (*time code*)	Returns the second referred to by the time represented by the *time code* or date–time code

Text Functions	Operation
CHAR (*number*)	Returns the character specified by the code *number*
CONCATENATE (*text1, text2*)	Joins several text items into one text item (The & operator can also be used for concatenation)
EXACT (*text1, text2*)	Checks to see whether two text values are identical. Returns TRUE if the text strings are identical, FALSE otherwise (case sensitive)
FIND (*text_to_find, text_to_search, start_pos*)	Finds one text value within another (case sensitive)
LEFT (*text, n*)	Returns the leftmost *n* characters from a text value
LEN (*text*)	Returns the number of characters in text string, *text*
LOWER (*text*)	Converts *text* to lowercase
MID (*text, start_pos, n*)	Returns *n* characters from a *text* string starting at *start_pos*
REPLACE (*old_text, start_pos, n, new_text*)	Replaces *n* characters of *old_text* with *new_text* starting at *start_pos*
RIGHT (*text, n*)	Returns the rightmost *n* characters from a *text* value
SEARCH (*text_to_find, text_to_search, start_pos*)	Finds one text value within another (not case sensitive)
TRIM (*text*)	Removes spaces from *text*
UPPER (*text*)	Converts *text* to uppercase

Function Name	Operation
VLOOKUP	Vertical lookup
(*value, table, N, matchType*)	Looks up a *value* in the left column of a *table*, jumps to column *N* of the table (to the right of the matched column), and returns the value in that location
	If *matchType* is set to TRUE, the lookup will fail unless the match is exact. If *matchType* is omitted or set to FALSE, Excel will use the next higher value as the match
HLOOKUP	Horizontal lookup
(*value, table, N, matchType*)	Looks up a *value* in the top row of a *table*, jumps down to row *N* of the same table (same column), and returns the value in that location

Statistical Functions	Description
AVERAGE (*range*)	Calculates the arithmetic average of the values in the specified *range* of cells
STDEV (*range*)	Calculates the sample standard deviation of the values in the specified *range* of cells
STDEVP (*range*)	Calculates the population standard deviation of the values in the specified *range* of cells
VAR (*range*)	Calculates the sample variance of the values in the specified *range* of cells
VARP (*range*)	Calculates the population variance of the values in the specified *range* of cells

Time-Value-of-Money Functions	Description
FV(*iP, Nper, Pmt, PV, Type*)	Calculates a future value, *FV*, given a periodic interest rate, i_p, the number of compounding periods, *N*, a periodic payment, *Pmt*, an optional present value, *PV*, and an optional code indicating whether payments are made at the beginning or end of each period, *Type*: *Type* = 1 means payments at the beginning of each period. *Type* = 0 or omitted means payments at the end of each period
PV(*iP, Nper, Pmt, FV, Type*)	Calculates a present value, *PV*, given a periodic interest rate, i_p, the number of compounding periods, *N*, a periodic payment, *Pmt*, an optional future value, *FV*, and an optional code indicating whether payments are made at the beginning or end of each period, *Type*
PMT(*iP, Nper, PV, FV, Type*)	Calculates the periodic payment, *Pmt*, equal to a given present value, *PV*, and (optionally) future value, *FV*, given a periodic interest rate, i_p, the number of compounding periods, *N*. Type is an optional code indicating whether payments are made at the beginning (*Type* =1) or end (*Type* =0) of each period

Internal Rate of Return and Depreciation Functions	Description
IRR(*Incomes, irrGuess*)	Calculates the internal rate of return for the series of incomes and expenses:
	Incomes is a range of cells containing the incomes (and expenses as negative incomes) (required)
	IrrGuess is a starting value, or guess value, for the iterative solution required to calculate the internal rate of return, optional
NPV (*iP, Inc1, Inc2, ...*)	Calculates the net present value, *NPV*, of a series of incomes (*Inc1, Inc2, ...*) given a periodic interest rate, i_P:
	Inc1, Inc2, etc., can be values, cell addresses, or cell ranges containing incomes (and expenses as negative incomes)
VDB (*Cinit, S, NSL, Perstart, Perend, FDB, NoSwitch*)	Calculates depreciation amounts using various methods (straight line, double-declining balance, MACRS)
	Cinit is the initial cost of the asset (required)
	S is the salvage value, required (set to zero for MACRS depreciation)
	NSL is the service life of the asset, required
	Perstart is the start of the period over which the depreciation amount will be calculated, required
	Perstop is the end of the period over which the depreciation amount will be calculated, required
	FDB is declining balance percentage, optional (Excel uses 200% if omitted)
	NoSwitch tells Excel whether to switch to straight-line depreciation when the straight-line depreciation factor is larger than the declining-balance depreciation factor, optional (set to FALSE to switch to straight line, TRUE to not switch; the default is FALSE)

Matrix Math Functions	Description
MMULT(*M1, M2*)	Multiplies matrices *M1* and *M2*. Use [Ctrl–Shift–Enter] to tell Excel to enter the matrix function into every cell of the result matrix
TRANSPOSE(*M*)	Transposes matrix *M*
MINVERSE(*M*)	Calculates the inverse of matrix *M* (if possible)
MDETERM(*M*)	Calculates the determinant of matrix *M*

PROBLEMS

1 Trigonometric Functions

Devise a test to demonstrate the validity of the following common trigonometric formulas. What values of A and B should be used to test these functions thoroughly?

a. $\sin(A + B) = \sin(A)\cos(B) + \cos(A)\sin(B)$

b. $\sin(2A) = 2\sin(A)\cos(A)$

c. $\sin^2(A) = \dfrac{1}{2} - \dfrac{1}{2}\cos(2A)$

Note: In Excel, sin^2(A) should be entered as `=(sin(A))^2`. This causes sin(A) to be evaluated first and that result to be squared.

2 Basic Fluid Flow

A commonly used rule of thumb is that the average velocity in a pipe should be about 1 m/s or less for "thin" fluids (viscosity about water). If a pipe needs to deliver 6,000 m³ of water per day, what diameter is required to satisfy the 1-m/s rule?

3 Projectile Motion II

Sports programs' "shot of the day" segments sometimes show across-the-court baskets made just as (or after) the final buzzer sounds. If a basketball player, with three seconds remaining in the game, throws the ball at a 45° angle from 4 feet off the ground, standing 70 feet from the basket, which is 10 feet in the air, as illustrated in Figure 55:

    a. What initial velocity does the ball need to have in order to reach the basket?
    b. What is the time of flight? and
    c. How much time will be left in the game after the shot?

Ignore air resistance in this problem.

Figure 55
Throwing a basketball.

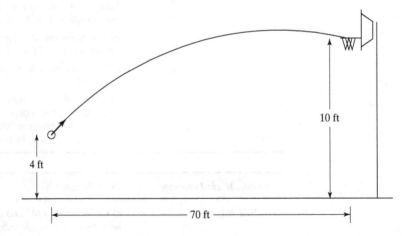

4 Pulley I

A 200-kg mass is hanging from a hook connected to a pulley, as shown in the accompanying figure. The cord around the pulley is connected to the overhead support at two points as illustrated in Figure 56.

Figure 56
Pulley supports.

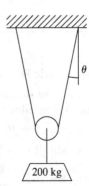

What is the tension in each cord connected to the support if the angle of the cord from vertical is

    a. 0°?
    b. 5°?
    c. 15°?

5 Force Components and Tension in Wires I

A 150-kg mass is suspended by wires from two hooks, as shown in the accompanying figure. The lengths of the wires have been adjusted so that the wires are each 50° from horizontal, as illustrated in Figure 57. Assume that the mass of the wires is negligible.

Figure 57
Forces and tensions in wires I.

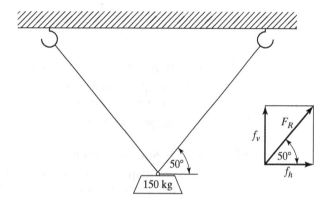

    a. Two hooks support the mass equally, so the vertical component of force exerted by either hook will be equal to the force resulting from 75 kg being acted on by gravity. Calculate this vertical component of force, f_v on the right hook. Express your result in Newtons.
    b. Compute the horizontal component of force, f_h, by using the result obtained in part (a) and trigonometry.
    c. Determine the force exerted on the mass in the direction of the wire F_R (equal to the tension in the wire).
    d. If you moved the hooks farther apart to reduce the angle from 50° to 30° would the tension in the wires increase or decrease? Why?

6 Force Components and Tension in Wires II

If two 150-kg masses are suspended on a wire as shown in Figure 58, such that the section between the loads (wire B) is horizontal, then wire B is under tension, but is doing no lifting. The entire weight of the 150-kg mass on the right is being held up by the vertical component of the force in wire C. In the same way, the mass on the left is being supported entirely by the vertical component of the force in wire A. What is the tension on wire B?

Figure 58
Forces and tensions in wires II.

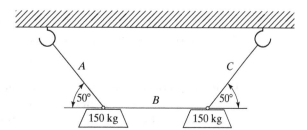

7 Force Components and Tension in Wires III

If the hooks shown in the previous problem are pulled farther apart, as illustrated in Figure 59, the tension in wire B will change, and the angle of wires A and C with respect to the horizontal will also change.

Figure 59
Forces and tensions in wires III.

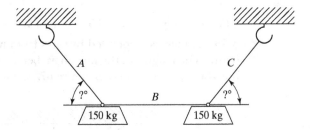

If the hooks are pulled apart until the tension in wire B is 2000 N, compute:

    a. The angle between the horizontal and wire C.
    b. The tension in wire C.

How does the angle in part (a) change if the tension in wire B is increased to 3000 N?

8 Finding the Volume of a Storage Bin I

A fairly common shape for a dry-solids storage bin is a cylindrical silo with a conical collecting section at the base where the product is removed (see Figure 60).

Figure 60
Storage silo.

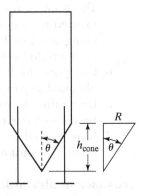

To calculate the volume of the contents, you use the formula for a cone, as long as the height of product, h, is less than the height of the conical section, h_{cone}:

$$V = \tfrac{1}{3}\pi r_h^2 h \qquad \text{if } h < h_{cone}, \tag{11}$$

Here, r_h is the radius at height h and can be calculated from h by using trigonometry:

$$r_h = h_{cone}\tan(\theta). \tag{12}$$

If the height of the stored product is greater than the height of the conical section, the equation for a cylinder must be added to the volume of the cone:

$$V = \tfrac{1}{3}\pi R^2 h_{cone} + \pi R^2(h - h_{cone}) \qquad \text{if } h > h_{cone}. \tag{13}$$

If the height of the conical section is 3 meters, the radius of the cylindrical section is 2 meters, and the total height of the storage bin is 10 meters, what is the maximum volume of material that can be stored?

9 Finding the Volume of a Storage Bin II

Consider the storage bin described in the previous problem.

    a. Calculate the angle θ as shown in the diagram.

    b. For a series of h values between 0 to 10 meters, calculate r_h values and bin volumes.

    c. Plot the volume vs. height data.

10 Pulley Problem II

A 200-kg mass is attached to a pulley, as shown in Figure 61.

Figure 61

Four-pulley system.

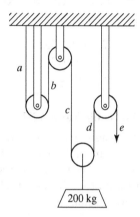

    a. What force must be exerted on cord e to keep the mass from moving?

    b. When the mass is stationary, what is the tension in cords a through e?

    c. Which, if any, of the solid supports connecting the pulleys to the overhead support is in compression?

11 Nonideal Gas Equation

The Soave–Redlich–Kwong (SRK) equation is a commonly used equation of state that relates the absolute temperature T, the absolute pressure P, and the molar volume $\hat{V}$ of a gas under conditions in which the behavior of the gas cannot be considered ideal (e.g., moderate temperature and high pressure). The SRK equation[1] is

$$P = \frac{RT}{(\hat{V} - b)} - \frac{\alpha a}{\hat{V}(\hat{V} + b)} \tag{14}$$

where R is the ideal gas constant and α, a, and b are parameters specific to the gas, calculated as follows:

$$a = 0.42747\frac{(RT_C)^2}{P_C}$$
$$b = 0.08664\frac{RT_C}{P_C}$$
$$m = 0.48508 + 1.55171\omega - 0.1561\omega^2 \tag{15}$$
$$T_r = \frac{T}{T_C}$$
$$\alpha = \left[1 + m\left(1 - \sqrt{T_r}\right)\right]^2$$

[1] *From Elementary Principles of Chemical Processes,* 3d ed., R. M. Felder and R. W. Rousseau, New York: Wiley, 2000.

Here,

T_C is the critical temperature of the gas,
P_C is the critical pressure of the gas, and
ω is the Pitzer acentric factor.

Each of these is readily available for many gases.
Calculate the pressure exerted by 20 gram-moles of ammonia at 300 K in a 5-liter container, using

a. the ideal gas equation,
b. the SRK equation.

The required data for ammonia are tabulated as follows:

$$T_C = 405.5\text{K},$$
$$P_C = 111.3 \text{ atm},$$
$$\omega = 0.25 \tag{16}$$

12 Projectile Motion III

Major-league baseball outfield fences are typically about 350 feet from home plate. Home run balls need to be at least 12 feet off the ground to clear the fence. Calculate the minimum required initial velocity (in miles per hour or kilometers per hour) for a home run, for baseballs hit at the angles 10°, 20°, 30°, and 40° from the horizontal.

Index